THE AMERICAN HISTORICAL SUPPLY CATALOGUE 2

Also by Alan Wellikoff

THE AMERICAN HISTORICAL
SUPPLY CATALOGUE
A
Nineteenth-Century
Sourcebook

THE AMERICAN HISTORICAL SUPPLY CATALOGUE 2

An Early-Twentieth-Century Sourcebook

Alan Wellikoff

SCHOCKEN BOOKS   New York

First published by Schocken Books 1986
10 9 8 7 6 5 4 3 2 1   86 87 88 89
Copyright © 1986 by Alan Wellikoff

Library of Congress Cataloging-in-Publication Data
Wellikoff, Alan.
The American historical supply catalogue 2.
Includes index.
1. Americana—Catalogs. 2. United States—Manufacturers—Catalogs.
I. Title.
TS199.W444 1986   745.1′075′073   86–6614

Design by Richard Erlanger

Manufactured in the United States of America
ISBN 0–8052–0819–4

Contents

Things are in the saddle
And ride mankind.

—RALPH WALDO EMERSON

Preface

AS what follows is a catalog, it's perforce a collection of things. As these are American things into the bargain, a catalog of them isn't as simple a matter as it may seem. For one thing, *things* have always been part of our national reason for being.

FROM the earliest European accounts depicting the North American landscape with drawings that posed monstrous alligators alongside Indian maidens plumed and languid as Raphaelite nymphs, it's been expected of the New World by the Old that it continually produce a succession of wonders to marvel at and enjoy. The first of these were necessarily native and agricultural—the corn, tobacco, cocoa, and odd aboriginal sachem that crossed the Atlantic to delight crowned heads at court. Eighteenth-century republicanism was naturally less well received, but by then, with our frontier-honed "Yankee ingenuity," we Americans had set ourselves to the task of creating, in the words of Tom Paine, a "New Beginning"—and one furnished with newly minted things.

FROM the American Bill of Rights to Thomas Jefferson's gadgety dumbwaiter, it's always been incumbent upon new things to provide the promise of independence and an easier life. By 1793, when the cotton gin anticipated the demise of slavery through the mechanization of labor, the entire notion of the perfectibility of man was being subtly reinforced. The Whitney gin and the wool-carding machine of 1794 found the country "at zero," according to industrialist and historian Chauncey M. Depew, and the starting gun for America's first industrial revolution had sounded. Steamships, electric lights, telegraphs, telephones, phonographs, and moving-picture machines successively helped confirm the promise of an impending utopia that could be glimpsed at places like the New York Crystal Palace in 1853 or the Chicago Columbian Exposition forty years later. In their 1936 book *Art and the Machine*, authors Sheldon and Martha Candler Cheney enthusiastically describe the material output that resulted from the merger of industry and science throughout this period:

> The water turbine, the high-pressure steam boiler, the fabrication of steel, perfection of motor and dynamo: these were factors. Morse, Bessemer, Roebling, Edison were figures. Inventions, discoveries, experiments, and always greater consolidation of capital, greater efforts towards industrial expansion, with more inventions, more discoveries, more experiments following each advance, ultimately inspired that first colossal dream of the machine in which it became an instrument of unparalleled material power, a national dream of an empire of steel and concrete.

BY the close of the nineteenth century, the stuff of a shining, mechanized, Columbian City on the Hill was being prepared with the help of such men as Henry Ford and the Wright brothers. Together, these unlikely Orometheans in boiled goods and eight-quarter caps forged the country's second industrial revolution—a time seen as one that would result in a society replete with things unimaginably modern and cunning.

BUT the rapid advance of American materialism also inspired its own reaction. The Arcadian myth of the late Victorian era that expressed itself in the popular interest in wildlife, parklands, and a kind of suburban pastoralism, dovetailed with art nouveau design, neo-Federalist architecture, and the Arts and Crafts guilds as manifestations of resistance to the seemingly headlong technological progress taking place. Still, the creation of greater buildings, steamships, airplanes, and automobiles could not be abated, and through the course of war and Depression other styles and movements—Prairie School architecture, art deco design, and the development of the skyscraper and streamliner—would eagerly embrace the "newness" of those things they shaped. By the time of the 1933 Chicago Century of Progress Exposition, hard times had charged every new thing with some grand promise, and the designs created to cooly reflect an object's function passionately proclaimed its historical aspirations at the same time. Long before mid-century Christopher Wren's famous epitaph, *Si historium requiris, circumspice* (If you seek history, look around you), would apply to just about every thing in 48 states from the *California Zephyr* to Burma Shave.

"I AM collecting the history of our people," wrote Henry Ford, "as written into the *things* their hands made and used." Insofar as this book is a collection of some 520 historical items that Americans have used (and still make) it harbors some of the same ambition; but as a sourcebook, it's the primary purpose of *The American Historical Supply Catalogue 2* to avail its readers of the opportunity also to acquire those products listed.

OVERWHELMINGLY, the items that follow are not antiques, but newly manufactured products replicating those first made during the period extending roughly from 1900 through 1945. As such, they bring the past into the present in a way that has a cultural curiosity all its own—and taken together they are intended to convey the impression of an early-twentieth-century trade catalog suddenly "come alive" from the past.

The American Historical Supply Catalogue 2: An Early-Twentieth-Century Sourcebook continues the practice begun by its predecessor, subtitled *A Nineteenth-Century Sourcebook* (New York: Schocken Books, 1984), in distinguishing between the varieties of period products that it contains. Thus, as described in this book, a *replica* is an item that has been copied, or replicated, from one once made in the past; a *reproduction* differs in that to make it, a company (usually the original company) has resurrected old molds, dies, formulas, patterns, or plans to produce again an item as it once did, using the same methods and materials; an item *in continual production* is one which, for all intents and purposes, has been uninterrupted in its production since it was first made early in the century; and last, a *remanufactured* item is one that has been rebuilt from predominantly original (but unused) parts to which reproduced or replicated parts have been added. Examples of these in this book are the Indian Chief motorcycles rebuilt by Jacob Junkers, and the Timmis Motor Company's remanufactured 1934 Ford roadsters.

"New York Crystal Palace," an 1853 lithograph by Nathaniel Currier

AS REBUILTS, reproductions, and items in continual manufacture are by nature authentic, it's the replicas in this catalog that bear watching. While it is invariably the shoddy replica that gives a bad name to this entire body of goods, for each manufacturer of such merchandise there is another who, as a result of good faith and devotion to the item and period it represents, makes a superior-quality replica of detailed authenticity. While I've tried to limit the replicas herein to the latter type, I've actually seen only a small portion of those described and (in most cases) have been forced to rely on the intuition I've developed over the course of writing these books. Where the suppliers are themselves quoted it is usually because their descriptions are interesting or succinctly informative, although sometimes a supplier's coyly worded copy is being passed along for the reader's own judgment. It must be noted that neither the author nor the publisher makes any claims about or guarantees the quality or authenticity of any items described in this sourcebook.

FINALLY, as many of the suppliers included in this book have small businesses, subject to the vagaries of the marketplace, prices may have changed without notice and suppliers may even have gone out of business by the time this book is in your hands. It is therefore strongly recommended that where suppliers have allowed their prices to be quoted, the reader use these to infer true current prices and correspond directly with the supplier before sending any money. All prices are quoted postpaid unless otherwise indicated; and when ordering the products described, kindly note any postage and handling charges, and include sales tax where appropriate.

Acknowledgments

THANKS FIRST to Emile Capouya, whose encouragement during the writing of the *American Historical Supply Catalogue* series has been as invaluable a part of its coming about as was his acquisition of it for Schocken Books; and also to my agent Nick Ellison, who encouraged *him*. Thanks as well to Pat Woodruff, my editor, against whose natural kindness and grace no tense situation can endure; to Millicent Fairhurst for first-rate production and art direction; to copy editor Fred Bidgood for not taking hardship pay; to Dick Borden at the Springfield, Massachusetts, post office; and to Ron Fraser, Sooky Goodfriend, Theodore Kelly, Joanne Meyer, Russell Piper, Jr., and Robert Wilson, whose suggestions above-and-beyond-the-call resulted in several excellent product listings.

I AM also grateful to Andrew Anspach of the Hotel Algonquin, Stephanie Bradford of Jenifer House, Janice Casali at Springfield's Lady in Red Antiques, Miles Clark of the Cumberland General Store, Warren Eberspacher at the Historical Aircraft Corporation, Jacob Junkers at Indian Motorcycle News, Bill Shelley at Laff-O-Graph Productions, Ray Wallgren at the Radio Steel Company, Gill Williams of the Vestal Press, and Russell Williams of Eberhard Faber for making my job easier with their intelligence and good natures.

I OWE A DEBT as well to those authors whose books provided me with much in the way of product sources, quotations, and historical lore, especially Betty Cornfeld and Owen Edwards for their *Quintessence*, John Dos Passos for the U.S.A. trilogy, Elizabeth Ewing for the *History of Twentieth Century Fashions*, Stuart Berg Flexner for his epic *Listening to America*, Bernard Grun for the *Timetables of History*, Robert Heide and John Gilman for their *Dime Store Dream Parade*, Bevis Hillier for his excellent *Style of the Century*, Geoffrey Perrett for *America in the Twenties*, and Mitford Mathews for the *Dictionary of Americanisms*.

AND FINALLY, for their suggestions, war stories, and other help, to my friends and family members—Chris Blair, Denis Boyles, George Comtois, Louise Comtois, Richard Erlanger, Katherine Esplin, Baer Frimer, Al Gross, David Kelly, Laura Rankin, Kathy Roche, Karen Spaulding, Ephriam Stein, David Szydlo, Tom Turner, Claire Wellikoff, and Jane Ziegler—my gratitude is warmly acknowledged. This goes particularly for my parents, Joseph and Anne Wellikoff, who over the course of my life have imparted a strong sense of the times through which they've lived; and for my friends Martha Landry and Alan Rose, who over the past several years have done the same for an era that ended before any of us was born.

A.W.

Modern Homes

"HONOR BILT" means a more Substantial Home—a Warm and Comfortable Home—Superior Home for you—and at a big saving in money and time!

They are permanent, high grade homes. "HONOR BILT" Homes are furnished ready cut and fitted. They have double floors, double walls and 2x4-inch studding.

Highest Quality Material

The lumber furnished for "Honor Bilt" homes is bright and new, fine, dry No. 1 framing, clear Cypress for outside finish, and clear siding. Expert mechanics, modern machinery and good materials insure perfectly made millwork. Oak, Birch, Fir or Yellow Pine (as specified) for interior finish—the kind of material that will prove to be a little better than generally used in home construction. Every detail is a quality product.

Easy Payments

If you own a good, well located building lot and have some cash, you can buy an "HONOR BILT" Modern Home, including the Heating, Plumbing and Lighting Fixtures; arrange Easy Monthly Payment Terms, and (in some instances) we will advance part of the cash for labor and such materials as we do not furnish—brick, cement, etc. The monthly payments shown do not include our low interest.

Many of our customers build their own "Honor Bilt" homes, doing part or all of the work themselves, in which case they do not need to put in much cash as we consider the value of their work the same as cash.

Prices for "HONOR BILT" Modern Homes shown on these pages include the ...

Lumber
Lath
Millwork
Doors
Windows

Shingles or Roofing as specified.
We guarantee enough material ... use complete, except cement ... and plaster.

You need ... "HONOR BILT" Modern Homes ... $2,000.00, dep ... for city, sub ... Floor plans are shown for every design. Just a few of the "Honor Bilt" Modern Homes are shown here.

Proofs of Satisfied Customers

We have thousands of letters from customers who have not only saved from $500.00 to $2,000.00, but who happily tell us that ours are the best homes in their locality.

Saved $1,500.00

Sears, Roebuck and Co.
I wish to take this opportunity to express my appreciation of the courtesy and fair treatment you have accorded me. As near as I can estimate I saved about $1,500.00 through building one of your "Honor Bilt" Homes and, as I know very little about carpenter work, I think that a very remarkable saving.

LESLIE F. DRESSLER.

Address Furnished on Request.

"Honor Bilt" Modern Home Conveniences

Above—"HONOR BILT" Kitchen De Luxe White Tile Sink and Drain Board. White Enamel Cupboards.

We feature in addition: A breakfast alcove, wardrobe, clothes closets, folding built-in ironing boards, coal chutes, wall safes, broom closets, etc.

The Puritan. SEVEN ROOMS AND BATH
$2,504 MONTHLY PAYMENTS **$40**

The Conway. FIVE ROOMS AND BATH
$1,614 MONTHLY PAYMENTS **$30**

Standard
Built Homes
From
$520 to $1,041
Choice of
4, 5 or 6
Rooms With Bath

The Grant. SIX ROOMS AND BATH
$1,041 MONTHLY PAYMENTS **$25**

This Free Book of 100 Homes!

Our "Book of Modern Homes, 598K," contains over 100 designs from $520.00 to $4,652.00. Choose from One and Two-story Houses, Bungalows, Income Bungalows, Two-Flat Buildings, Colonials, English, Mission and American types.

It explains our free Architectural Service, Easy Payment Plan, and our successful "Honor Bilt" System.

A magnificent book! Many pages of beautiful color illustrations of exteriors, rotogravure illustrations of furnished interiors and floor plans.

Included are: Sectional Summer Cottages, designed for woods or seashore, from $298.00 up; also 31 wood and steel garages for $86.50 and up.

Ask for "Book of Modern Homes, 598K."

Free Home Exhibits in These Cities

Chicago, Ill., Store, Arthington St. and Central Park Ave. Downtown Exhibit, 10 N. Dearborn St.
Cincinnati, Ohio, 131 W. 4th St.
Cleveland, Ohio, 1013-1017 Euclid Ave., Wurlitzer Bldg.
Columbus, Ohio, 78 S. Third St.
Dayton, Ohio, 49 East 2d St., Columbia Bldg.

Detroit, Mich., 704 Penobscot Bldg., 143-147 Fort St. W.
New York, N. Y., 115 Fifth Ave.
Philadelphia, Pa., Store, 4640 Roosevelt Blvd. Downtown Exhibit, 313 S. Broad St.
Pittsburgh, Pa., 3016-3018 Jenkins Arcade.
Washington, D. C., 704 Tenth St., N. W.

Get this FREE Book of HOMES

Honor Bilt MODERN HOMES Sears, Roebuck and Co.

Ask for 598K

House Plans

FROM SUPERMARKETS to shopping malls, the descendants of the traditional American general store live today in their several overly air-conditioned forms. One place where you can find the real thing still in operation is at the Cumberland General Store in Crossville, Tennessee.

Crossville lies at the heart of the 1933 Homesteads Project, a Roosevelt administration plan to develop acres of surrounding timberland into subsistence farms for the Depression-weary people of the Tennessee mountains. Eleanor Roosevelt, who would address the assembled homesteaders from the back of a lumber truck, was considered the project's "highly placed friend" for her interest in it.

The first ten families moved into Cumberland Homestead's cottage-style houses on December 1, 1934. In her book, *Looking Back: Cumberland Homestead's Golden Anniversary Album*, Emma Jean Pedigo Vaden describes these cottages' unique construction and design:

> The building materials utilized were the timber and stone cleared from the land. The solid masonry walls are 12 inches thick. The interiors are of natural finished tongue-and-grooved panelling with hardwood floors throughout. Project blacksmiths fashioned traditional spade-patterned latches and hinges for all the doors. Each kitchen had a double-basin sink, and a hand-pump over the well. A water-storage tank, located in the attic, provided a gravity-fed water supply to both kitchen and bathroom. Mrs. Roosevelt insisted the houses have bathrooms even though most homes in the region had only outside privies. All houses were electrically wired in anticipation of the TVA electrical power system which was several years in arriving. Designers believed a wood-burning fireplace and a cookstove would sufficiently heat the homes, but the families found them cold during the bitter winter months.

The Cumberland General Store's "Wish and Want Book" offers plans for the "authentic Homestead house," as well as for other early-twentieth-century homes.

"Wish and Want Book," $3.75.

Cumberland General Store

Route 3
Crossville, TN 38555
Tel. 615/484-8481

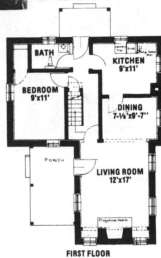

FIRST FLOOR

SECOND FLOOR

Pressed Metal Building Products

OPERATING out of the same building that it moved into at the turn of the century, the W. F. Norman Company manufactures a line of pressed-metal sidewalls, ceilings, wainscoting, and roofs that are unassailable in their authenticity. This is because both the company's production techniques and equipment—which include the use of antique rope-drop hammers—are as unchanged as the factory itself. Many of the dies used are more than 80 years old, and when working in concert with the drop hammers, control quality better than do their modern hydraulic counterparts, says the firm.

Illustrated here is W. F. Norman's Rococo ceiling plate along with several sidewall and cornice designs. Overall, nearly 140 items—including ceiling centers, friezes, and borders—are available in more than forty styles ranging from the late-Victorian period to the early twentieth century. Their material can be painted any color, and either brass or copperplated.

In addition, W. F. Norman has recently reintroduced its 1908 line of Spanish, Mission, Normandie, and Victorian-style pressed-metal roof tiles.

Brochure available.

W. F. Norman Company

P.O. Box 323
Nevada, MO 64772

Dumbwaiters

HAND-OPERATED dumbwaiters have been offered by the Vincent Whitney Company of Sausalito, California, since 1929.

Brochure available.

Vincent Whitney Company

P.O. Box 335
Sausalito, CA 94966
Tel. 415/332-3260

Tin Ceilings

AA ABBINGDON Affiliates of Brooklyn, New York, offers a large line of metal ceilings in turn-of-the-century and modern designs.

Brochure available.

A A Abbingdon Affiliates

2149 Utica Ave.
Brooklyn, NY 11234
Tel. 212/477-6505

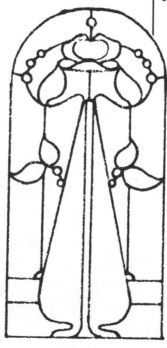

Leaded Art Glass

Don't flinch, don't foul, hit the line hard.

—THEODORE ROOSEVELT

PRESIDENT Theodore Roosevelt (who once delivered a speech in Milwaukee with a would-be assassin's bullet lodged in his chest) had a robust manliness that reflected the mood of turn-of-the-century American culture. Many historians relate both the rise of "jingoism" and women's suffrage to the national tilt toward this "new masculinity," with the decorative arts also strongly affected. This period might be marked from the time when the sinuously curvilinear art nouveau style of the "decadent" 1890s was supplanted by a new, rectilinear style during the first decade of this century.

In stained glass the (curvilinear) art nouveau designs of Louis Comfort Tiffany (1848–1933) not only established the art form domestically, but won for it worldwide recognition.

G. B. Alberts, a follower of Tiffany, founded the Alberts Stained Glass Studio in 1892, a firm considered an important link in the transition of art nouveau design toward the rectilinear. Early in the twentieth century Alberts sold his company to one Edward Penna, an Englishman, who then established the Louisville Art Glass company in Kentucky. Continually in business from that time to this, Louisville Art Glass offers stained-glass sidelights, transoms, and windows in a complete range of art nouveau patterns and designs.

Literature available.

Louisville Art Glass Studio

1110 Baxter Ave.
Louisville, KY 40204
Tel. 502/585-5421

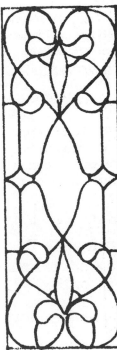

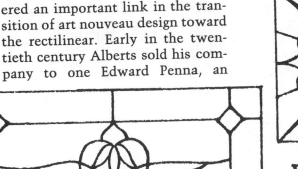

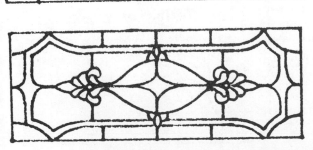

House Paint

DURING the nineteenth and early twentieth centuries the exterior colors of homes were applied in a deliberately architectural way. Combinations of color were seen as aids to enhancing the appearance of a house by further delineating its form.

As outlined in the Sherwin-Williams Company brochure "Heritage of Colors," the period from 1820 to 1920 was marked by six phases during which gradual shifts in the use of exterior colors altered the character of the homes they decorated:

Colors in vogue during the Neoclassic and Early Victorian periods were light and delicate. Richer, deeper, colors evolved in the high and late Victorian eras. The Edwardian period was characterized by a general lightening of the palette. During the Colonial Revival period, colors became even lighter and cleaner.

Sherwin-Williams, which was founded in 1866 and has likely been responsible for the color of more houses than any other company, loaned the use of its archives to Dr. Roger Moss, executive director of the Philadelphia Athenaeum, for the purpose of selecting forty authentic colors representing these architectural periods. Available today through all Sherwin-Williams stores, the "Heritage Colors Collection" includes several colors brought back from our own century's Bungalow and Prairie School (c. 1915), Arts and Crafts (c. 1890–1920), neo-Georgian, and neo-Federal periods (c. 1920).

"Heritage of Colors" brochure, $2.

The Sherwin-Williams Company

101 Prospect Ave. NW
Cleveland, OH 44115

Roycroft Wallpaper

ELBERT HUBBARD, "The Sage of East Aurora," was founder of the Roycroft crafts complex that is still in that pretty Buffalo, New York, suburb. Prior to his untimely death in the sinking of the S.S. *Lusitania,* Hubbard was more than anyone else responsible for the emergence of widespread interest in the American Arts and Crafts movement.

Hubbard, who said "Art is not a thing, it's a way," founded the Roycrofters commune which, although never numbering more than 500 artists and artisans, produced a tremendous amount of finely printed and bound books, artwork, handmade copper, brass, silver, leather and terracotta wares, and furniture. These works are now treasured collector's items, and constitute one of America's most significant episodes in the exercise of design philosophy.

Reproductions of Roycroft wallpaper are available through Craftsmen Design of Boston. The wallpaper is obtainable in one of four color combinations: green and brown, brown and gray, blue and gold, or gray and pink.

Brochure available.

Craftsmen Design (a.k.a. Craftsmen Gallery, Inc.)

P.O. Box 173
Boston, MA 02173
Tel. 617/227-9484

Original Wallpaper

ORIGINAL early-twentieth-century wallpaper is available in limited quantities from the Wallpaper Works of Toronto, Canada.

Price: $20 per roll (plus shipping and insurance).

19- by 19-inch sample books are obtainable with a deposit of $100.

The Wallpaper Works

749 Queen St. West
Toronto, ON M6J 1G1
Canada
Tel. 416/366-1790

Bathroom Fixtures from S. Chris Rheinschild

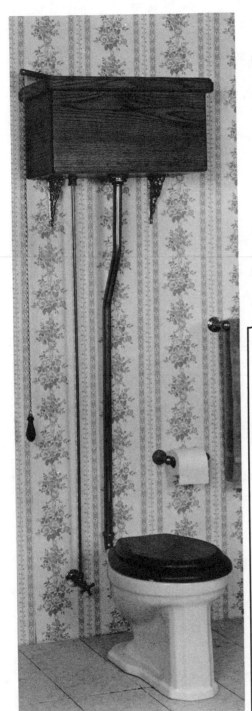

Pull-Chain Toilet

THE RHEINSCHILD pull-chain toilet is a replica of a turn-of-the-century model, updated through the use of materials and construction methods unavailable eighty-five years ago.

The toilet's box tank is made of top-quality solid oak, and is lined with heavy-gauge stainless steel. The valve and flush mechanisms are solid brass pieces.

The toilet comes with a hardwood flush handle and brass pull chain. The flush pipe is also brass, cast in the original offset shape.

Price: $410.

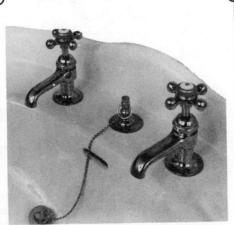

Basin Faucet Set

MADE from polished brass and bearing china insets marked for hot and cold water, this set appears the same as those faucets shown in the Sears catalog of 1908.

Dimensions: height, 4 inches; spout projection, 3 inches.

Price: $82.

All orders require a 50% deposit; the balance, plus packing and shipping charges, is C.O.D.

Oak Medicine Cabinet

IN THE Turn-of-the-century style, this medicine cabinet may be finished to match the pull-chain toilet's seat and box tank. The cabinet has a plate-glass mirror and three adjustable shelves.

Dimensions: 17 inches by 26 inches.

Price: $125.

Brochure available, $1.

S. Chris Rheinschild
2220 Carlton Way
Santa Barbara, CA 93109
Tel. 805/962-8598

From Sunrise Specialty

Clawfoot Bathtubs and Showers

SUNRISE SPECIALTY of Berkeley, California, offers clawfoot bathtubs of the type commonly used early in this century. These are not replicas but salvaged antiques, restored and refitted with new brass fixtures and oak rims. Sunrise Specialty uses the Chicago Faucet Company's taps exclusively. These have been continually manufactured since the late nineteenth century and are the best available.

Also shown are the firm's replica brass shower ring and tub and shower set, the latter including a swivel china-and-brass shower head, separate tub and shower valves, and heavy-walled solid-brass pipe.

Prices: antique tub, $2,050 (crated, shipped freight collect); shower ring with three 24-inch ceiling supports, $125 prepaid; wall shower and tub combination, $365 prepaid.

Oak Low-Boy Water Closet

A MORE conventional-looking commode, and one already replacing the pull-chain w.c. by 1908. Supplied with china bowls, oak seat, and brass flush elbow. **Price:** $550, freight collect.

Pedestal Sink

THIS is the only replica of a late Victorian (c. 1900) pedestal sink on the market. Cast in vitreous china with a porcelain glaze, it fits a 12-inch widespread faucet (not included).

Dimensions: 32 inches high, 24 inches wide, and 20 inches deep.

Price: $400, freight collect.

VISA, MasterCard, American Express, and personal checks accepted. Orders can be shipped C.O.D. with a 50% deposit.

Catalog available, $3.

Sunrise Specialty and Salvage Company

*2210 San Pablo Ave.
Berkeley, CA 94702
Tel. 415/845-4751*

Galvanized-Steel Bathtubs

I was sorry that he was gone . . . and sorrier still that he had carried off my red blanket and my bath-tub.

—MARK TWAIN, *GHOST STORY*, 1896

THESE BATHTUBS, manufactured by the Cumberland General Store, are sometimes considered more comfortable than their enameled counterparts since their (26-gauge) galvanized-steel basins warm faster and their shape allows for a more comfortable reclining position.

The tubs are supported by cradle legs of 2½-inch golden oak, which terminate in curved feet; the rim is capped with the same wood, 3 inches wide. The basin has cutouts for an old-style standard tub faucet, waste drain, and overflow.

Overall dimensions: height, 21¾ inches; length, 59½ inches; width at top of rim, 27 inches.

Price: $450, F.O.B. Crossville, Tennessee.

"Wish and Want Book," $3.75.

Cumberland General Store

*Route 3
Crossville, TN 38555
Tel. 615/484-8481*

Commode Seat

AS PART of their line of products that "you can bet your assets on," DeWeese Woodworking of Philadelphia, Mississippi, offers a solid-oak commode seat with solid-brass hinges. Standard and elongated styles are available.

Brochure available.

DeWeese Woodworking Company

*P.O. Box 576
Philadelphia, MS 39350
Tel. 601/656-4951*

Renovator's Supply, Inc.

THE REMARKABLE success of Renovator's Supply places it at the point position of contemporary interest in quality turn-of-the-century hardware replicas.

Renovator's Supply began business in 1978 when, frustrated by their inability to find a source of authentically replicated fixtures with which to restore their colonial farmhouse in western Massachusetts, Claude and Donna Jeanloz became that source, and set up a mail-order business to supply others. So well were they received that after a single year they had to move the operation into larger quarters (an old Model-T garage with a restored Victorian facade). Since 1985 the Jeanlozes have been posting more than three million copies of their mail-order catalog each year.

This catalog includes solid-brass plumbing fixtures, brass and oaken bath accessories, copper weather vanes, curtains, braided rugs, fireplace accessories, and more. Listed below are samples of some of the items appropriate to this book.

Sussex Widespread Lav Set

THIS SET features porcelain "hot" and "cold" handles with a polished-brass spout and porcelain pop-up knob, and is intended for sinks with their hot and cold water pipe holes set 8–15 inches apart. Includes brass drain. Polished and lacquered.

Dimensions: center of faucet to spigot, 5¼ inches; diameter of porcelain "bells," 3¼ inches.

Price: Renovator's catalog #93015, $390 ($350 each for orders of three or more).

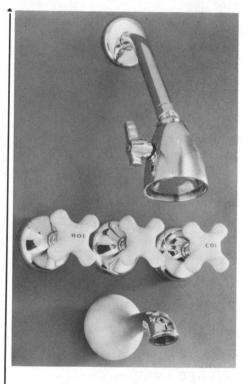

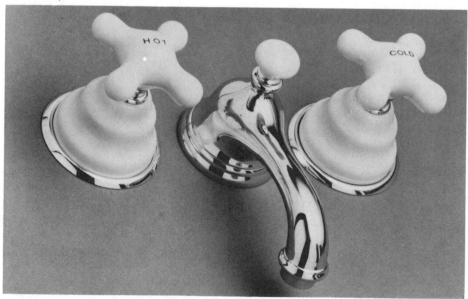

Philadelphia Tub and Shower Set

A POLISHED - BRASS THREE - valve tub and shower set with porcelain cross handles. It comes with a wall-mounted tub spout and shower head.

Price: Renovator's catalog #97519, $205 ($185 each for orders of three or more).

Black Rimlocks

THESE black rimlocks with their white porcelain knobs are really handsome, and, as Renovator's Supply puts it, "a classic combination." They feature working parts of brass and steel, skeleton keys, privacy latch locks, and field-reversible handling. The horizontal rimlock measures 5 inches by 3 inches by ⅝ inch; the vertical rimlock, 4½ inches by 4 inches by ⅝ inch. The knobs of each project 2¾ inches.

Prices: For both the horizontal (Renovator's catalog #26003) and vertical (Renovator's catalog #26004) rimlocks, $34.95 ($29.95 for orders of eight or more, $26.95 for 12 or more).

Pull-Out Plugs

AN OLD-FASHIONED black rubber stopper complete with brass chain and drain ring.

Dimensions: length, 8 inches; pipe diameter, 1¼ inches.

Prices: brass pull-out plug, Renovator's catalog #99079, $15.95 ($11.65 each for orders of three or more); chrome pull-out plug, Renovator's catalog #93047, $8.50 each ($7.65 each for orders of three or more).

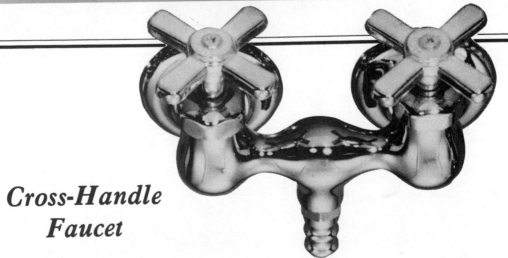

Cross-Handle Faucet

THIS FAUCET OF polished chrome plate over brass is intended for use in clawfoot bathtubs. The hot and cold valves measure 3⅜ inches from center to center. The set is 4½ inches wide and projects 2 inches. A ⅝-inch-diameter spout connects to a hand-held shower. Also available in polished brass.

Price: Renovator's catalog #34551, $39.95 each ($32.75 each for orders of three or more).

Orders of $20 or less require a $2 handling charge.

Color catalog, $2.

The Renovator's Supply
182 Northfield Rd.
Millers Falls, MA 01349
Tel. 413/659-2211

Lighting Fixtures

Satin Brass Finish

These fixtures are very appropriate for those who desire neat appearing, serviceable fixtures at extremely low prices.

The pans and ceiling canopies are made of heavy weight brass nicely finished in brush satin brass and carefully coated with lacquer to preserve the finish. All of these fixtures are equipped with key switches.

Like all of our fixtures these are made in accordance with the requirements of the proper authority for proper installation and the highest grade of material is used throughout and reflected in price.

Satin brass finish. Length, 36 inches. Oval pan of round pan. Frosted glassware. Shipping weight.

34K5912—3 lights............................**$3.50**
Satin brass finish. Length, 36 inches. Top canopy, 4½ inches wide. Frosted glassware. Shipping weight, 8 lbs.

34K5913—3 lights............................**95c**
Satin brass finish. Round pan, 14 inches wide. Use our 34K6825 Lamps shown on page 659. Shipping weight, 8 lbs.

34K5731—5 lights............................
Satin brass finish. Length, 36 inches. Frosted fancy glassware. Shipping weight, 3 pounds.

34K5914—1 light............................**97c**
Satin brass finish. Length, 36 inches. Oval pan, 12 inches long, 6 inches wide. Frosted glassware. Shipping wt., 12 lbs.

34K5915—2 lights............................**$2.50**

34K5916—3 lights............................**$3.00**
Satin brass finish. Length, 36 inches. Round pan, 12 inches wide. Use our 34K6825 Lamps shown on page 659. Shipping weight, 8 lbs.

............................**$2.50**
White frosted glass.............................**$1.00**
Round pan, 12 inches wide. Frosted glass. Shipping weight, 15 pounds.

34K5918—3 lights............................**$2.75**
Satin brass finish. Oval pan. Oval pan, 12x6 inches. Frosted glass. Shipping weight, 10 pounds.

34K5919—2 lights............................**$1.85**

(Image fixture labels: 34K5917 1-Light $1.00; 34K5915 2-Light $2.50; 34K5913 3-Light $1.85; 34K5918 3-Light $2.75; 34K5912 3-Light $3.50; 34K5916 3-Light $3.00; 34K5913 1-Light 95c; 34K5914 1-Light 97c; 34K5731 5-Light $3.50; 34K5734 1-Light $2.50)

Genuine Silver and Black

Silver and black have always been effective in the decorative scheme of the room, not only for its beauty, but also because of its appropriateness. Genuine silver plate, combined with the effect of embossed parts brought out in black, give to these fixtures a strikingly rich, distinctive appearance. Indeed, the long, graceful curves, the scroll designing and the clever embossing, will more than please you. You can rest assured you are offered a real bargain and, as usual, Sears quality is of the best. Length, 36 inches; width, 20 inches. Lamps not included in price. Use our Lamp 34K6825 on 34K5466, 34K5163 and 34K5164 and 34K6878 on 34K5463. Lamps shown on page 659. The fixtures cannot be shipped by parcel post. The brackets match the fixtures. Height, 10 inches; width of wall plate, 4½ in. Each bracket is equipped with a switch.

34K5164—2-Light Bracket. Shipping weight, 5 pounds............................**$3.00**

34K5163—1-Light Bracket. Shipping weight, 4 pounds............................**$2.25**

34K5463—5-Light Ball Lamp Fixture. Shipping weight, 30 pounds.............**$8.50**

34K5466—5-Light Candle Fixture. Shipping weight, 30 pounds.............**$7.95**

(Image fixture labels: 34K5164 2-Light $3.00; 34K5163 1-Light $2.25; 34K5463 5-Light $8.50; 34K5466 6-Light $7.95)

Glass Bowl Fixtures

Metal parts satin brass finish. Length, 36 inches. Frosted glass, fancy design 14x16-inch bowl, and side lights to match.

34K5946—Has one keyless socket inside of bowl, but no side lights. Shipping weight, 15 pounds............................**$3.00**

34K5947—Has one keyless socket inside of bowl, and three side lights with key sockets. Shipping weight, 23 pounds............................**$5.00**

(Image fixture labels: 34K5946 1-Light $3.00; 34K5947 4-Light $5.00)

Bedroom Lighting Fixtures

These fixtures have been specially designed for the lighting of bedrooms. They are also very appropriate for sun parlors and breakfast rooms. Beautifully embossed cast metal, finished in old ivory, with dainty decorations of green leaves and pink flowers. The ball lamps are not included in the price. Use our lamps 34K6825 on 34K5155, and lamp 34K6878 on 34K5325, 34K5327 and 34K5216. For lamps see page 659.

34K5155—1-light bracket. Wall plate, 9½x4¾ inches. Extends 4¼ inches. Equipped with switch. Shpg. wt., 5 lbs. Less lamps............................**$2.00**

34K5216—1-light ceiling fixture. Length, 5 inches; width, 7 inches. Keyless socket. Shipping weight, 3 pounds. Less lamps............................**$1.15**

34K5325—2-light. Length, 5 in. Oval cast plate, 11½x5¼ inches. Keyless socket. Shipping weight, 5 pounds. Less lamps............................**$2.00**

34K5327—3-light. Length, 5 in.; width, 10¾ inches. Triangular shaped cast plate. Keyless socket. Shipping weight, 5 lbs. Less lamps............................**$2.75**

(Image fixture labels: 34K5325 2-Light $2.00; 34K5327 3-Light $2.75; 34K5155 1-Light $2.00; 34K5216 1-Light $1.15)

Genuine Silver Plate Fixtures

You have only to look at the illustration to see the grace and charm of the designing of these fixtures, and you can easily imagine the soft and lovely effect of Genuine Silver Plate. These fixtures are very popular, as their simple lines harmonize with the majority of homes, and add to the loveliness of the room.

These fixtures are 36 inches long and 19 inches wide. Lamps not included in price. 34K5472 and 34K5473 take 34K6878 lamps and 34K5444 and 34K5445 take 34K6825 lamps, shown on page 659. These fixtures are not mailable. Shipping weight, 17 pounds.

34K5472—4 lights............................**$7.45**
34K5473—Same as above, but 5 lights.......**8.79**
34K5444—4 lights............................**6.75**
34K5445—Same as above, but 5 lights.......**8.25**

(Image fixture labels: 34K5444 4-Light $6.75; 34K5473 5-Light $8.79)

Street Lamps

They went way out Rhode Island Avenue and circled round back by the Old Soldiers' Home. There was no air anywhere and the staring identical street-lights went by on either side, lighting segments of monotonous rustling trees.
—JOHN DOS PASSOS, *THE 42ND PARALLEL*, 1929

FULLY RESTORED original 1920s street lamps are available from Lamp Light Industries of Elyria, Ohio. Featuring an earlier, turn-of-the-century design, these lamps were handmade by skilled craftsmen a generation ago. They are available today in limited numbers featuring cast-iron fluted columns ranging in height from 10 to 22 feet, with three styles of lanterns. The lenses can be either Lexan or glass, and are fitted with a standard mogal base socket for the incandescent bulb.

Price: including cast-iron fluted pedestal, decorative center and top castings, tapered cast-steel column, cast aluminum, copper and brass lantern with Lexan or glass lens and fixture, and installation instructions, $1,495, F.O.B. Elyria, Ohio.

Literature available.

Lamp Light

135 Yorkshire Court
Elyria, OH 44035
Tel. 216/365-4954
(phone collect when ordering)

Churchill Desk Lamp

THE ORIGINAL of the replica lamp we see here was made around 1900 when Winston Churchill was a 26-year-old correspondent covering the Boer War. During World War II, while he occupied posts as Britain's chairman of the Armed Services Committee, prime minister, minister of defence, and First Lord of the Treasury, it occupied a place on his desk. The Orvis company's replica lamp is made of solid brass and has a hand-blown triplex shade consisting of three layers of glass: one clear, one white, and one green. It stands 15 inches high and weighs 4½ lbs.

Price: $130 (plus $3.50 for shipping and handling).

Gift and clothing catalog available.

Orvis

Manchester, VT 05254
Tel. 802/362-1300

Aladdin Mantle Lamps

When he was well past [the cabin] he saw that the light on the window was not the light of the moon. A lamp burned inside, and out of the walls came the low outcry of voices.

—ELIZABETH MADOX ROBERTS, "DEATH AT BEARWALLOW," 1927

WITH a new burner that improved upon the old wick oil lamp's candlepower while reducing its smokiness, "mantle lamps" were developed by Victor Samuel Johnson in 1909. Marketing his invention through the Mantle Lamps Company, Mr. Johnson chose a name to imbue his lamp's evident powers with an Arabian mystique.

But this was not enough to sustain the Aladdin Mantle Lamp after the Rural Electrification Administration brought 60 cycles into every remote bayou, flat, and mountain holler in 1936. There would be no mass market for any mantle lamp after the 1928 Model No. 12—not until lately, that is.

Today Aladdin sells the old No. 12 as the "Brass Heritage Lamp," a 23-inch reproduction available in a choice of three period shades. This time around, you can get an electrical converter too.

Suggested retail **prices:** Brass Heritage Lamp with opal white shade (catalog #B2301-653), $109.95; with crystal champagne shade (catalog #B2301-672), $116.95; with dogwood shade (catalog #B2301-661), $127.95. Electric converter kit (catalog #N185B), $21.95 (plus $2.20 for postage and handling).

Color brochure available.

Obtainable through local retail outlets or from:

Aladdin Service & Products

P.O. Box 100960
Nashville, TN 37210
Tel. toll free 800/251-4535

Aladdin's Brass Heritage Mantle Lamp with (contemporary) Morning Glory shade

Art Nouveau Lamps

WHEN THE Paris-based art nouveau movement first arose in the 1880s, the electric light was still a relative novelty. As a result the art nouveau household accorded lighting fixtures a unique status as quasi-scientific *objets d'art* that enriched the organic motif of their setting by assuming the forms of gracefully arched flowers and plants.

The Elegant Cat company of Eureka, California, offers a line of replica art nouveau lamps that can serve as inexpensive alternatives to the originals. The firm can provide customers with a selection of bases and shades for both floor and table models.

Brochure available.

The Elegant Cat

1440 B St.
Eureka, CA 95501
Tel. 707/445-0051

Ceiling and Wall Fixtures

The Oregon-based Rejuvenation House Parts Company has been in operation replicating turn-of-the-century fixtures since 1977. Their line of gas and electric shades, sconces, ceiling lights, and chandeliers is handcrafted in the same manner and using the same materials as the originals they follow.

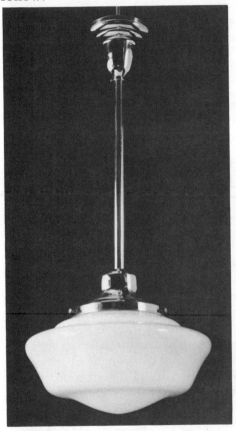

The Overlook

THIS four-light chandelier is modeled after one described as "very appropriate for those who desire neat-appearing, serviceable fixtures at extremely low price" by the Sears, Roebuck and Company catalog of 1927. The fixture has a diameter of 18 inches and a standard length of 36 inches (minimum length: 26 inches). The Overlook accepts 60-watt bulbs and is also available in a three-light unit.

Price: Rejuvenation catalog #CN4E, $120, lacquered.

The Mount Tabor

ON THE SAME 1927 page is the original Mount Tabor, a three-light fixture with an 18-inch diameter and a 10-inch length. As replicated by Rejuvenation House Parts, this fixture is also available with two, three, four, or five lights, each accepting 60-watt bulbs.

Prices: Mount Tabor two-light electric, Rejuvenation catalog #CT2E, $88 unlacquered, $97 lacquered; three-light electric, Rejuvenation catalog #CT3E, $96 unlacquered, $106 lacquered; four-light electric, Rejuvenation catalog #CT4E, $104 unlacquered, $114 lacquered; five-light electric, Rejuvenation catalog #CT5E, $112 unlacquered, $123 lacquered. Add $10 each for postage and handling.

Model CL6

THE "SCHOOLHOUSE" fixture popular from 1905 into the 1930s. Standard length is 35 inches; standard width, 12 inches. Accepts a 150-watt bulb.

Price: Rejuvenation catalog #CL6, $39 unlacquered, $43 lacquered (plus $8 for each lamp for postage and handling).

The Ladd's Addition

AN early-twentieth-century bowl light fixture with a diameter of 14 inches and a standard length of 30 inches (minimum length: 22 inches). The Ladd's Addition accepts three 60-watt bulbs.

Price: Rejuvenation catalog #CDB, $122 unlacquered, $134 lacquered.

VISA and MasterCard accepted. All orders must be accompanied by a check, money order, or charge card number. Unless otherwise specified, all items require an additional 10% of the cost to cover postage and handling.

Catalog, $3.

Rejuvenation House Parts Co.

901 N. Skidmore
Portland, OR 97217
Tel. 503/249-0774

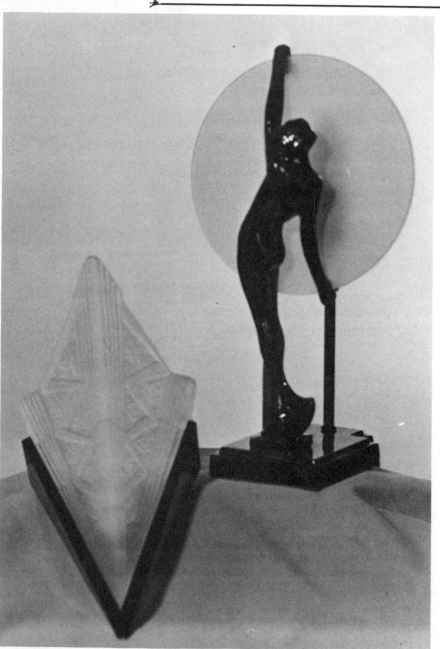

Art Deco Lighting

FRANKART, INC., was a small New York company that specialized in the manufacture of stylized art deco clocks, lamps, ashtrays, cigarette boxes, candy containers, fishbowl stands, bookends, vases, candle holders, floor ashtrays, and coffee tables. Using one or more nude statuettes, the furnishings were spray-painted in either gunmetal black enamel or "Depression green," a patina intended to suggest aged copper or bronze. These were generally sold in department stores and the better gift shops.

Frankart lamps were particularly the rage during the 1930s and invariably showed a nude dancer posing reverentially with the sun. The Sarsaparilla company's replica of a circa-1927 Frankart piece is a "shadow lamp" showing its nymph in silhouette for greater dramatic effect. Sarsaparilla's Nymph with Glass Disc lamp is shown here along with their replica French deco wall sconce, circa 1922.

Prices: Sarsaparilla #132B1, Frankart lamp, $130; Sarsaparilla #117B1, deco wall sconce, $85.

Sarsaparilla Deco Designs, Ltd.

5711 Washington St.
West New York, NJ 07093
Tel. 201/863-8002

From Bradford Consultants

Tungsten Lamps

> To find a filament for his electric lamp that would work . . . he tried all kinds of paper and cloth, thread, fishline, fibre, celluloid, boxwood, cocoanutshells, spruce, hickory, bay, mapleshavings, rosewood, punk, cork, flax, bamboo, and the hair out of a redheaded Scotchman's beard.
>
> —JOHN DOS PASSOS, *THE 42ND PARALLEL*, 1929

THOMAS EDISON first went with the bamboo, then with carbon, which could sustain only enough heat to produce an amber light—good enough for the 1800s perhaps, but the centenary demanded far more brilliance. Edison's research showed that only filaments made of tungsten, then a rare and intractable metal, could provide the necessary candlepower. New methods were then developed to win commercial quantities of tungsten from the ore to which it clung.

The Mazda bulb—a tungsten lamp named for the Persian goddess of light—was introduced in 1909 and quickly replaced its crepuscular predecessor. The Mazda was so successful that versions of it remained in use through 1930. Straight-sided, and possessing a zigzag tungsten filament, Bradford Consultants' Eureka is an authentic replication of this historic bulb. It is 60 watts, 120 volts, with a standard medium base.

Prices: Type "T" (for the period 1909–1920), $6 each ($5.75 each for orders of 12 or more, $5.50 each for orders of 72 or more); Type "P" (for the period 1920–1930), $5.80 each ($5.55 each for orders of 12 or more, $5.30 each for orders of 72 or more).

Thomas Edison strains to hear Henry Ford during ceremonies honoring the 50th anniversary of the invention of the incandescent light, October 21, 1921.
CREDIT: PICTORIAL PARADE

Silk Fabric Lamp Cord

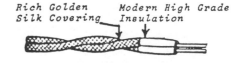

"TWISTED" fabric lamp cords, almost universal until World War II, have been replicated by Bradford Consultants of Collingswood, New Jersey.

Bradford's Apollo Golden lamp cord combines modern high-grade insulation with a covering of woven "Old Gold" silk to combine safety and authenticity. The Apollo cord is intended for use at a maximum of 120 volts, and for low power loads not exceeding 3 amps or 360 watts incandescent lamp load at 120 volts.

Price: $1.95 per foot (plus $2 shipping per order).

Literature available.

Bradford Consultants

*16 East Homestead Ave.
Collingswood, NJ 08108
Tel. 609/854-1404*

Windsor Style Matched Chair and Rocker

Sold for Cash Only

Just different enough in design to add a distinctive note to the furnishings of your living room. You'll like the solid appearance of the wide spread legs supported by the double cross stretchers. The slanting back rail that helps to form the sides is exceptionally comfortable. The backs are just the right height for complete relaxation. The saddle shape seats are deep and comfortable. In these pieces, in typical colonial style, the seats are lower. Strongly, carefully constructed of hardwood, in choice of mahogany or walnut finishes. Size of seat, 19x17½ inches. Height of the back, 24 inches. Height of seat from floor, 17½ inches. Shipping weight, each piece, 25 lbs.

	Mahogany Finish	Walnut Finish
1K1461—Chair	$6.25	$6.35
1K1462—Rocker	6.35	6.45

See page 685 for the new Electric Fireplace Grate.

Furniture

Our Finest Rocker Built for Style and Comfort

Sag Seat Style

$13.45

The sag seat is supported on a criss-cross webbing base. Upholstered in an attractive pattern of velour in choice of blue or mulberry. The back of the back is plain velour. The frame is of fine hardwood finished in dark walnut. Very strongly constructed; the arms are connected to the front posts by steel braces. Size of seat, 22½x12½ inches. Height of back, 22½ inches. Shipping weight, 30 pounds. Be sure to state choice of upholstery color.

1K546—Cash only $13.45

Comfortably Designed —Beautifully Upholstered

Spring Cushion Seat

$8.95

Cash Only

Has a genuine auto type spring seat, upholstered in fine quality blue velour, and supported by 9 cushion springs. The frame is of fine kiln dried hardwood finished in dull walnut. The frame is exceptionally well made with steel corner angle braces supporting the underconstruction of the seat and the arms and front posts. High comfortable back. Size of seat, 19x17 inches. Height of back, 22 inches. Shipping weight, 24 pounds.

1K1469 ....$8.95

Auto Type Spring Filled Cushion

$9.35

Tapestry

Full box type of upholstered cushion with 9 springs in the seat. The center spring is extra deep, allowing extra "give" at the center of the cushion. Form fitting curved back. The runners are broad, long and smoothly turned, allowing smooth rocking action. The frame is made of quality hardwood, finished in walnut. The seat is upholstered in tapestry or choice of blue, taupe or mulberry velour. Seat, 19x18 inches. Height of back, ... Shipping weight, 27 pounds.

Tapestry seat $9.35
... seat. State choice of color. 9.45

Genuine Leather Seat Rocker

Genuine Auto Type Spring Seat

$9.95

Cash Only

Every home has need of such a restful, decorative rocker. It is just one outstanding example of the savings you can make when you buy furniture here. Solidly constructed of kiln dried hardwood, satin finish in walnut. Two-tone back. The seat is supported by 9 springs and is upholstered in genuine leather, brown Spanish grained. Size of seat, 18¾x17 inches. Height of back, 22¼ inches. Shipping weight, 28 pounds.

1K1458 ....$9.95

$5.00 DOWN
$5.00 MONTH

Cash Only

Comfortable Deep Upholstered Wing Rocker

Neat in appearance and very comfortable. Deep padded wings and back; the seat is supported by 8 coil springs fastened to steel bands. The back is reinforced by steel bands. The frame is of kiln dried hardwood richly finished in mahogany. Upholstered all over in artificial leather, brown Spanish grained, or with the back, the seat and arms in genuine leather, brown Spanish grained, and the balance in artificial leather. Size of seat, 22x20 in. Height of back, 25 in. Shipping weight, 65 pounds. Packed to secure lowest transportation charges. Easily put together.

1K1471—Artificial leather $11.25
Genuine leather 17.35

Cash Only

Relax in This Rocker

Has an Extension Foot Rest and Reclining Back

The reclining back is adjustable to three positions; the foot rest, which folds out of sight when not in use, is extended to a comfortable "stretch out" length. The seat is supported by 4 deep spiral springs. The seat and back are softly padded. Mahogany finish hardwood frame. Upholstered in choice of imitation or genuine leather, brown Spanish grained, or blue or taupe velour. Seat, 19x18 in. Height of back, 23½ in. Shipping weight, 55 pounds. Packed to secure lowest transportation rates. Easily put together.

1K1429—Imitation leather $12.55
Genuine leather 17.85
Blue or taupe velour. State color 16.35

This rocker suggests luxurious rest. So wide, deep and inviting, and so softly upholstered. The cushion seat has 9 springs; the back has 11 springs. All parts are softly padded. The frame is of kiln dried hardwood, finished in mahogany. Upholstered in genuine leather, brown Spanish grained, with the outside of the arms and back in artificial leather. Size of seat, 20x18 inches. Height of back, 25 inches. Shipping weight, 95 pounds. Shipped set up.

Spring Filled Seat and Back

1K1479—Genuine brown Spanish leather. Cash price....$30.85
Genuine brown Spanish leather. Easy payment price 33.95

Terms: $5.00 down and $5.00 a month. Use Time Payment Order Blank on page 1092.

Murphy Beds

WILLIAM L. MURPHY, born in Stockton, California, in the 1870s, went to San Francisco near the turn of the century to find a wife. As he could afford only one room, Murphy devised a way of sticking his bed up into the wall so he could entertain his intended while at the same time allaying any fears *she* might have entertained concerning his honor. In 1900 Murphy secured a patent for the "Murphy-In-A-Door-Bed."

While it wouldn't be long before the flapping Murphy bed would become a standard silent-film-comedy prop, for both its economy and common sense the Murphy bed caught on big. The bed helped some during the Depression, but soon postwar prosperity would make it seem old-fashioned.

Today, while the Murphy Door Bed Company is run by Clark M. Murphy (grandson of William L. and his San Francisco bride), the postwar generation that's come of age to find rental space again dear has rediscovered the hide-away bed.

Prices: from $260 for a Murphy bed accommodating a 39- by 70-inch mattress with no headboard, to $890 for a panel-bottomed bed accommodating a 54- by 80-inch mattress and box spring.

Literature and price list available.

Murphy Door Bed Company

40 E. 34th St.
New York, NY 10016
Tel. 212/682-8936

1926 Model Murphy Bed

Adirondack Lawn Chair

THEY ARE immortalized in artist Fairfield Porter's painting *July* —three white Adirondack lawn chairs contemplating a landscape of evergreens and lawn. Highly apparent here are their most salient features: the slanted, high-slat backs and the continuous pieces that both support the seat and become the rear legs.

While their specific origin remains murky, what evidence there is places the first Adirondack lawn chairs in the New York forest for which they are named. They can be remembered there gracing the broad porches and lawns of the clubs, summer retreats, and sanitariums that were built at the beginning of the century. Painted white, red, or dark green, they share a resemblance to the Arts and Crafts chairs that were their contemporaries, and their ingenious design makes them far more comfortable than seems possible for so hard and inexpensive a seat.

The Adirondack Store's lawn chairs are made from seasoned oak (knotty pine was the original material, which explains the inevitable paint job) and must be assembled from four pieces. All necessary hardware is included.

Dimensions: 39 inches high, 23 inches wide, and 35 inches deep.

Price: $88, plus $10 for shipping ($14 to the West Coast).

Brochure available.

Adirondack Store and Gallery

109 Saranac Ave.
Lake Placid, NY 12946
Tel. 518/523-2646

Office Furniture Kits from Craftsman's Corner

Roll-Top Desk

It was a relief to get back to the office where the enlisted men were moving in newly arrived American rolltop desks.

—JOHN DOS PASSOS, *NINETEEN NINETEEN, 1930*

THIS turn-of-the-century roll-top desk kit has been sized down from the period office furniture that it replicates, and is billed as suitable for home use as well as office. Craftsman's Corner claims that in its pigeonholing, fully finished back, S-curve top, and shaped oaken drawer pulls the desk otherwise duplicates original versions.

Dimensions: 54 inches wide, 45 inches high, and 26 inches deep.

Price: Craftsman's Corner catalog #223S, $1,389, freight collect.

Swivel Chair

"Even at this moment, my friends, we are under fire ready to make the supreme sacrifice that civilization shall not perish from the Earth." Major Wood leaned back in his swivel chair and let out a squeak that made everybody look up with a start and several people looked out of the window as if they expected to see a shell from Big Bertha hurtling right in on them.

—JOHN DOS PASSOS, *NINETEEN NINETEEN, 1930*

"**R**EVOLVING office chair with Bank of England arm" reads the 1908 Sears catalog's description of the swivel chair most resembling that offered by Craftsman's Corner in kit form. Both chairs are made of solid oak, but the unfinished modern replica kit costs about twenty-five times as much! The chair is intended as a companion to their roll-top desk kit.

Dimensions: 23 inches wide, 24 inches deep, with adjustable height.

Price: Craftsman's Corner catalog #062S, $239.95, freight collect.

Filing Cabinets and Stacking Barrister's Bookshelves

CRAFTSMAN'S CORNER offers these two- and three-drawer filing cabinets, and the stacking barrister's bookshelves—all made of oak in kit form—as companion pieces to the swivel chair and roll-top desk kits above.

Prices: Craftsman's Corner catalog #235S, two-drawer filing cabinet kit, $229.95 (plus $28 for shipping and handling); catalog #084S, three-drawer filing cabinet kit, $299.95 (plus $34 for shipping and handling); catalog #963S, barrister's cabinet single-shelf-unit kit, $94.95 (plus $12 for shipping and handling); catalog #962S, barrister's cabinet base and top trim kit, $34.95 (plus $6.50 for shipping and handling).

Color catalog available.

Craftsman's Corner Woodcraft Collection
4012 N.E. 14th St.
Des Moines, IA 50302

Alvar Aalto
Furniture

AT FIRST GLANCE the stools depicted here seem altogether too commonplace to warrant the recognition they've received by the Museum of Modern Art and other arbiters of what goes for the best in twentieth-century design. But look again and their practical form emerges—distinct enough to dispel their memory as fixtures in the homes of bohemian 1950s suburbanites.

While familiarity may breed contempt, ubiquity (at least in this instance) need not connote commonness. For in one of those rare instances where the quality of a designer's work has not been sullied by his wide appeal, Alvar Aalto, one of the early twentieth century's greatest designers, is today one of its most popular.

Aalto, a Scandinavian who died in 1976, was committed to a type of modernism that departed from the austerity of the Bauhaus School to incorporate, for all its functionalism, a welcome friendliness. "To be surrounded by Aalto's furniture," writes Paul Goldberger, architectural critic for the *New York Times*, "is to be bathed in a kind of warm, confident glow." This effect is attributable to Aalto's use of biomorphic curves and lightly colored wood veneers.

In addition to his three- and four-legged stools, several of Alvar Aalto's chairs and tables are manufactured by Artek, a Finnish company that has made all the Aalto pieces since they first went into production in the late 1920s. All are marketed in the United States by ICF (formerly International Contract Furnishings), Inc., of New York.

For further information, contact:

ICF, Inc.
305 E. 63rd St.
New York, NY 10021
Tel. 212/750-0900

Arts and Crafts Furniture

THE Arts and Crafts movement, begun in England by William Morris (1834–1896), combined with several kindred notions in the theory of design to flourish early in the twentieth century.

Arts and Crafts theory was derived from Morris's belief that a society debilitated by the Industrial Revolution could be regenerated by a return to the production of hand-crafted goods though a system of medieval-style guilds. Strongly influenced by Celtic (some also say Dutch, others Spanish) antecedents, Arts and Crafts (or "Mission," as it popularly came to be called) furniture was identified by its use of bracingly clean, rectilinear forms, warmly executed in fumed oak. By the turn of the century the aesthetic of Morris and others among the movement's founders began to dovetail with the notions of still more men. Notable among these was Charles Rennie MacIntosh (1868–1928), a Scotsman generally recognized as the supreme genius of European design throughout this

Stickley armchair by Craftsmen Design

period. MacIntosh was the leading advocate of the use of straightforward rectilinear lines to replace the Paris-based 1890s art nouveau curvilinear, which he characterized as "melted margarine."

While MacIntosh's most devoted American follower was Elbert Hubbard—an eccentric Chicagoan whose Roycroft Institution employed 500 workmen by the 1920s—the leading domestic exponent of Mission design is generally recognized to be Gustav Stickley. Stickley's book, *What Is Wrought in the Craftsman Workshops,* is discussed later in this section.

Boston's Craftsmen Design began the production of its "Renaissance Furniture"—custom replicas of MacIntosh, Stickley, Limbert, and Roycroft designs—when it was asked to produce several Stickley prototypes for the Greene and Greene Interiors 1983 Exhibit in Pasadena, California. Each of Craftsmen Design's replicas is branded and dated to avoid being mistaken for original pieces.

Craftsmen Design also replicates the furniture of Frank Lloyd Wright, the influence upon whom by MacIntosh et al. appears evident in the accompanying photos of Craftsmen Design replicas of his and Stickley's spindle chairs. But fearful of being too closely identified with the advocacy of handicrafts, the ever-irascible Wright denounced such comparisons with passion, making the point that the Industrial Age's influence on his "organic" design was a welcome one. Machinery, said Wright, was his God, and if the architecture of the machine age was rubbish, then the machine was the victim and not the cause. Wright scorned Mission furniture for being "plain as a barn door," while vaunting his own work as "truly simple" in comparison.

Despite the arcane posturing and

Frank Lloyd Wright oak spindle side chair with leather slip seat

theorizing behind it, Arts and Crafts furniture grew to become extremely popular early in the century when it could be found throughout the great houses of the rich, the bungalows of the bohemian, and the Colonial revival homes of the middle class alike.

Craftsmen Design's custom work relies on the customer's selection of specific original pieces for replication. Company president Roger L. Conant Williams recommends two books—*The Collected Works of Gustav Stickley* by Stephen Gray and Robert Edwards, and *The Mission Furniture of L. & J. G. Stickley*, edited by Stephen Gray (both published by Turn of the Century editions and available through Craftsmen Design)—as suitable starting points for research.

Brochure obtainable.

Craftsmen Design (a.k.a. Craftsmen Gallery, Inc.)

P.O. Box 173
Boston, MA 02173
Tel. 617/227-9484

The Furniture of Frank Lloyd Wright

FRANK LLOYD WRIGHT, (1867–1959), America's most famous (and as he himself once testified under oath, America's greatest) architect, designed more than 600 commercial and residential buildings in his lifetime, of which 400 were built. These include such celebrated structures as Chicago's 1909 Robie House, Pennsylvania's 1936 Falling Water, and New York City's 1956 Guggenheim Museum. Despite being abandoned in the rush to adore the imported German Bauhaus School of design, the "organic" style and open, flowing space, horizontal planes, integrated structure, and use of local materials that characterized Wright's Prairie School was long the standard for indigenous American design, and has had an influence on modern residential architecture unlike that of any other style.

Wright generally worked alone, and his approach to design was intensely personal. Among its tenets was the belief that furnishings should complement the buildings that they furnish. This led Wright to create a great deal of the decorative designs used in his buildings— and the owner of one of his houses

was once even required to wear a Wright-designed dress.

Today, because of Wright's grand reputation, and due to the increasingly high level of public interest in architecture, interior design, and classic decorative design objects generally, originals of Wright's decorative designs have been selling for record prices—one of the stained-glass windows Wright designed for the Martin House in Buffalo, New York, recently brought $110,000. Now, authenticated reproductions of several pieces of Frank Lloyd Wright's furniture will for the first time become available through Atelier International of New York City.

As part of Atelier's "Masters Collection"—which includes reproductions of modern classic furniture by Le Corbusier, Charles Rennie MacIntosh, Gerrir Thomas Rietveld, and Erik Gunnar Asplund—Atelier will begin selling reproductions of Wright's furniture in the spring of 1987. This line was created with the cooperative research, design, and licensing of the Frank Lloyd Wright Foundation of Scottsdale, Arizona.

For further information, contact:

Atelier International

595 Madison Ave.
New York, NY 10022
Tel. 212/644-0400

Institutional-Style Chairs

"**T**HEY WERE ORIGINALLY used for institutions —government agencies, hospitals, and schools," writes former fashion designer Deborah Donchian of the Thirties-era aluminum chairs she now replicates. "The old ones can usually be found with a greenish-silver coating of enamel paint. Once the paint is removed chemically, underneath lies a beautiful aluminum chair!"

Made in the United States, the chairs are 100% welded aluminum. They are available in both armchair and armless versions, with either a clear lacquer finish or anodyzed in a series of colors.

Prices: $230 each (armchair), $200 (armless). Anodyzed blue, turquoise, violet, emerald, red, or black: $50 additional (minimum order of four chairs per color).

DecoTech

148 E. 89th St.
New York, NY 10128
Tel. 212/860-7627

Frankart Statues

"**I**F YOU WATCH THE Busby Berkeley films *Gold Diggers of 1933, Dames* (1933), or *Footlight Parade* (1933) closely you will notice a Frankart 'greenie' [a Depression-green-colored statue] on a mirrorized coffee table, vanity, or nightstand in Ruby Keeler's or Joan Blondell's apartment," Robert Heide and John Gilman wrote in their 1979 book, *Dime-Store Dream Parade.* In 1933 a Frankart standing-lady ashtray similar to the one shown here was sold through the L. & C. Mayers merchandise catalog for $14.

Prices: Sarsaparilla #105BC, aluminum-alloy ashtray or planter, $125; Sarsaparilla #190, replica 1927 aluminum Frankart nymph-and-frog bookend statue, $45.

Sarsaparilla Deco Designs, Ltd.

5711 Washington St.
West New York, NJ 07093
Tel. 201/863-8002

National Trust for Historic Preservation

Statuettes by Daniel Chester French

Chartered by Congress in 1949 to encourage public participation in the "preservation of districts, sites, buildings, and objects significant to American history and culture," the National Trust for Historic Preservation not only provides advisory, financial, and educational assistance to appropriate organizations and individuals, but owns many historic properties as well. Membership in the National Trust and the purchase of the items below aids the organization in its efforts on behalf of our national heritage.

SCULPTOR DANIEL CHESTER FRENCH (1850 – 1931), best known for the seated but nonetheless monumental sculpture of Abraham Lincoln (1922) that fills the Lincoln Memorial in Washington, D.C., also produced statuary on a less grandiose scale. Reproductions of two of these, *Rip Van Winkle* (1925) and the plaster *Andromeda Maquette* (1929), are available from the National Trust.

Of *Andromeda* French once wrote, "I still believe that the beauty of woman is beauty at its best and highest." The reproduction of the plaster maquette he created to express this view measures 5¼ inches and is priced at $35 (plus $2.25 for shipping). *Rip Van Winkle*, the original of which is near the entrance to Washington Irving's Irvington-on-Hudson, New York, estate, is made of bonded bronze and measures 18 inches in height.

The **price** for the *Rip Van Winkle* statuette is $105 (plus $12.50 for shipping).

Catalog available, $1.

Preservation Shops

Dept. AH
National Trust for Historic
* Preservation*
1600 H St. NW
Washington, DC 20006
Tel. 202/673-4200

Arts & Crafts Furniture Books from the American Life Foundation

The American Life Foundation is a nonprofit educational institution devoted to the study of how the social functions of artifacts from the American past relate to those of today. In recent years the foundation has been republishing many nineteenth- and early-twentieth-century books concerning architecture and the decorative arts to assist restorers of old buildings.

What Is Wrought in the Craftsman Workshops

by Gustav Stickley

BEGINNING WITH Stickley's apt-as-ever dictum "Richness does not entail luxury nor simplicity cheapness," this 1904 publication lards its documentation of the early Arts and Crafts style with the movement's companion philosophy.

Paperback, 96 pages, 7 by 10 inches.

Price: $7.

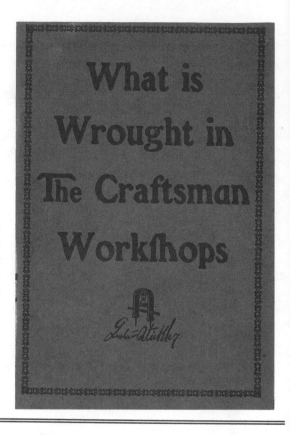

The Arts & Crafts Furniture of Charles P. Limbert

TWO CATALOGS (originally published in 1904 and 1910 respectively) of Charles P. Limbert's Holland Dutch Arts and Crafts furniture show the entrepreneurial side of the popular Mission style. The philosophical musings of the Arts and Crafts movement's early proponents here take on a more commercial pitch as Limbert's copy rails against "the vulgarly ornate and elaborately carved and fretted monstrosities of the mid-Victorian age." Introduction by Robert L. Edwards.

Paperback, 128 pages, 7 by 10 inches.

Price: $9.

The Arts & Crafts Furniture of CHARLES P. LIMBERT

Two catalogues with an introduction by Robert L. Edwards

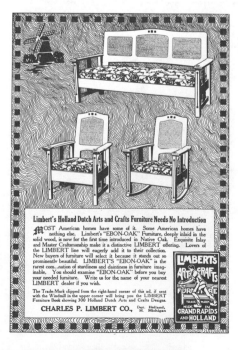

From The Wicker Revival by James Lazear

The Wicker Revival

by James Lazear

NEARLY 200 different kinds of wicker furniture from the nineteenth and twentieth centuries, of which more than 150 are from the rare 1904 catalog of Joseph P. McHugh, one of the Mission style's most successful innovators.

Paperback, 80 pages, 5½ by 8½ inches.

Price: $6.

Include $2 on all orders to cover the cost of shipping.

Brochure available.

American Life Foundation and Study Institute

P.O. Box 349
Watkins Glen, NY 14891

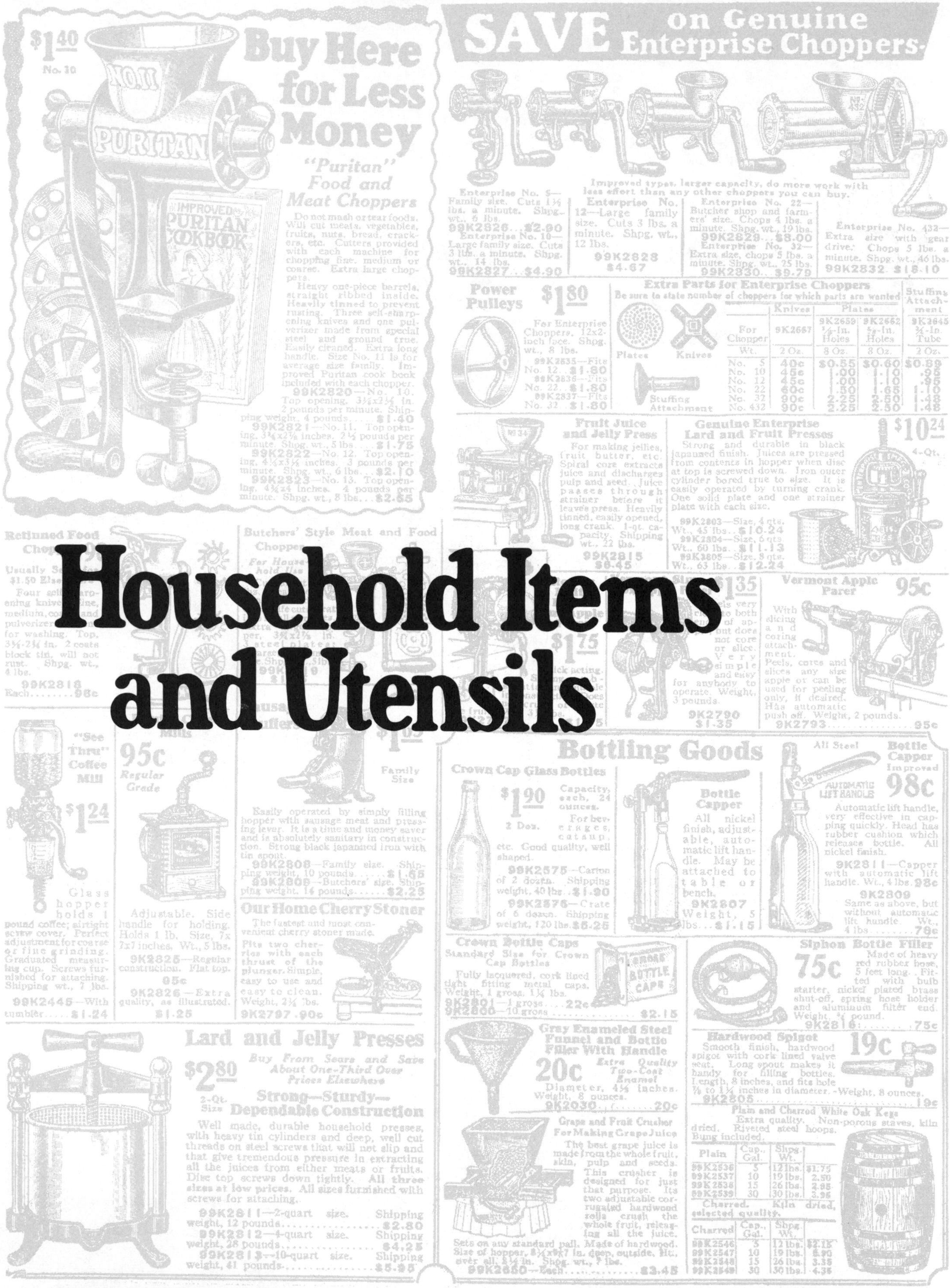

Buy Here for Less Money

$1.40
No. 10

"Puritan" Food and Meat Choppers

Do not mash or tear foods. Will cut meats, vegetables, fruits, nuts, bread, crackers, etc. Cutters provided with each machine for chopping fine, medium or coarse. Extra large choppers.

Heavy one-piece barrels, straight ribbed inside. Heavily tinned to prevent rusting. Three self-sharpening knives and one pulverizer made from special steel and ground true. Easily cleaned. Extra long handle. Size No. 11 is for average size family. Improved Puritan cook book included with each chopper.

99K2820—No. 10. Top opening, 3¼x2¼ in. 2 pounds per minute. Shipping weight, 4 pounds $1.40
99K2821—No. 11. Top opening, 3¼x3¼ inches, 2½ pounds per minute. Shpg. wt., 5 lbs. .. $1.75
99K2822—No. 12. Top opening, 4¼x3½ inches. 3 pounds per minute. Shpg. wt., 6 lbs. ..$2.10
99K2823—No. 13. Top opening, 4¾x4 inches. 4 pounds per minute. Shpg. wt., 8 lbs...$2.55

Enterprise No. 5—Family size. Cuts 1½ lbs. a minute. Shpg. wt., 6 lbs.
99K2826......$2.90
Enterprise No. 10—Large family size. Cuts 3 lbs. a minute. Shpg. wt., 14 lbs.
99K2827—$4.90

Improved types, larger capacity, do more work with less effort than any other choppers you can buy.

Enterprise No. 12—Large family size. Cuts 3 lbs. a minute. Shpg. wt., 19 lbs.
99K2828 $4.67

Enterprise No. 22—Butcher shop and farmers' size. Chops 4 lbs. a minute. Shpg. wt., 19 lbs.
99K2829...$8.00
Enterprise No. 32—Extra size, chops 5 lbs. a minute. Shpg. wt., 25 lbs.
99K2830...$9.79

Enterprise No. 432—Extra size with gear drive. Chops 5 lbs. a minute. Shpg. wt., 45 lbs.
99K2832..$18.10

Power Pulleys $1.80

For Enterprise Choppers, 12x2-inch face. Shpg. wt., 8 lbs.
99K2835—Fits No. 12 ..$1.80
99K2836—Fits No. 22 ..$1.80
99K2837—Fits No. 32 ..$1.80

Extra Parts for Enterprise Choppers

Be sure to state number of choppers for which parts are wanted.

For Chopper	Wt.	Knives 9K2657	Plates 9K2659 ¼-In. Holes	Plates 9K2662 ½-In. Holes	Stuffing Attachment 9K2645 ¾-In. Tube
		2 Oz.	8 Oz.	8 Oz.	2 Oz.
No. 5	40c	$0.55	$0.60	$0.89
No. 10	45c	1.00	1.00	.95
No. 12	45c	1.00	1.00	.95
No. 22	60c	1.50	1.65	1.10
No. 32	90c	2.25	2.50	1.25
No. 432	90c	2.25	2.50	1.48

Fruit Juice and Jelly Press

For making jellies, fruit butter, etc. Spiral core extracts juice and discharges pulp and seed. Juice passes through strainer before it leaves press. Heavily tinned, easily opened, long crank. 1-qt. capacity. Shipping wt., 22 lbs.
99K2815 $6.45

Genuine Enterprise Lard and Fruit Presses

Strong and durable in black japanned finish. Juices are pressed from contents in hopper when disc at top is screwed down. Iron outer cylinder bored true to size. It is easily operated by turning crank. One solid plate and one strainer plate with each size.

$10.24
4-Qt.

99K2803—Size, 4 qts. Wt., 45 lbs. $10.24
99K2804—Size, 6 qts. Wt., 60 lbs. $11.13
99K2805—Size, 8 qts. Wt., 63 lbs. $12.24

Vermont Apple Parer 95c

With slicing and coring attachment. Peels, cores and slices any size apple or can be used for peeling only, if desired. Has automatic push off. Weight, 2 pounds.
9K2793 ....95c

Retinned Food Chop

Usually sell $1.50 elsewhere.

Four self-sharpening knives, cutters for fine, medium, coarse and pulverizer for washing. Top, 3¼-2¼ in. 2 coats block tin, will not rust. Shpg. wt., 4 lbs.
99K2818 Each.........98c

Butchers' Style Meat and Food Chopper

For house-hold use

"See Thru" Coffee Mill

$1.24

Glass hopper holds 1 pound coffee; airtight screw cover. Perfect adjustment for coarse or fine grinding. Graduated measuring cup. Screws furnished for attaching. Shipping wt., 7 lbs.
99K2445—With tumbler.....$1.24

Mills 95c
Regular Grade

Easily operated by simply filling hopper with sausage meat and pressing lever. It is a time and money saver and is absolutely sanitary in construction. Strong black japanned iron with tin spout.
99K2808—Family size. Shipping weight, 10 pounds $1.68
99K2809—Butchers' size. Shipping weight, 16 pounds $2.23

Our Home Cherry Stoner

The fastest and most convenient cherry stoner made.

Fits two cherries with each thrust of the plunger. Simple, easy to use and easy to clean. Weight, 2½ lbs.
9K2797 .90c

Adjustable. Side handle for holding. Holds 1 lb. Size, 7x7x7 inches. Wt., 5 lbs.
9K2825—Regular construction. Flat top. 95c
9K2826—Extra quality, as illustrated. $1.25

Lard and Jelly Presses

$2.80

Buy From Sears and Save About One-Third Over Prices Elsewhere

2-Qt. Size

Strong—Sturdy— Dependable Construction

Well made, durable household presses, with heavy tin cylinders and deep, well cut threads on steel screws that will not slip and that give tremendous pressure in extracting all the juices from either meats or fruits. Disc top screws down tightly. All three sizes at low prices. All sizes furnished with screws for attaching.

99K2811—2-quart size. Shipping weight, 12 pounds $2.80
99K2812—4-quart size. Shipping weight, 28 pounds $4.25
99K2813—10-quart size. Shipping weight, 41 pounds $5.95

Bottling Goods

Crown Cap Glass Bottles

$1.90
2 Doz.

Capacity, each, 24 ounces. For beverages, catsup, etc. Good quality, well shaped.
99K2575—Carton of 2 dozen. Shipping weight, 40 lbs. $1.90
99K2576—Crate of 6 dozen. Shipping weight, 120 lbs. $5.25

Crown Bottle Caps

Standard Size for Crown Cap Bottles

Fully lacquered, cork lined tight fitting metal caps. Weight, 1 gross, 1¼ lbs.
9K2801—1 gross.....22c
9K2800—10 gross.....$2.15

Gray Enameled Steel Funnel and Bottle Filler With Handle

20c

Extra Quality Two-Coat Enamel. Diameter, 4¼ inches. Weight, 8 ounces.
99K2030 .....20c

Grape and Fruit Crusher For Making Grape Juice

The best grape juice is made from the whole fruit, skin, pulp and seeds. This crusher is designed for just that purpose. Its two adjustable corrugated hardwood rolls crush the whole fruit, releasing all the juice.

Sets on any standard pail. Made of hardwood. Size of hopper, 8½x9½? in. deep, outside, etc., over all, 8½ in. Shpg. wt., 7 lbs.
99K2660—Each.........$3.45

Bottle Capper

All nickel finish, adjustable, automatic lift handle. May be attached to table or bench.
9K2807 Weight, 5 lbs.....$1.15

Bottle Capper Improved 98c
All Steel
Automatic Lift Handle

Automatic lift handle, very effective in capping quickly. Head has rubber cushion which releases bottle. All nickel finish.
9K2809—Capper with automatic lift handle. Wt., 4 lbs. 98c
Same as above, but without automatic lift handle. Wt., 4 lbs. 76c

Siphon Bottle Filler 75c

Made of heavy red rubber hose, 5 feet long. Fitted with bulb starter, nickel plated brass shut-off, spring hose holder and aluminum filter end. Weight, ¾ pound.
9K2816.........75c

Hardwood Spigot 19c

Smooth finish, hardwood spigot with cork lined valve seat. Long spout makes it handy for filling bottles. Length, 8 inches, and fits hole ⅞ to 1¼ inches in diameter. Weight, 8 ounces.
9K2805.........19c

Plain and Charred White Oak Kegs

Extra quality. Non-porous staves, kiln dried. Riveted steel hoops. Bung included.

Plain	Cap. Gal.	Shpg. Wt.	
99K2536	5	12 lbs.	$1.75
99K2537	10	19 lbs.	2.50
99K2538	15	26 lbs.	2.98
99K2539	30	50 lbs.	3.95

Charred, Kiln dried, selected quality.

Charred	Cap. Gal.	Shpg. Wt.	
99K2546	5	12 lbs.	$2.15
99K2547	10	19 lbs.	2.90
99K2548	15	26 lbs.	3.38
99K2549	30	50 lbs.	4.35

Household Items and Utensils

Housewares from the Chop-Rite Manufacturing Company

Chop-Rite of Pottstown, Pennsylvania, manufactures several traditional kitchen utensils.

Cherry Stoner

"**P**ITS every cherry—will not miss." The Chop-Rite cherry stoner will pit the fruit without otherwise disfiguring it. The stoner cleans easily, and will not rust since it is heavily tinned.

Sausage Stuffer, Lard or Fruit Press

THIS is actually three implements in one: it stuffs sausage casings, presses lard or cheese, and squeezes fruit and vegetables. It features cast-iron cylinders bored perfectly true. The tin cylinder lies within the cast cylinder to enable the operator to remove hot cracklings without inconvenience. Nontoxic black finish. Capacity: 8 quarts. Height: 22 inches.

Wholesale price list and retailer information available.

Chop-Rite Manufacturing Company

P.O. Box 294
Pottstown, PA 19464
Tel. 215/326-5970

Meat Chopper

THE Chop-Rite meat chopper is available with a one-piece cast-iron stand, cylinder, and hopper. It is heavily tinned and will not be affected by rust or acids. All parts are easily removed and cleaned.

Old Dutch Cleanser

UNLIKE its earlier pejorative connotation in phrases like "Dutch treat," the word "Dutch" was associated with domestic hygiene early in this century. The Old Dutch Cleanser woman and the Dutch Boy Paint boy first appeared then (she's unchanged), and when the Colgate company illustrated an ad for its antiseptic powders, it was careful to use figures wearing traditional Dutch costume.

Available at retail stores throughout the country.

Old Dutch Cleanser is a registered trademark of Purex, Inc.

Waffle Iron

THE 1908 EDITION of the Sears, Roebuck & Company catalog, "The Great Price Maker," sold a waffle iron looking just like this one for 78¢. Then, of course, they were the most mundane of household items. The John Wright company's waffle iron has a 20-inch diameter and incorporates a later twentieth-century innovation—hollow "teeth" on the baking plates.

For dealer information, contact:

John Wright, Inc.

*North Front Street
Wrightsville, PA 17368
Tel. 717/252-3661*

1931 Waffles

For the Basic Recipe You'll Need:

2 cups flour	2 eggs
4 teaspoons baking powder	1¼ cups milk
½ teaspoon salt	⅓ cup melted butter

Sift and measure your flour, and then add the dry ingredients and sift again. Now beat just the egg yolks and add them to the milk. Stir the liquid ingredients into the dry ones, and add your melted butter. Beat your egg whites until they are stiff, and fold them into the batter just before baking. Bake in your preheated waffle iron for 2 or 3 minutes. Make sure the iron is nice and hot. Increase your milk if the batter is too thick.

Try these variations to the Basic Recipe.

Cheese Waffles:
Reduce butter to 2 tablespoons and add ½ cup grated cheese. Fold in the cheese last.

Bacon Waffles:
Add 4 slices of uncooked bacon which have been cut into small pieces. Sprinkle the bacon over the batter after it has been poured in the waffle iron. Try this recipe using cooked bacon if you prefer.

Ham Waffles:
Reduce your butter to 3 tablespoons and add ½ cup of cooked ham (chopped). Fold in the ham last.

From FORGOTTEN RECIPES, compiled by Jaine Rodack. Reprinted with the permission of Wimmer Brothers Books, Memphis, Tennessee.

Ironware

THE Lodge Manufacturing Company is a fourth-generation family business incorporated in 1896. The extensive selection of ironware it produces includes skillets, old-style griddles, country and straight kettles, and cornstick and muffin pans.

Price list and order form available.

Lodge Manufacturing Company

*P.O. Box 380
South Pittsburgh, TN 37380
Tel. 615/837-7181*

Cumberland General Store Housewares

Soapsaver

Save soapsuds if you have a garden, for they form a very useful manure for flowers, as well as shrubs and vegetables. It is well to have a sunk tub in every garden where the soapy water can stand until required for gardening.

— "USEFUL HINTS" FROM THE 1900 *FARMER'S ALMANAC*

CUMBERLAND'S soapsaver, a once-common device for making use of soap slivers, can help here. "Swish it in your water for lots of suds," says Cumberland.

Price: $5.63, F.O.B. Crossville, Tennessee.

Kitchen Pump

CUMBERLAND'S OLD - style kitchen pump is made of cast iron and is completely functional. Easily installed by any plumber or handyman, the pump hooks right up to the cold-water lines and will not interfere with any other faucets. It stands 15 inches high, with a shipping weight of 25 lbs.

Price: $160, F.O.B. point of origin.

Round Dinner Pail

THE following is reprinted from the Cumberland General Store "Wish and Want Book":

W. Smith, of Sharp Place, Tennessee, hewed out railroad ties for a living. . . . After felling a white oak and forming it to proper dimensions with a broad axe, he would hoist it on his shoulder and carry it out of the woods to a mule trail. At times, ties brought as much as 15¢ apiece. Each day, he carried a four lb. lard bucket full of pinto beans and corn bread. Now you may not have to replenish as much energy as old Smith did but you're sure to enjoy this miner's dinner pail fashioned after his old lard bucket. Made from extra-hard cold-rolled aluminum. Sanitary seamless construction. Capacity, five quarts.

Price: $16, F.O.B. point of origin.

Lovell Clothes Wringer

THE LIFE of a wringer," proclaimed the Sears catalog of 1908, "largely depends upon its rolls." Quite right, too. Cumberland's Lovell wringer employs semi-soft "balloon" rollers for just this reason. These, in addition to the wringer's all-steel frame, gray baked-enamel finish, rustproofing, and hard maple bearings, make for a durable appliance.

It can be attached to stationary or portable tubs (round or square), its clamps open to 1¾ inches, and it's equipped with 12- by 1⅝-inch rollers.

Price: $88.92.

Ceiling Fans

AS BOTH the year during which the Wright brothers first flew an airplane and the year the Hunter ceiling fan was introduced, 1903 saw great strides take place in the art of cooling oneself off. Of the two approaches, it's the fan that's far and away the more energy efficient, requiring no more juice to operate than does a lightbulb. The fan is quieter as well, and its thrust-type ball-bearing construction provides trouble-free operation.

All Hunter ceiling fans offered feature circulating oil bath, fixed blades, and two speeds controlled by a pull chain.

Prices for a 36-inch ceiling fan (325 rpm, 80 watts): with pecan blades, a brown-painted motor, and a shipping weight of 35 lbs., $210.57; for the same unit with cane-inset blades, a brass-plated motor and blade mounts, and a shipping weight of 45 lbs., $350.58; for the same unit with pecan-finished blades, a brass-plated motor and blade mounts, and a shipping weight of 45 lbs., $336.92.

Prices for a 52-inch ceiling fan (220 rpm, 120 watts): with pecan-finished blades, a brass-plated motor and blade mounts, and a shipping weight of 70 lbs., $455.83; for the same unit with white-painted blades, a white motor, and a shipping weight of 70 lbs., $293.62; for the same unit with pecan-finished blades, a brown motor, and a shipping weight of 64 lbs., $293.62.

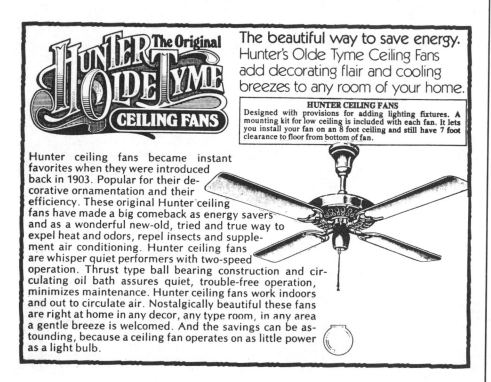

The beautiful way to save energy. Hunter's Olde Tyme Ceiling Fans add decorating flair and cooling breezes to any room of your home.

HUNTER CEILING FANS
Designed with provisions for adding lighting fixtures. A mounting kit for low ceiling is included with each fan. It lets you install your fan on an 8 foot ceiling and still have 7 foot clearance to floor from bottom of fan.

Hunter ceiling fans became instant favorites when they were introduced back in 1903. Popular for their decorative ornamentation and their efficiency. These original Hunter ceiling fans have made a big comeback as energy savers and as a wonderful new-old, tried and true way to expel heat and odors, repel insects and supplement air conditioning. Hunter ceiling fans are whisper quiet performers with two-speed operation. Thrust type ball bearing construction and circulating oil bath assures quiet, trouble-free operation, minimizes maintenance. Hunter ceiling fans work indoors and out to circulate air. Nostalgically beautiful these fans are right at home in any decor, any type room, in any area a gentle breeze is welcomed. And the savings can be astounding, because a ceiling fan operates on as little power as a light bulb.

Ostrich Feather Duster

GRAY, South African ostrich feathers with a wooden handle in four lengths. Shipping weight: 2 lbs.

Prices: 12-inch feather duster, $7; 15-inch, $9.63; 19-inch, $10.50; 28-inch, $12.83.

All prices are quoted F.O.B. Crossville, Tennessee.

"Wish and Want Book," $3.75.

Cumberland General Store
Route 3
Crossville, TN 38555
Tel. 615/484-8481

Shoeshine Foot Rest

A PRE-WORLD WAR I "star" design, Woodcraft Supply Corporation's shoeshine foot rest is 7 inches long and includes a heel step to support both small and large shoes. When the prebored feet are screwed into a box, the foot rest's open design permits it to function as a handle. Black enamel finish.

Price: Woodcraft catalog #11S42-UH, $4.95.

Tool catalog, $3 (refundable with order).

Woodcraft Supply Corporation
41 Atlantic Ave.
Woburn, MA 01888
Tel. 617/935-5860

Two-Tub Laundry Stand

M ADE OF a "heavily galvanized material that has been hot-dipped in molten zinc after forming to give a longer-lasting protective coating to surfaces and seams," Cumberland's two-tub laundry stand has rounded corners and a double-seamed metal drain. It comes complete with hose, hook, and fittings.

Capacity: 15½ gallons each tub.
Dimensions: tubs, 20⅛ by 20 inches each; depth, 11⅛ inches.

Plans for an Oaken Ice Box

W ELL, *ALMOST* an ice box. The Hammermark company's plans lack the tin insulation and other features that would enable the cabinet to store ice, but they do closely follow the design of iceboxes advertised in the Sears catalog of 1904.

Product sheet available, $1 (refundable with order).

Hammermark Associates
P.O. Box 201-SC
Floral Park, NY 11002

Length of stand, 42 inches; width, 16½ inches. Overall height, 32 inches. Shipping weight: 35 lbs.
Price: $100.94.

Lehman Hardware & Appliances, Inc.

In 1935 brothers J. E. and Dave Lehman began their hardware store to supply "the tools, utensils, and appliances used in rural homes and on Amish farms." Responding to the recent interest in this type of merchandise, Lehman's "Non-Electric 'Good Neighbor' Heritage Catalog" is available well beyond Amish country, overeager title and all.

Tin Match Box

THIS wall-mounted container will hold an entire box of Blue Tips. Available in either light blue, pale yellow, or dark green.

Dimensions: 6 inches high, 3¼ inches wide, and 3¼ inches deep.

Price: Lehman catalog #MB, $4.95.

Gas Hotplates

THESE ARE DESCRIBED by Lehman Hardware as perfect for canning, cooking, and laundry work on hot summer days. Their gas hotplate has heavy round cast-iron burners with ported holes and air mixers. The burners can be individually adjusted through the use of "Stay-Cool" bakelite knobs. The hotplate can be converted from LP to natural gas with a screwdriver, and comes with a heavy-gauge steel frame. The Lehman hotplate is not AGA approved.

Prices: single-burner gas hotplate, $31.95; double-burner, $48.95; triple-burner, $64.95.

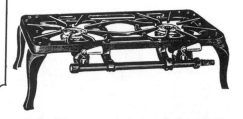

Two-Piece Sad Iron

BASED on the turn-of-the-century Potts sad irons that first featured detachable handles, an innovation that allowed the ironer to keep one base warming while the other was in use, the Lehman sad iron has a hand-ground bottom to ensure snag-free operation, a hollow cast-iron base, and a wooden handle.

Prices: sad iron bases, $15.95 apiece; handle, $15.95 (Lehman Hardware recommends that you purchase two bases with a single handle).

James Hand Washer

A DEVOLUTIONARY washday miracle, the James Hand Washer is lever-activated—a turn-of-the-century innovation (in 1908, Sears called *its* lever washer the "New-Way"). The James washer's "pendulum action" ensures that your washload is fully submerged, and requires only seven minutes' thrashing.

The James tub and dasher are both made from high-grade stainless steel. The dasher hand is ⁵⁄₁₆-inch steel with a hardwood grip. Black wooden legs with a reinforcing crossbar run the length of the tub, which has a rust- proof drain.

Specifications: tub height, 25½ inches; length, 22½ inches; width, 16¼ inches; capacity, 16 gallons.

Price (with wringer): $239.

Soda-Pop Bottle Openers

F ROM the days of Vin Fiz, Bevo, and Nesbitt's California Orange, these cast-iron drugstore bottle openers read "Drink Coca-Cola," "Pepsi-Cola," "7UP, You Like It, It Likes You," and "Drink Dr. Pepper" in red letters on a silver background.

Price: $4.95 each.

Pyramid Toaster

Toast
Cut stale bread into slices one-fourth inch thick; dry in the oven. Then put on a toaster or fork, move it gently over heat until dry, then allow it to become a light brown by placing it nearer the heat and turning constantly; or, light gas oven and heat five to eight minutes. Place bread in toaster or pan, one inch from gas, in lower or broiling oven. When brown on one side turn and brown on the other. Bread cut into triangles and toasted are called toast points, and are used for garnishing.
—FROM THE 1903 "SETTLEMENT" COOKBOOK, COMPILED BY MRS. SIMON KANDER AND MRS. HENRY SCHOENFELD

Whew! Lehman Hardware's early-twentieth-century pyramid toaster can put you right into this picture, diffusing its heat for even browning and "all-the-way-through" crispness. The pyramid toaster works equally well on an open fire, a woodstove, or over a gas burner, toasting two slices at a time.

Price: Lehman catalog #2-T, $4.50.
VISA, MasterCard, and personal checks accepted.

"Non-Electric" catalog, $2.

Lehman Hardware & Appliances

4779 Kidron Rd.
Kidron, OH 44636
Tel. 216/857-5441

Pioneer Place Housewares

Copper Wash Boiler

THIS copper wash boiler was built for Pioneer Place by the same company that developed the original boilers a century ago. Excellent for water-bath canning, it will fit over two burners, holds almost ten imperial gallons, and comes complete with lid.

Dimensions: length, 22 inches; width, 12 inches; height, 13 inches.

Price: $55.25, ppd.

Grandma's Economy Washboard

THIS "labor-saving device" comes complete with back drain and standard-size rubbing surface and is very serviceable. Its overall size is 23 by 12½ inches.

Price: $10.50, ppd.

Catalog available.

The Pioneer Place
Route 2, 9938 County Road 39
Belle Center, OH 43310

Paper Doilies

"The practically impossible-to-find paper lace doilies you've been searching for are finally here!" presumes the color catalog put out by Brookstone. The doilies come 150 to the box, assorted into 8-, 10-, and 12-inch diameters.

Price: Brookstone catalog # 07065, $5.95 (plus $2.25 for shipping).

Catalog available.

Brookstone Company
641 Vose Farm Rd.
Peterborough, NH 03458

From the Vermont Country Store

The Vermont Country Store was founded in 1946 by Vrest Orton and is now run by his son, Lyman—a proud storekeeper who operates his business out of a wood-frame building along Route 100 in Weston. The store posts a mail-order catalog that delights in selling many once-familiar products which, like summer fireflies, vanish without notice and are only missed when they first reappear.

Linen Toweling

THE OLDTIME standard for roller and hand towels, this toweling's smooth, thickly woven linen is also excellent for dish drying. Please specify choice for either red, yellow, or blue stripes when ordering.

Dimensions: 18 inches wide. Shipping weight: ¼ lb. per yard.

Price: Vermont Country Store catalog #13249, $3.25 per yard (1 yard minimum length).

Compact Orange Juicer

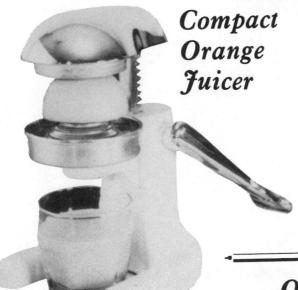

"**M**ANY OF US remember our mothers using this lever orange juice squeezer," relates the Vermont Country Store. "It used to be called 'Shorty' because when closed it stands only 8 inches tall." Made of solid metal, this juicer features a rack-and-pinion gear mechanism. Its bottom stand is made of baked enamel and its top is polished chrome. Available in white only. Shipping weight: 7 lbs.

Price: Vermont Country Store catalog #14931, $44.95.

Oakleaf Pinstripe Sheets

A 1920s DESIGN, with light-gray oak leaves and pinstripes set against a white background. Made of 200-count cotton. Shipping weight: 2 lbs. each.

Prices: flat twin sheet (72 inches by 102 inches) Vermont Country Store catalog #14359 "leaf," $23.50; flat double (81 inches by 102 inches), Vermont Country Store catalog #14361 "leaf," $29.95.

White Enameled Steel Breadbox

A VANISHED DOMESTIC U.S. product whose manufacture lingers in Canada, this breadbox comes complete with a single adjustable shelf, side vent holes, and a hinged front door.

Specifications: 16½ inches wide, 10 inches high, and 10½ inches deep. Shipping weight: 11 lbs.

Price: Vermont Country Store catalog #14912, $23.95.

Cotton Bedspread and Shams

I N continual manufacture for sixty years, these patterned bedspreads are made of 100% cotton and are machine washable. Their traditional circle design has been created by looping the yarn to make a permanent bas-relief pattern. Specify white or natural color.

Shipping weights: twin, 6 lbs.; double, 7 lbs.

Prices: twin (80 inches by 110 inches), Vermont Country Store catalog #14874, $39.95; double (96 inches by 110 inches), Vermont Country Store catalog #14875, $45.95; pillow sham (20 inches by 26 inches), Vermont Country Store catalog #14878, $16.95 apiece.

Goose-Down Pillows

T HESE PILLOWS are made with sterilized white feathers and have traditional striped-ticking covers of 100% cotton. Please specify your preference for a soft, medium, or hard pillow.

Dimensions: 26 inches by 20 inches. Shipping weight: 3 lbs.

Price: Vermont Country Store catalog #15158, $60.00.

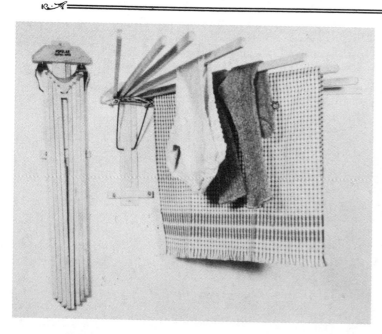

Folding Wall Clothes Dryer

S TILL made of the same rugged hardwood as was the original model fifty years ago, this dryer's eight 22-inch arms fold up out of the way when not in use. Folded, the rack stands 27 inches tall and 6 inches wide. Shipping weight: 4 lbs.

Price: Vermont Country Store catalog #14020, $13.50.

Electrolux Slide-Along Vacuum Cleaner

VIRTUALLY *anything* **called a vacuum cleaner will suck up dirt adequately enough** to keep dust devils from the point of spontaneous generation. But when it comes to war toys, no vacuum (or appliance, for that matter) can hope to compare to the 1920s-designed Electrolux Slide-Along. From its flying-bridge handle to its all-terrain runners, the streamlined 'Lux's Swedish designers successfully anticipated the *Star Wars* AT-AT in both adaptability and invincibility; and its louvered troop doors are a radical feature only recently adopted by the designers of the famed Israeli Merkava tank. These, plus the fact that its huge bay can receive most toy tanks and trucks (once the dust bag has been re-moved and discarded, of course), makes the Slide-Along the essential C-5A transport in any boy's Arsenal of Preparedness.

The Electrolux Slide-Alongs sold by the Vermont Country Store are fully reconditioned models featuring many new parts, including bearings, gaskets, cord, handle, and hose. Rechroming helps the vacuum look like new, and a rebuilt motor sees to it that it works that way as well. The Electrolux flip-over rug/floor brush, dusting brush, and crevice tool are also included.

Dimensions: 23 inches long by 8½ inches high. Shipping weight: 25 lbs.

Price: Vermont Country Store catalog #15032, $139.95.

Delivery charges (based on shipping weight) required in advance.

Seasonal catalog, "The Voice of the Mountains," available from The Vermont Country Store, Catalog Request, Route 100, Weston, VT 05161.

The Vermont Country Store
Mail Order Office
P.O. Box 3000
Manchester Center, VT 05255

In Memoriam: A Dead Wringer

The Henry Ford of the laundry room, Fred L. Maytag began the production of wringer-washers back in 1909 when the "Hired Girl" (shown here) was introduced. With a pulley mechanism that allowed the washers to be operated from an outside power source, the Hired Girl eliminated hand operation.

The Maytag company continually made improvements on their wringer-washers, introducing their last model ("the first white appliance") in 1939. Production of this model peaked in 1948, only to decline thereafter until its November 22, 1983, demise.

The 1909 Maytag "Hired Girl"

Doughboys and their "Hired Girl," Plattsburg, New York, 1917

$4.50 — 32-Piece Set

$4.75 — 32-Piece Set

Ivory Body Floral Dinner Set

Floral decorated dinnerware at exceptionally low prices. Decorated with a conventional floral design of yellow flowers with burnt orange colored centers, slate colored stems and small leaves which adds contrast to the beautiful color of the flowers. Made of the new ivory semi-porcelain in an octagon shape.

35K338—Ivory Body Floral Dinnerware. Complete sets and open stock. For list of pieces in the complete sets see page 914.

32-Piece Dinner Set. Wt. 26 lbs.	$4.50	53-Piece Dinner Set. Wt. 42 lbs.	$8.60		
66-Piece Dinner Set. Wt. 51 lbs.	12.65	90-Piece Dinner Set. Wt. 75 lbs.	15.85		

	Size Abt.	Set of Six		Size Abt.	Each
Tea Cups and Saucers		$1.48	Covered Vegetable Dish		$1.35
Coffee Cups and Saucers		1.71	Gravy or Sauce Boat		.49
Bread and Butter Plates	6 in.	.66	Platter, small	11¼ in.	.35
Pie Plates	7 in.	.75	Platter, medium	13¾ in.	.58
Tea or Breakfast Plates	8 in.	.93	Platter, large	15¾ in.	.92
Dinner Plates	9 in.	1.18	Cream Pitcher		.37
Dinner Plates, extra large	9¾ in.	1.40	Pitcher	3½ pts.	.62
Soup Plates (coupe shape)	8 in.	1.15	Bowl	1 pt.	.48
Sauce Dishes	5 in.	.50	Covered Sugar Bowl		.68
Oatmeal Dishes	6 in.	1.03	Pickle Dish		.22
Oyster Bowls		1.30	Covered Butter Dish	9 in.	.85
			Oval Open Vegetable Dish	9 in.	.61
			Round Deep Salad Bowl	9¼ in.	.88

Garden Flower and Blue Line Dinner Set

A popular style of dinnerware decorated with sprays of blue, pink and yellow garden flowers and buds with green leaves connected with a blue line forming a border. Made of American pure white semi-porcelain in a plain edge shape.

35K340—Garden Flower and Blue Line Dinnerware. Complete sets and open stock. For list of pieces in the complete sets see page 914.

32-Piece Dinner Set. Wt. 26 lbs.	$4.75	53-Piece Dinner Set. Wt. 42 lbs.	$10.65		
66-Piece Dinner Set. Wt. 51 lbs.	12.98	90-Piece Dinner Set. Wt. 75 lbs.	16.35		

	Size Abt.	Set of Six		Size Abt.	Each
Tea Cups and Saucers		$1.55	Covered Vegetable Dish		$1.25
Coffee Cups and Saucers		1.83	Gravy or Sauce Bowl		.55
Bread and Butter Plates	6 in.	.73	Platter, small	11¼ in.	.36
Pie Plates	7 in.	.80	Platter, medium	13¾ in.	.60
Tea or Breakfast Plates	8 in.	.98	Platter, large	15¾ in.	.95
Dinner Plates	9 in.	1.23	Pitcher	3½ pts.	.67
Dinner Plates, extra large	9¾ in.	1.48	Bowl	1 pt.	.52
Soup Plates (coupe shape)	8 in.	1.20	Covered Sugar Bowl		.72
Sauce Dishes	5 in.	.53	Pickle Dish		.23
Oatmeal Dishes	6 in.	1.08	Covered Butter Dish		1.09
Oyster Bowls		1.38	Oval Open Veg. Dish	9 in.	.61
			Round Deep Salad Bowl	9¼ in.	.90

China and Glassware

Bright or Yellow Matte Gold Dinner Sets

Choice of either bright gold or 18-karat yellow matte gold dinnerware. No. 35K246 Dinnerware is a bright gold band with bright gold traced handles. No. 35K234 Dinnerware is an 18-karat yellow matte gold band, handles heavily covered with gold.

The matte gold is the satin finished gold used on the highest priced sets. The ware of both sets is of first quality American pure white semi-porcelain in a plain edge shape. Complete sets and open stock. For list of pieces in the complete sets see page 914.

	35K246	35K234			35K246	35K234
32-Piece Dinner Set. Wt. 26 lbs.	Bright Gold. $4.45	Matte Gold. $7.75	66-Piece Dinner Set. Wt. 51 lbs.		Bright Gold. $12.50	Matte Gold. $21.75
53-Piece Dinner Set. Wt. 42 lbs.	Bright Gold. 10.35	Matte Gold. 17.75	90-Piece Dinner Set. Wt. 75 lbs.		Bright Gold. 15.75	Matte Gold. 25.75

		35K246	35K234			35K246	35K234
	Size Abt.	Bright Gold Set of Six	Matte Gold Set of Six		Size Abt.	Bright Gold	Matte Gold
Tea Cups and Saucers		$1.53	$2.63	Sauce Dishes, Set of 6	5 in.	$0.49	$0.98
Coffee Cups and Saucers		1.78	3.08	Oatmeal Dishes, Set of 6	6 in.	1.08	1.75
Bread and Butter Plates	6 in.	.70	1.14	Oyster Bowls, Set of 6		1.35	2.15
Pie Plates	7 in.	.78	1.38	Covered Vegetable Dish, Each		1.22	2.40
Tea or Breakfast Plates	8 in.	.95	1.63	Gravy (Sauce) Boat, Each		.45	.96
Dinner Plates	9 in.	1.19	.88	Platter, small, Each		.32	.49
Dinner Plates, extra large	10 in.	1.45	2.85	Platter, medium, Each	13¾ in.	.55	.89
Soup Plates (coupe shape)	8 in.	1.20	1.88	Platter, large, Each	15¾ in.	.86	1.54
				Cream Pitcher		$0.37	$0.60
				Pitcher	3½ pts.	.60	1.25
				Bowl	1 pt.	.22	.37
				Covered Sugar Bowl		.45	1.35
				Pickle Dish		.20	.37
				Covered Butter Dish		1.08	1.85
				Oval Open Veg. Dish	9 in.	.38	.60
				Round Deep Salad Bowl	9¼ in.	.56	.90

The Beautiful Colonial Shape Gold Band Set

$4.50 — 32-Pc. Set

Ivory Body Gold Band Dinner Set

Reminiscent of rare ivory, grown mellow with the touch of years is this beautiful Gold Band Dinner Set. The bright gold band on the cream colored ivory semi-porcelain body blends most harmoniously, giving the appearance of a rich matte gold. Handles of each piece are traced in gold. The dinnerware is made in the popular octagon shape.

35K242—Ivory Body, Gold Band Dinnerware. Complete sets and open stock.

32-Piece Dinner Set. Wt. 26 lbs.	$4.50	66-Piece Dinner Set. Wt. 51 lbs.	$12.75		
53-Piece Dinner Set. Wt. 42 lbs.	10.75	90-Piece Dinner Set. Wt. 75 lbs.	16.25	For list of pieces in the complete sets see page 914.	

	Size Abt.	Set of Six		Size Abt.	Set of Six
Tea Cups and Saucers		$1.49	Dinner Plates (extra large)	10 in.	$1.43
Coffee Cups and Saucers		1.75	Soup Plates (coupe shape)	8 in.	1.23
Bread and Butter Plates	6 in.	.62	Sauce Dishes	5 in.	.52
Pie Plates	7 in.	.78	Oatmeal Dishes	6 in.	1.06
Tea or Breakfast Plates	8 in.	.93	Oyster Bowls		1.33
Dinner Plates	9 in.	1.20	Covered Vegetable Dish, Each		1.39

	Size Abt.	Each		Size Abt.	Each
Gravy, or Sauce Boat		$0.50	Bowl	1 pt.	$0.37
Platter, small	11¼ in.	.36	Covered Sugar Bowl		.70
Platter, medium	13¾ in.	.58	Pickle Dish		.38
Platter, large	15¾ in.	.92	Covered Butter Dish	9 in.	1.05
Cream Pitcher		.38	Oval Open Veg. Dish	9 in.	.48
Pitcher	3½ pts.	.65	Round Deep Salad Bowl	9¼ in.	.60

Roycroft China

REPRODUCTION Arts and Crafts Roycroft Inn china is available through Craftsmen Design of Boston, Massachusetts.

Brochure obtainable.

Craftsmen Design (a.k.a. Craftsmen Gallery, Inc.)

P.O. Box 173
Boston, MA 02173
Tel. 617/227-9484

A Roycroft setting complete with the china and wallpaper sold through Craftsmen Design of Boston, Massachusetts

Imperial Hotel Dinnerware

IN 1913 the imperial household of Japan commissioned Frank Lloyd Wright to design a Western-style hotel to be located in Tokyo. Completed in 1922, the Imperial Hotel miraculously survived an earthquake that destroyed nearly all of the city's buildings the following year. But what, in forty-five years, God and Jimmy Doolittle couldn't do was ultimately accomplished in 1968, when Wright's architectural and engineering masterpiece fell before the wrecker's ball.

For the Imperial Hotel, Wright designed a dinnerware pattern that reflected his use of strong geometric forms. Now faithfully reproduced by Chicago's Heinz & Company (architect Thomas Heinz is also the editor of the *Frank Lloyd Wright Newsletter*) through an agreement with the dinnerware's original Japanese manufacturer, the settings are now being sold through Buffalo's Albright-Knox Art Gallery, among others.

Price: $170 for each seven-piece setting (plus $5 per set to cover shipping and insurance).

Albright-Knox Gallery

Gallery Shop
1285 Elmwood Ave.
Buffalo, NY 14222

Diner Mugs

DINERS began making their appearance early in the 1900s after one Patrick Tierney got the idea for upgrading the ill-reputed lunch car (a restaurant converted from a horse-drawn streetcar after electricity came in) by providing them with booths and the tonier look of a railroad dining car. This worked well, and by the 1910s in-town diners were being joined by roadside ones converted from genuine railcars.

Between this modest beginning and the garish "Wurlitzer" diners now going up, there have been a lot of art deco diners built by the side of the road. These streamlined eateries helped to create the *haute* vernacular in American architecture and cuisine.

Designed to resemble a railcar, Palmer, Massachusetts' 1927 Day And Night Diner is pre-dawn art deco. CREDIT: ALAN ROSE

In true proletarian spirit, art deco diners are usually all steel and factory made—and in their slab sides and compound curves there's always a reminder of their rolling-stock heritage. Inside, an arrangement of glass brick, etched and tinted mirrors, and chromed urns tells the road-weary that here's a place where the coffee ought to be good; but what confirms this feeling is the mug in which the muck arrives—the classic diner mug.

The Vermont Country Store's diner mugs are made of white enameled china, green-banded in the authentic style. They're so sturdy you can shoot baskets with them, and as I can personally attest, they're great for all-nighters at the typewriter.

Dimensions: 3½ inches high by 3¼ inches in diameter. Capacity: 7 ounces. Shipping weight: 2 lbs.

Price: Vermont Country Store catalog #13068, $6.95 each.

Delivery charges (based on shipping weight) required in advance.

"Voice of the Mountains" catalog available from The Vermont Country Store, Catalog Request, Route 100, Weston, VT 05161.

The Vermont Country Store

Mail Order Office
P.O. Box 3000
Manchester Center, VT 05255

Depression-Era Diner Doughnuts

A mid-1930s recipe for mocha-java's favorite on-the-skids companion

2 cups sifted flour	½ cup sugar
2 level teaspoons baking powder	1 tablespoon melted shortening
¾ teaspoon salt	1 egg, well beaten
½ teaspoon nutmeg	½ cup milk
½ teaspoon cinnamon	

Sift the flour three times with the baking powder, salt, and spices. Combine the sugar, melted shortening, and beaten egg; add dry ingredients alternately with the milk. Turn out on a well-floured board and roll to a ⅛-inch thickness. Cut with a doughnut cutter and fry in deep hot fat until a golden brown. Sprinkle with powdered sugar.

Reprinted from DIME-STORE DREAM PARADE: POPULAR CULTURE 1925–1955 *by Robert Heide and John Gilman (originally published by E.P. Dutton, N.Y., in 1979).*

Figurine Saltshakers

ALONG WITH cookie jars, whimsical saltshakers would **invariably** be found atop the porcelain tables of Depression-era kitchens. Many of these figures were made by the Nelson McCoy Pottery Company, which also successfully marketed a Hattie MacDaniel cookie jar (to compete with the famous Aunt Jemima version) modeled after the unforgettable actress who played Mammy in 1939's *Gone With the Wind*.

Prices: Sarsaparilla #923, porcelain baker boy salt and pepper shakers, $9; Sarsaparilla #920, earthenware airplane salt and pepper shakers, $7; Sarsaparilla #925, earthenware bellhop salt and pepper shakers, $9.

Sarsaparilla Deco Designs Ltd.

5711 Washington St.
West New York, NJ 07093
Tel. 201/863-8002

Replica Fiesta Ware

WHEN YOUR restaurant is located within one of art deco's most sacred temples, dime-store dishes are just what's called for. At least that's what Rockefeller Center's American Festival Café must have been thinking when they commissioned the Rego China Company of Queens, New York, to replicate Fiesta ware, the pottery designed by Frederick Rheade in 1936.

Fiesta ware originally came in five brilliant colors: Chinese red, indigo blue, green, yellow, and ivory. It was intended that these could be mixed and matched—a blue cup, say, atop an ivory saucer—without ever risking any loss of appetite. Doing this may have been only a feeble form of fun, but the result was festive—just as the name implied. Fiesta ware was sold by department stores mostly, although cheaper lines in different patterns were brought out for sale by the five-and-dimes. Woolworth's Harlequin was the best known of these, and was sold by the chain right into the 1970s.

While the Rego China replicas are china—and not just pottery—they've duplicated the rounded deco look and characteristic rings of authentic Fiesta ware. Mysteriously, though, the most salient feature of the originals has been abandoned. "American Festival Café China" is available only in a kind of deadpan white—per order, no doubt, of the Bureau of Approved Trendiness.

American Festival Café China is ovenproof and can be used in both home and commercial dishwashers. It is available through Savories, a Rockefeller Center store.

Prices: five-piece place setting (cup, saucer, bread-and-butter plate, soup bowl, and 10½-inch plate), $40; service for four, $150; completer set (covered sugar bowl, creamer, sauceboat, platter, salt and pepper shakers), $83.

Prices for individual pieces: 10½-inch plate, $14.25; 9-inch plate, $10.50; 6¼-inch plate (bread-and-butter plate), $5.95; cup, $6.50; saucer, $5.95; rim soup bowl, $7.75; two-handed soup bowl, $13.50; small tray (narrow), $8; small tray (wide), $9.25; large tray, $15; oval platter, $23.50; salt and pepper shakers, $6.75 each; covered sugar bowl, $14.50; creamer, $12.25; sauceboat, $19.75; ramekin, $5; demitasse set (cup and saucer), $12.25.

Telephone orders and American Express cards are accepted. On orders of $125 or more within New York City, delivery is free.

Savories

30 Rockefeller Plaza
New York, NY 10020
Tel. 212/246-6457

Carnival Glass

ACCORDING to Frank M. Fenton of the Fenton Art Glass company, what is known today as Carnival glass was first produced in 1907 when his firm introduced a line of glassware that it called Iridill. This glass, iridescent as a dragonfly's wing, fit in well with the swampy feel of curvilinear art nouveau's thickset tendrils. Pressed into figurines and plates and bells with "highly figured patterns," Fenton's iridescent glass sold well, and by 1910 several other companies were producing Carnival glass.

In 1970 Fenton Art Glass resumed production of their iridescent glass following a forty-one-year hiatus. Ever since, the company has annually issued several reproductions of its early-twentieth-century Carnival glass. These are distinguished from the originals by having the name "Fenton" inscribed on the bottom of the piece.

A publications list of retail Fenton glass catalogs is available.

The Fenton Art Glass Company
Williamstown, WV 26187
Tel. 304/375-6122

Glassware from Jenifer House

Standing on Massachusett's Route 7 in Great Barrington, Jenifer House is a cluster of red barns packed to their rafters with country clothing, gifts, and assorted Americana. This makes the place something of a Berkshire tourist attraction in the summertime, although the Jenifer House gift catalog will provide a semblance of the same fun at home.

Ice Cream Parlor Ware

IN THE 1890s, when carbonated water couldn't be sold on the Lord's Day, the sundae is said to have been first concocted as a kind of soda-less ice cream soda. In those times, Sunday was the only day you could buy one. It took until the Thirties for the banana split to appear—slower than one of the United Fruit scows that began hauling bananas up from the Caribbean in 1899.

Jenifer House's ice cream parlor glassware comes in a style that's prewar and Dairy Queen, both. Available in sets of four are: an 8½-inch banana split dish, a 12-ounce soda glass, a 5½-ounce tulip sundae glass, and a 4½-ounce footed sherbet dish.

Grocery Provision Jars

"PRACTICAL, heavy-glass see-through storage jars. Complete with easy-to-handle functional lids," writes the adjective-mad Jenifer House of their grocery storage jars. These are available in ½-, 1-, and 2-gallon sizes; and in a set consisting of one of each size.

Penny Candy Jars

"NIGGER BABY!" the rebel yell for an incoming Union artillery shell, by the 1890s had become the name for the country's most popular penny candy. By 1905 both Tootsie Rolls and jelly beans had joined the baby-shaped chocolates in ample glass jars that were placed high up out of the reach of covetous kids. These jars are still available from Jenifer House in 8-, 18-, 36-, and 62-ounce sizes ranging from 5 to 9 inches in height.

Gift catalog available.

Jenifer House

New Marlboro Stage
Great Barrington, MA 01230
Tel. 413/528-1500

Locomotive Container

THE Margaret Woodbury Strong Museum of Rochester, New York, claims status as the nation's leading museum of nineteenth- and early-twentieth-century Americana, its collection reflecting the life of the American middle class from 1820 to 1940. The museum is dedicated "totally to collecting, preserving, and exhibiting popular objects," writes the director, William T. Anderson, and to interpreting "the social and cultural development that took place in the Northeast during the era of industrialization."

The Margaret Woodbury Strong Museum selects items from its collection for replication by craftsmen especially licensed for this purpose. Before going on sale in the museum shop, items such as the turn-of-the-century locomotive container depicted here must conform to the museum's strict requirements for quality and authenticity.

Dimensions: approximately 2 inches by 4½ inches.
Price: Museum Shop #4207, $4 (plus $2.25 for shipping).

Color gift folder available.

Museum Shop

The Margaret Woodbury
Strong Museum
One Manhattan Square
Rochester, NY 14607

Mantel Clocks

Beauty-Accuracy

Select with care the clock that is to grace your mantel. On these pages you will find guaranteed clocks made by the foremost clockmakers of America. They have reliable movements that will give unfailing service. Each case is splendidly finished with exceptional care even to minute details. Unless specified otherwise, these clocks strike the hours and half hours on a soft tone cathedral gong. With ordinary care any of our clocks should give years of satisfaction. It will pay you to purchase one of these fine mantel clocks from the World's Largest Store.

The Major

Mantel Clock. The new Florentine russet finish, so popular just now. This russet (golden brown) finish, with a novel and exceedingly attractive crystallized effect, is not only soft and pleasing in appearance but contrasts splendidly with the handsome gilt metal trimmings. It will neither be affected by dust nor moisture. Clock runs eight days with one winding. It is 15 inches long and 10 inches high. Has a 5-inch dial, with clean cut numerals and hands and is protected by a fine bullseye glass. Strikes hours and half hours on deep cathedral gong. Shipping weight, 15 pounds.

5K9101¼.......................... **$5.50**

The Saracen. Dignity and beauty are reflected in the Saracen, one of the finest examples of American craftsmanship. Although the case represents a departure from the conventional black enameled wood clock, it will harmonize with the furnishings of any living room. This handsome blackwood clock with its high polish finish is sure to win your approval. Side ornaments, feet, columns, caps and bases are finished in gilt. The columns are marble-like in appearance. Above the columns are two mahogany finish panels with two-tone inlay effect. Hours and half hours are struck on a cathedral gong. The 8-day movement is reliable. The 5-inch porcelain dial with a bullseye glass is especially easy to read. Clock is 20 in. long, 10¾ inches high. Shpg. wt., 17 lbs.

5K9105¼.......................... **$6.90**

$8.40

The Associate

Mantel Clock. The most popular pattern on the market and our highest grade black enameled clock. Highly polished, 18¾ inches long and 12 inches high. The 5-inch dial is covered with an exceptionally clear bullseye glass, framed with a gilt metal sash. Front is decorated with gilt metal ornamentations and engraved scroll. Sides are attractively finished with variegated red ornamentation and fine imitation (white) onyx columns, set in gilt metal caps and bases. The movement, the most important part of the clock, runs 8 days with one winding. Strikes hours and half hours on a cathedral gong. We recommend The Associate as one of the best values offered in clocks. Shipping weight, 19 lbs.

5K9104½

The Protector

Mantel Clock. Black enameled wood, polished to a high finish. 16½ inches wide, 10⅛ inches high and has 5-inch dial. Bullseye glass with gilt finish metal sash. Has six silver finish columns, capped with gilt metal tops and bases, gilt metal side ornaments and feet. The movement runs 8 days with one winding. Strikes the hour and half hour on a soft tone cathedral gong. Shipping weight, 15 pounds.

5K9107¼—Clock only.............. **$5.38**

An Ornament for Your Clock

The attractive silver plated Elephant, shown on the clock above, will enhance the beauty of any Blackwood Mantel Clock. Heavily lacquered to prevent tarnishing. The elephant stands 8¼ inches high and is 9¾ inches long. Shipping weight, 7 pounds.

5K9000—Ornament only.............. **$3.65**

5K9002¼—Clock and Ornament, complete.............................. **8.95**

The Valencia

A popular black enameled wood clock attractively decorated with green top and bottom moldings. Four ivory-like columns. Has gilt metal feet, side ornaments and trimming. The 5-inch dial is protected by a bullseye glass. Reliable 8-day movement. Beautiful cathedral gong strikes hours and half hours. 16¾ inches long, 11¼ inches high. Shipping weight, 15 pounds.

5K9108¼. **$6.35**

Clocks

$5.00 AND UP

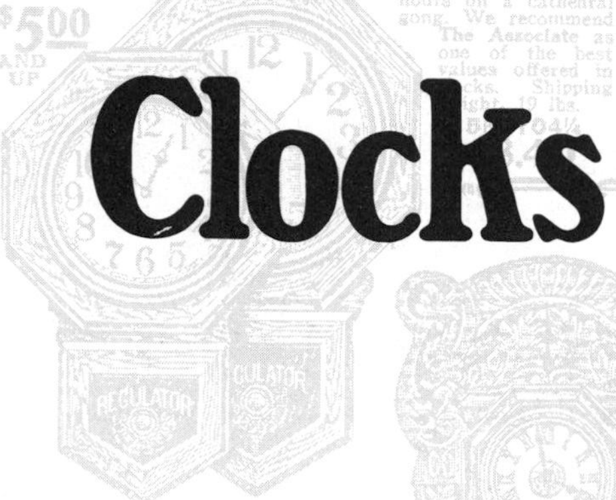

Oak Wall Clock for Church, School, Shop or Factory

Runs 8 days. 22¾ inches high, 10-inch dial. Shipping weight, 16 lbs.

5K9135¼—Time only. **$5.00**

5K9137¼—Time with calendar...................... $5.55

5K9139¼—Time with strike on wire gong...................... $6.20

Same as above with 12-inch dial; height, 26 inches. Shipping weight, 20 pounds.

5K9140¼—Time only..... $5.80

5K9142¼—Time with calendar...................... $6.35

5K9144¼—Time with strike on wire gong...................... $6.70

White Enamel Kitchenette Eight-Day Wall Clock. Every home should have one. White enamel with nickel-plated trimmings makes the most pleasing appearance. 13¾ inches high, 8 inches wide; 5-inch dial. Shpg. wt., 7 lbs.

5K9115¼ **$5.25**

Kitchen Clocks of Quality at Unusually Low Prices

Oak Front Eight-Day Kitchen Clock

Strikes the hour and half hour. Has alarm attachment. Fancy embossed case. Stands 22½ inches high and 15 inches wide. 5¼-inch dial. Fitted with thermometer to tell temperature; also a barometer that predicts the changes in the weather. Shpg. wt., 15 lbs.

5K9121¼. **$5.35**

Oak Kitchen Clock

One of the latest models from the factory. It is a small but beautifully designed and accurate kitchen clock. Is 13⅝ inches wide. Stands 13¾ inches high. Has an 8-day movement. Strikes the hours and half hours on a wire gong. Shpg. wt., 10 lbs.

5K9129¼......... **$3.30**

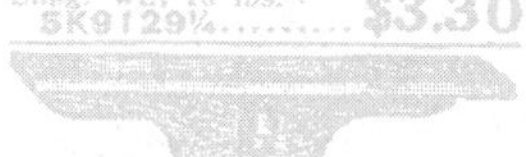

Hardwood Oak Clock Shelf

Fits shelf clocks only; 16½ inches long and 5 inches wide. Shipping wt., 2 lbs.

5K8595.............. **75c**

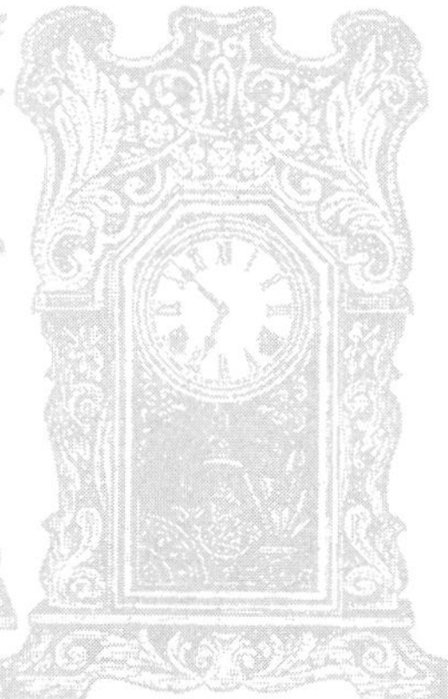

Shelf Clock

Oak finish. Embossed in beautiful scrolls and leaves. Light oak with heavy varnish finish. Runs 8 days with one winding; 22¼ inches high and 15⅛ inches wide; 5⅜-inch dial. Shipping wt., 16 lbs.

5K9123¼—Wire bell strike....... **$3.65**

5K9125¼—Wire bell strike with alarm.. **$4.15**

5K9127¼—Gong bell strike with alarm. **$4.60**

Regulator Clock for Office, Factory or Store

Hanging Wall Regulator Clock

Oak. Runs 8 days with one winding. 35 inches high; 12-inch dial. Shipping weight, 30 pounds. Not mailable.

5K9232¼—Time only **$7.15**

5K9234¼—Time and strike........................ $8.00

5K9236¼—Time, strike and calendar attachment.... 8.50

Kitchen, School or Hall Clock

A clock for church, school, factory, shop or home. 17⅛ in. in diameter and finished with a front of hand rubbed oak. Has 12-inch dial. Minute hand is 5⅛ in. long. We guarantee the 8-day pendulum movement for accuracy under almost any conditions. This clock registers the time only. Ideal for public or domestic use. Shipping weight, 15 pounds.

5K9111¼ Oak front................ **$5.98**

Mission-Style Regulator Clock

FROM the part of the country where Gustav Stickley's domestic Arts and Crafts movement originated today comes this "Mission-style" regulator clock. It's encased in beveled glass and quarter-sawn white oak and has a nonstriking, eight-day movement.

Dimensions: 37 inches high, 9 inches wide, and 6 inches deep.

Price: $195, F.O.B. Addison, New York.

Purple Island Design

R.D. #1, Box 109
Addison, NY 14801
Tel. 607/359-2731

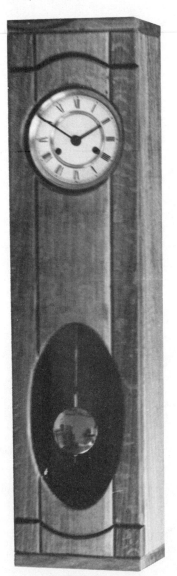

Airplane Clocks

THE amalgamation of time, flight, and the future: above, a replica 1940 AT-6 Radial Clock with a 1-rpm sweep hand, an aluminum-alloy spinoff of the famous AT-6 Texan advanced trainer that helped many World War II U.S. Army Air Corps pilots get their wings; at right, a low-wing monoplane clock suggesting a desk-bound Lockheed Electra, circa 1938.

Prices: Sarsaparilla #555P, aluminum airplane alarm clock, $95; Sarsaparilla #104H, marble and brass airplane desk and alarm clock, $95.

Sarsaparilla Deco Designs, Ltd.

5711 Washington St.
West New York, NJ 07093
Tel. 201/863-8002

Store Calendar Clock

CUMBERLAND general store's calendar clock replicates one first made by the Sessions Clock Company of Forestville, Connecticut, in 1903. Its cabinet is solid walnut into which rosettes have been carved on the door and upper pediment. The clock's face has an antiqued dial with black roman numerals to indicate the hour and red arabic ones to indicate the day.

Dimensions: 28 inches high by 14 inches wide.

Price: Cumberland catalog #8228, $250 F.O.B. Crossville, Tennessee.

"Wish and Want Book," $3.75.

Cumberland General Store

Route 3
Crossville, TN 38555
Tel. 615/484-8481

Our Elite Porcelain Enameled GAS RANGE and KITCHEN HEATER Combined

Made by the world's largest and most exacting stove builders.

$77.85 Cash

Priced Unusually Low

A beautiful white enameled pearl gray trimmed four-burner gas range with a fine, dependable oven and broiler! A practical and thoroughly efficient kitchen heater and rubbish burner of equal beauty! Combined into one solid utility unit to meet the needs and desires of thousands of housewives. The heater uses a minimum of fuel and disposes of waste and rubbish that would be a nuisance to destroy otherwise. Does wonders in the way of cooking and heating and will keep the kitchen warm and comfortable in zero weather. Burns Hard or Soft Coal, Coke or Wood.

Notice the roomy gray enameled UTILITY DRAWER of a thousand and one uses. You will greatly appreciate the convenience of this handy compartment for keeping the knives, forks, and other cooking equipment close to the stove, where they belong. This stove has the same easy sliding grates, the same rounded, smooth flowing surfaces as described on page 942 under our ELITE Gas Range.

The gas section has four heat diffusing burners, including three full size burners and one large giant burner, an oven that bakes as beautifully as it looks and has all the features of the up to date stove. If you have been considering either a kitchen heater or a new beautiful gas range, why not get both in one? At our price the cost is very low and the satisfaction great. The space under the cooking burners is white porcelain enameled, easy to keep clean and convenient for storing cooking utensils.

Measurements: Baking oven, 16x17½x13 inches; broiling oven, 16x17½x8 inches; cooking top, 32x19½ inches, including end shelf. Height to cooking top, 33½ inches. Length, over all, 52 inches. Floor space, 20x32 inches. Take 6-inch pipe. Heater has special drop coal feed door; top, 14½x19½ inches. Two 8-inch lids. Length for wood, 15½ inches. Shipping wt., 370 lbs.

Terms: $5.00 with order and $5.00 a month until full price has been paid. The easy and pleasant way to pay for kitchen comfort. Use Time Payment Order Blank on page 1092. Shipped promptly from our factory in NEWARK, OHIO.

22K99—Water coil to fit fire box to heat boiler. Shipping weight, 20 pounds..... 25

Made only with ......

22K1310—Combination, as illustrated. ......
Cash price......
Time payment price......

New and Improved ......
cooking by scientific ......
to order your sample ......
trohon and describe ......
Price only ......

Freight charges for shipping this unusual combination ......

Sanitary Clear Glass Stove Casters, not included in price. Protect floor, rugs or linoleum from being marred. Easy to clean. Order a set for your stove.

$63.50 Cash Price With Enamel Front

$58.50 Cash Price With Black Front Nickel Trimmed

$5.00 Down

$5.00 a Month

A—White porcelain enameled splasher cleans like a china dish.
B—Extra wide cooking top. Slide-easy top grates for gas section, two lids in coal section for cooking. Cook and heat with the same stove and fuel.
C—Large ashpan easily removed without fuss or mess.
D—Roomy utility drawer for storing cooking accessories.
E—Roomy shelf on top with back rail, making it safe and convenient to hold dishes and utensils.
F—Never fail, heat retaining oven constructed to insure the heat reaching all parts of the oven. Even heat for baking or roasting assured.
G—Note white enameled broiling pan.
H—Strong and sturdy legs. Easy to clean under the stove.

Combination GAS RANGE and KITCHEN HEATER With White Porcelain Enameled Front

$63.50 CASH

Exactly as Illustrated

And White Porcelain Enameled Mantle Shelf

This range is a combination of a kitchen heater and a gas range built into a single body. Very compact, takes up only a small amount of space.

Gas baking oven operates entirely independent from the coal section of the range. Guaranteed to do very fine work, both baking and roasting. It is not a combination oven and cannot be heated by the coal fire. The coal and wood fire cooks and heats, but does not bake. Uses gas only for baking.

You can cook with two fuels at the same time, using all six lids at a time when desired. Has two coal and wood lids and four gas cooking burners, including three full size and one Giant burner.

The coal and wood compartment may be used as an incinerator as well. Burn all your refuse, garbage and waste without odor; an easy, profitable way to dispose of such refuse.

Fire box burns hard or soft coal, coke, short wood, corn cobs, rubbish and kitchen waste. Cooks quickly and will furnish plenty of heat to warm your kitchen in the coldest weather.

The stove body is made of heavy gauge steel. Oven, 18x19 inches. Top, 34½x21½ inches. Fire box length for wood, 16 inches. Takes 6-inch stovepipe. Shpg. wt., 360 lbs.

Be sure to state whether you burn manufactured or natural gas. Range will not burn acetylene or gasoline gas. We will ship range for manufactured gas unless otherwise specified.

Range With White Enameled Front and Mantle Shelf.
22K1310—Range, as illustrated. Cash price...... **$63.50**
22K1310—Range, as illustrated. Time payment price...... $69.50
Range, Plain Black, Nickel Trimmed, and Mantle Shelf.
22K1311—Range. Cash price...... $58.50
22K1311—Range. Time payment price...... 64.50
22K1900—Automatic Lighter for top burners...... 1.20

When you consider the great saving our factory prices give you, it is easy to figure the difference between our low prices and those asked by others.
Shipped promptly from our factory in NEWARK, OHIO.

You need not Pay Cash in full. Terms: $5.00 with order, $5.00 a month until time payment price is paid. Use Time Payment Order Blank on page 1092.

22K97—Water front to fit in fire box to heat hot water boiler. **$4.75**
Shipping weight, 20 pounds.

Sanitary Clear Glass Stove Casters. Protect floor, rugs or linoleum from being marred. Easy to clean. Be sure to order a set for your stove. Shipping weight, per set of four, 4 lbs.
22K2929—Set of 4 Casters...... 40c

Ranges and Stoves

You need not pay cash in full.
$5.00 DOWN
$5.00 A MONTH

The Queen Atlantic Kitchen Range

AT THE center of every turn-of-the century home was a wood- or coal-burning kitchen range. The stove was used not only for cooking and baking, but also to provide the household with hot water and to heat adjoining rooms. By the early twentieth century full-size kitchen ranges were being built by the hundreds of thousands all across the country.

Portland Stove's Queen Atlantic has been in continual production since its introduction in 1906. From among such royalty of the time as the Star Kineo, the Home Comfort, the Crown Acorn, and the Glenwood stove, only she still reigns. The Queen Atlantic is made of 100% cast iron, and has long, deep fireboxes to accommodate loads of either wood or coal. She also features a six-lid top, deep ash pits, an optional hot-water reservoir, and a warming oven. The Queen Atlantic is the largest cast-iron kitchen range now made.

Dimensions: 32¼ inches high (to range top), 30 inches deep, and 57 inches wide (including end shelf).

Price: Queen Atlantic Cook Stove with single high shelf and end shelf, $2,091; with hot water reservoir, add $375; with warming oven, add $275; crating charge, $45. Specify wood or coal range.

A 25% deposit is required with each order, with balance due prior to shipment. Shipping charges are collected by the shipping company. Approximately 16 weeks is required for delivery from date of order as all stoves are individually handcrafted.

Portland Stove Company
P.O. Box 377
Fickett Road
North Pownal, ME 04069
Tel. 207/688-2254 or 775-6424

The Elmira Oval Cookstove

THE Elmira Oval is an airtight replication of the Findlay Oval stove, first introduced in 1908 by the Findlay Brothers Foundry near Ottawa, Ontario. Until its demise in 1956, the Findlay Oval was sold as the "Queen of the Cookstoves" to three generations of Canadian Mennonites. It was, in fact, their devotion to the Oval cookstove that brought about its remanufacture.

In the early 1970s Tom Hendrick, a hardware dealer from Elmira, Ontario, was doing all he could to scrounge old Findlay Oval replacement parts for stoves owned by area Mennonites. Hardly a day would pass when an Amish customer wouldn't pull his horse and buggy up to Hendrick's place to inquire after these parts and then extoll the old Oval's virtues.

So with the idea of having parts remanufactured, Hendrick went over to the Findlay foundry one day in 1976 to find the stove's original castings rusting away behind the plant. The wood stove revival of the late 1970s was only an ember then, undetected by the Findlay people, and they were uninterested in Hendrick's suggestion that they bring the stove back. So after mulling the idea over for a while, he decided that he'd go it alone. Hendrick slapped down the money for parts for about fifty stoves, and the Elmira Stove Works was born.

Today the Elmira operation is housed in a 35,000-square-foot factory and employs more than a hundred people. The requirements of the local Mennonites that made this all possible haven't been forgotten, but the "buxom-beauty" Oval and her more modest newly designed sisters, the Julia and the Sweetheart, now enjoy accolades from throughout the world.

In the course of remanufacturing the old Findlay Oval, Elmira has made several modifications to eliminate faults and otherwise provide improvements: the new Oval is airtight and provides a 25% longer burn; areas of wear discovered in the original have been reinforced; and many parts that were originally painted-over steel have now been porcelainized.

Also, the stove top has been thickened for better heat retention and the grates now have a summer and winter level. An optional water jacket that replaces a portion of the firebox can now heat from eight to ten gallons of water an hour. A coal-burning conversion package, and almond and gold porcelain colors are available.

Literature obtainable.

Elmira Stove Works

22 Church St. West
Elmira, ON N3B 1M3
Canada
Tel. 519/669-5103

Queen Cookstove

Four bottles, with corks partly drawn, were on the cold cooking stove.
—P. L. FORD, THE HON. PETER STIRLING AND WHAT PEOPLE THOUGHT OF HIM, 1899

THE SQUAT cookstove, its firebox stepping up by way of burners to the warming oven, was unchanged for generations. The famous Baltimore cookstove, patented by William T. James in 1815, shared its basic configuration with the Cumberland Store's 1907 Queen, shown here. The Queen is made entirely of cast iron, and features a large 24-inch by 24-inch cooking top. The oven is 21 inches deep by 12½ inches high, and has swing-away doors on either end. A cast-iron rack under the stove serves as a storage and drying area.

Specifications: width, 24 inches; depth, 45 inches; height to cooking surface, 20 inches; height to top, 34½ inches. Shipping weight: 335 lbs.

Price: $995, F.O.B. Crossville, Tennessee.

"Wish and Want Book" available, $3.75.

Cumberland General Store

Route 3
Crossville, TN 38555
Tel. 615/484-8481

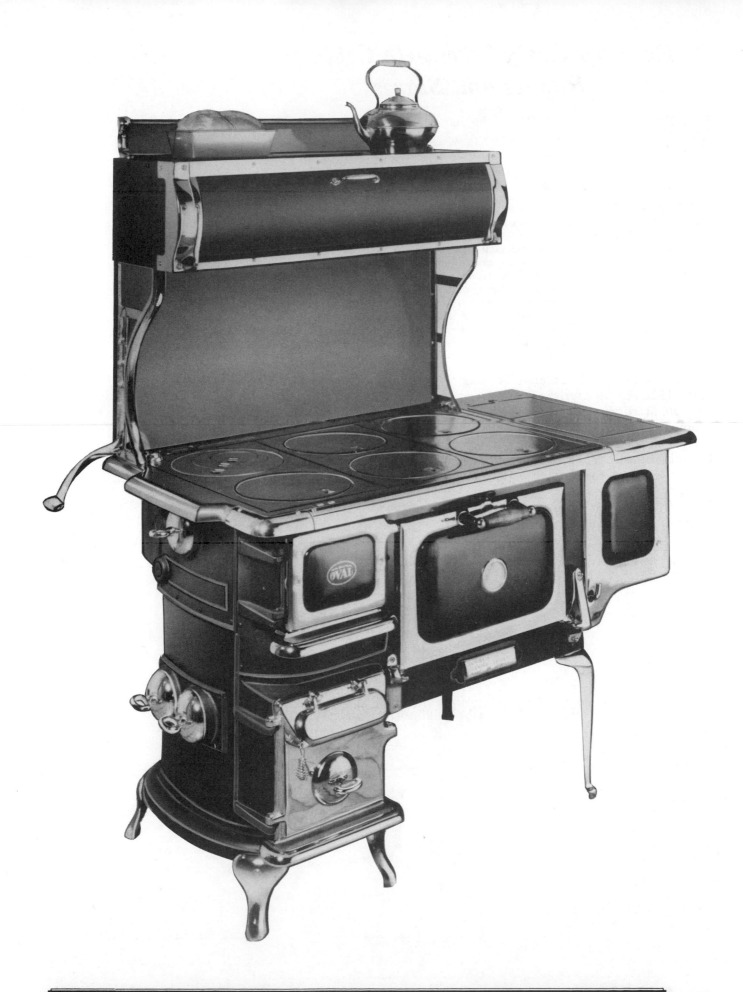

Restored Early-Twentieth-Century Ranges and Stoves

RICHARD RICHARDSON—who has earned the sobriquet "Stove Black" by dint of his 14 years' work in the restoration and sale of nineteenth- and early-twentieth-century parlor stoves, kitchen ranges, potbellies, and others—supplies us with the following regarding the restored cook ranges that he sells:

During the 1920s enamel stoves became popular. For the first time the cook had a variety of colors to choose from, plus the convenience of a stove that could be cleaned with a damp cloth. Typical colors were gray, beige, white, and pale greens in combination. Some spectacular blue models were also produced.

It was around this time that the gas and wood combination range was also made available. Early gas attachments were separate units that could be added to an existing range for operation independent of the wood or coal end of the stove. These ranges had no thermostats—only a heat indicator on the door—and had to be regulated manually. The addition of the gas "summer kitchens" was welcomed by cooks used to having to endure hot wood fires in the summertime. Gas-wood combinations as a single unit also began production during this period, with thermostatic controls introduced in the 1930s.

Depicted here is the Emerald Sterling, a restoration of a gas stove built in the 1920s by the Sterling Range Company of Troy, New York. Original Emerald Sterlings were available in combinations of either gray-on-white enamel or green-on-ivory. Among the other early-twentieth-century stoves offered by Good Time at this writing is a 1920s Sterling Gas-Wood Combination Range, a 1920 Hadley Dual gas-wood combination range, and a Victor gas-coal range.

Catalog available.

Good Time Stove Company

Route 112, P.O. Box 306
Goshen, MA 01032
Tel. 413/268-3677

Compare this Money Saving Price

Dilution Cream Separator

You get more cream, get it quicker, easier and more conveniently than when you resort to the old skimming methods.

Does the Work Quickly

Separates in three to four hours, and gives a sweet diluted milk that is much better for stock feeding than sour milk. Add an equal quantity of water to the milk. Cream separates and rises to top. You can watch separation through glass gauges in side of tank. Milk is drawn off through deep cone bottom faucet without disturbing cream.

Made of heavy tin plate. Seamed and well soldered throughout. Beautifully blue enameled outside. Prices include tank, tin tubes, strainer faucet and hardwood legs.

Can You Afford to Overlook These Values?

$3.25 10-Gal.

	Cap.	Shpg. Wt.	
99K2550	10 gal.	14 lbs.	$3.25
99K2551	*14 gal.	16 lbs.	4.—
99K2552	*18 gal.	20 lbs.	4.75
99K2553	*24 gal.	26 lbs.	6.30
99K2554	*32 gal.	31 lbs.	6.90

*Not mailable.

For Other Dairy Goods See Page 646

EQUIP YOUR DAIRY AT BIG SAVINGS

Double Can Cream Separators

$5.50 4-Gal.

Keeps cream cold and separates cream from milk in four to six hours in warm or cold weather. Removable inner can makes cleaning easy. Glass gauges show depth of cream. Water does not mix with milk or cream. Has separate faucets for drawing off milk and water. Inner can heavy tin plate. Outer can galvanized iron.

	Capacity of Inner Can	Shipping Weight	
99K2562	4 gal.	14 lbs.	$5.50
99K2563	*6 gal.	17 lbs.	6.20
99K2564	*8 gal.	20 lbs.	6.90
99K2565	*10 gal.	21 lbs.	7.25
99K2566	*12 gal.	23 lbs.	7.80

*Not mailable.

Our Improved Milk Coolers and Aerators

Milk Keeps Better If Cooled as Soon as Milked!

$6.40 Size No. 2

Pour milk or cream in at top through strainer and it comes out cool, sweet and clean. Cools milk quickly; aerates it, removing animal odors. Simple in construction. Easy to clean. Heavy tin plate with galvanized steel bottom. Use ice or cold running water. With double cheesecloth strainer, spring holding pins and directions. Not mailable.

99K2532—Size No. 2. Receiver holds 18 quarts. For 5 to 25 cows. Shipping weight, 25 pounds.............$6.40
99K2533—Size No. 3. Receiver holds 34 quarts. For 25 to 50 cows. Shipping weight, 33 pounds.............$7.80
99K2534—Size No. 4. Receiver holds 52 quarts. For 50 to 100 cows. Shipping weight, 40 pounds.............$9.30

Elgin Metal Churn

$2.65 2-Gal.

Gets all the butter from the cream in from 3 to 10 minutes. A well constructed churn with can of heavy steel, triple tinned and rustproof. Cover is of natural finish, selected hardwood. Frame is of steel. Castings have aluminum finish. Legs and standards strongly riveted steel. The gears, wheels and top castings are accurately fitted and run smoothly. Has removable dasher, making it easy to clean. Our prices are the lowest.

	Cap.	Shpg. Wt.	
99K2613		9 lbs.	$2.65
99K2614		13 lbs.	3.45
99K2615*		14 lbs.	3.95
99K2616*		18 lbs.	4.70

Holstein Dairy Scales

$3.50 40-Lb. Size

Milk Record Blank Included

Comply With Department of Weights and Measures Requirements

7-inch dial. Adjustable pointer permits obtaining exact weight of milk in pail. Directions furnished. Wt. 4 lbs.
9K2898—Cap. 40 lbs. by tenths of a lb......$3.50
9K2899—Cap. 60 lbs. by tenths of a lb. 4.50
9K2897—Milk Record Blanks. Seven-day sheet for keeping daily record of milk output for each cow. Wt. 1 lb. Per 100 sheets......48c

Babcock Milk Testing Outfit

$6.85

Dairy authorities recommend the Babcock Test. Prices include test bottles, brush, acid measure, pipette and directions for making tests. Acid not included. Shpg. wt., 19 lbs.
99K2573—Four-bottle size......$6.85

Extra Glassware for Babcock Testers
9K2882—50 per cent cream bottles. Wt. 2 oz......30c
9K2884—10 per cent milk bottles. Wt. 2 oz......28c
9K2886—Set of 1 per cent skim milk bottles. Wt. 2 oz......75c
9K2888—17.6-18-C.C. combination milk and cream pipetta. Weight, 6 ounces......24c
9K2890—17.5-C.C. acid measure. Weight, 1 oz......15c

"STAR" BARREL CHURNS

$5.40 6-Gal.

Barrel of oak. Varnished. Not mailable.
99K2592—Holds 6 gallons. Churns 1 to 3 gallons. Shipping weight, 30 pounds......$5.40
99K2593—Holds 10 gallons. Churns up to 5 gallons. Shipping weight, 36 lbs......6.15
99K2594—Holds 15 gallons. Churns up to 7 gallons. Shipping weight, 45 lbs......7.00
99K2595—Holds 20 gallons. Churns up to 10 gallons. Shipping weight, 55 lbs......8.25

Has 4-paddle dasher, making butter quickly. Made of clear straight grained cedar. Hoops are electric welded. Legs and frame from hardwood.

$3.70 3-Gal.

	Cap.						
	13	7	60	$17.75			
99K8348½	20	10	70				
99K8349½	25	12	90	6.50			
99K8350½	35	16	100				
99K8351½							

*Not mailable.

Farm and Garden

Picket or Tie Out Chains

42c And Up

Heavy gauge steel chain with swivel snap on one end and 1¼-inch ring on other. Swivel in center to avoid tangling.
9K6036—Size 0 or about ⅛ in. diam., 20 feet long. Wt. 4 lbs......42c
9K6037—Size 2-0 or about ³⁄₁₆ in. diam., 30 feet long. Wt. 6 lbs......65c
9K6038—Size 3-0 or about ¼ in. diam., 30 feet long. Wt. 7 lbs......80c

For Cattle Halters and Ropes see page 1083.

Electric Welded Straight Link Cow Ties
23c

Links are extra strong. Size 2-0. About ⅛ inch in diameter, 4½ ft. long. Weight, 2 pounds.
9K6034 73c | $1.63

Sensible Cattle Leaders
Malleable iron. Length, 8¼ inches.
9K6086—With 10 ft. ½-in. rope......35c
9K6087—Leader only......25c

Self Piercing Bull Ring
25c

Copper. Better than old style rings. ¼x2¼ inch. Weight, 6 ounces.
9K6076......25c

Prize Bull Ring
45c

Large size, self piercing, extra heavy solid copper, beautifully finished. Size, ⅝x3 in. Weight, 6 ounces.
9K6075......45c

Buy An ANTI-KICKING COW CHAIN HERE FOR LESS MONEY

48c

Metal collar bands fit around hind legs of cow. Strong heavy weight chain can be drawn through lock, making any adjustment desired to prevent cow from kicking or side stepping while being milked.
9K6043—Wt. 1½ lbs......48c

Genuine Kentucky Loud Speaker Cow Bells
25c And Up

Can be heard twice as far as ordinary pressed steel bells. Will not easily dent or crush out of shape. Without straps.
9K6011—State size.

Height In.	Size No.	Size Mouth	Takes Strap	Wt. Lbs.	Each
					26c
					30c
					35c

Swiss Pattern Cow Bells
48c And Up

Finest Swiss bell metal, musical tone, sounding different than ordinary bells. Will give years of service. Comes without straps.

	Diam. Mouth	Takes Strap	Weight Lbs.	
9K6013	3¼ in.	1¼ in.	½	$0.48
9K6014	3¾ in.	1½ in.	¾	.85
9K6015	5 in.	2½ in.	1	1.24

Leather Cow Bell Straps, 20 Inches Long

Width, Inches	1¼	1½	2½
Weight	7 oz.	8 oz.	9 oz.
10K2601	30c	45c	54c

Turkey Bell
15c

Solid brass, polished. Diameter, 1¾ in., with leather strap and buckle as shown. Wt., each, 3 oz.
9K6062 15c $1.75 Each | Doz.

Sheep Bell With Strap
30c

Diameter, 2⅝ inches, with strap as shown. Wt., each, 5 oz.
9K6004 30c $2.90 Each | Doz.

Cow Poke
72c 2 for

Will not chafe. Strong, light and comfortable long forks. Length, over all, 36 in. Spur points stop animal from forcing way through fence.
99K6274
Shipping weight, 3½ lbs. 2 for 72c

Safety Weaners
35c No. 2

Permits calf to grass or drink. Does not go through calf's nose nor make it sore. Galvanized metal. Side protection prevents calf sucking sidewise. Parcel post weight, 1 pound.
9K6094—State size.

Size	For	Wt.	
1	Large Calves	4 oz.	35c
2	Yearlings	6 oz.	35c
3	2-Yr. Olds and Cows	8 oz.	45c

Wire Basket Weaners
29c and Up

Steel wire heavily tinned. Price includes web straps.
9K6096—Calves. Weight, 8 ounces...29c
9K6097—Yearlings. Weight, 12 ounces...33c
9K6098—Cows. Weight, 1 pound...40c

Sure-Cure Weaners
Positively Prevents Sucking

Adjustable nose ring fitted with smooth ball tips. Easily applied. Made of malleable iron and steel, heavily tinned.
9K6092—Calves. Weight, 4 ounces...40c
9K6093—Cows. Weight, 8 ounces...55c

The Baker Run-In-Oil Windmills and Towers

THE following have been reproduced from the Heller-Aller catalog: Price list and literature available, $1.50.

The Heller-Aller Company, Inc.

Corner of Perry and Oakwood
Napoleon, OH 43545
Tel. 419/592-1856 or 592-3216

BAKER RUN-IN-OIL WINDMILLS

"Old Reliable"

Thousands of users have nicknamed the Baker Windmills W h y? Because they have proven themselves capable of giving a life time of economical and dependable water pumping service. All working parts are running in a bath of oil. Requires oiling but once a year. More sails to the wheel. Simple and sturdy throughout. Will fit any make tower.

For Sale By

BAKER RUN-IN-OIL WINDMILLS

Real Service

Baker Windmills have proven themselves capable of giving a life time of uninterrupted service. All working parts are within the oil bowl and running in a bath of oil. Double gears equally distribute the load. More sails to the wheel. Oil but once a year. Strong and sturdy. You will appreciate it's many advantages. Will fit any make tower.

For Sale By

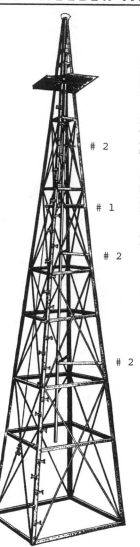

\# 2

\# 1

\# 2

\# 2

* NO. 4 — HEAVY DUTY — TOWERS

For use in extremely windy situations. Also recommended for use with electric generating units. Heavy corner post angles (3/16'' x 2½'' x 2½'') to the top.

THE HELLER-ALLER CO., NAPOLEON, OHIO, U.S.A.

Four Post Galvanized Steel Towers

Heller-Aller Towers are extra well braced and banded, thus giving added strength and security. All tension is taken care of at our factory and so no adjustment or alignment is left to the erector who may be inexperienced. We use flat steel bands for braces, which once erected, draw the tower firm and rigid. There is nothing to work loose or cause the tower to lose alignment.

Select a tower high enough to carry the mill 8 to 10 feet above all surrounding houses, barns, trees or wind obstructions within a 300 foot radius. This permits a clean sweep of the wind from all directions to the mill, giving greatest efficiency. A high tower also protects the mill from damaging swirling winds coming off close surrounding objects.

The tower illustration shows the type of construction used in the Heller-Aller Co. towers. Corner posts are fabricated from heavy galvanized angles, 2 inch angles in the No. 1 tower and 2½ inch angles in the No. 3 towers. The bands, horizontal pieces, are fabricated of either 1 inch or 1¼ inch galvanized angles. The braces are fabricated of 7/8 inch flat galvanized steel. For Pull-Out details, see page 18.

At figure No. 2 you will note how the pump rod guides are installed. The purpose of these guides is to keep the wood pump rod straight and in the center of the tower.

No. 1 Towers—For 8-Foot Mills and smaller. Corner posts are built of 2 inch angle.
* No. 4 Towers—For 12-Foot Mills and smaller. Corner posts are 2½ inch angle.

Tower Height Feet	No. 1 TOWERS			No. 4 TOWERS		
	Weight Pounds		List Price	Weight Pounds		List Price
15	320		$	420		$
20	390			520		
30	500			690		
35	570			780		
40	600			860		
50				1,030		
60				1,235		

Anchor posts, anchor plates, wood pump rods, pullout lever, and wood platform are always shipped with the tower. In ordering, always give the number of tower and height.

For repairs see page 39

Fig. 578

Steel Stub Tower

For erecting windmills on top of other make towers and buildings consisting of four top corner angles.

Fig. Number	Article		List Price
ST65	6½-ft. Stub with Platform.........		$
ST5	5 -ft. Stub with Platform.........		
ST4	4 -ft. Stub, less Platform.........		
ST3	3 -ft. Stub, less Platform.........		
WP	Wood Platform only, Painted		
575	Wood Pull-out Lever with Spring..		

BACK GEAR **BAKER** RUN-IN-OIL WINDMILLS

Fig. 906

6, 8, 10, 12 Foot Sizes

Phantom View

Entire Mechanism

The "Baker" Windmill is a powerful and sturdy mill with smooth and easy running qualities.

The wheel is designed with a multiplicity of blades correctly curved and pitched to convert the maximum amount of energy from the prevailing winds to pumping power. Through the back gear arrangement, the wheel makes three revolutions to produce one complete pumping stroke.

The back gear design provides two pinion gears pinned to the main shaft against the interior sides of the oil bowl. The pinion gears drive the two large gears mounted on the stud shafts which project into the bowl from the hubs on either side of the bowl. The use of two sets of gears, one on either side of the bowl, distributes the load evenly assuring less wear and longer life of the mechanism. The pitman is connected from the offset hub of the large gears to the center of the rocker arm. The rocker arm, which is connected to boss provided at the back end and is an intergral part of the bowl, carries the side straps which run upward and are secured to the pump rod casting. As the wheel turns the main shaft, the train of the mechanism produces the up and down stroke of the pump rod.

The vane made of high grade galvanized steel, is of larger area and long so as to serve postively as a rudder to keep the wheel into the wind.

DISTINCTIVE FEATURES OF THE BACK GEARED BAKER WINDMILL

1. A Perfect Product - Over 80 years experience in windmill production results in the finest. Simple in design and use of the best materials available.

2. Gray iron castings and cold rolled shafting team up to provide the most rigid construction, and the best wearing surfaces in this windmill.

3. The complete operating mechanism runs in the pool of oil contained in the bottom of the one piece cast iron bowl, lubricating all moving parts and bearing surfaces. There are no parts above the bowl to become dry. This is POSITIVE OILING.

4. Leverage Advantage - The underslung rocker arm gives the Baker Windmill direct upward lifting motion providing the greatest power transferal and resulting in an easy operating windmill.

5. Two pinions and 2 large gears on either side of the pump rod distributes the load, giving smoother action and longer life.

6. Compact and Simple Design - A minimum of working parts, all brought together within the bowl, produce the most compact train of power transmission.

7. Bearings - All bearings are made of the best grade of cast iron and because of the graphitic content of gray iron, an excellent bearing surface is created in this useage. The main removeable bearing is provided with an oil grove the full length of the bearing surface permitting the oil which is picked up by the pinion gear, to move through the bearing to the oil seal at the far end where the oil is trapped and dropped into an oil return channel taking the oil back to the bowl.

8. The Baker Wheel - After many years of experience and thorough testing, this wheel was developed to capture the maximum amount of energy from the wind and transform it into pumping power. The result is a windmill easily able to activate a pump in a slight wind.

9. The Baker Vane - Extra long and with Maximum area of galvanized steel to serve as a rudder to keep the wheel into the wind under variable conditions. The vane is "Automatically Self Governing" so that when the wind reaches a high velocity, it will take the windmill out of gear to avoid damage.

10. Ball Bearing Turntable - Two iron castings with chilled ball bearing races are provided to accept a complete ring of ½" ball bearings. The main casting is secured to the top of the tower and the second casting rides on the ring of ball bearings. The mast pipe of the windmill goes through the center of the two castings and is thereby free to revolve easily on the tower so that the wheel may always face the wind.

11. Will Fit Any Make of Existing Tower - Different styles of turntables and truing centers are available to fit many towers. If the Baker turntable cannot be adapted to the existing tower we can furnish, at small additional cost, stub towers which can be added to any tower and which will accommodate our equipment.

12. Easily Erected - Baker windmills are simple to assemble and erect.

Old-Style Dairy Tinware

For dealer information contact:

Louisville Tin & Stove Company

P.O. Box 1019
Louisville, KY 40201

TIN WARE

IX HEAVY CREAM CANS

APPROVED

MEETS RIGID SANITARY REQUIREMENTS OF STATE HEALTH AUTHORITIES

Made of IX bright tin, seamed and full soldered. Plain body. Heavy tinned ears—riveted on. Tinned wire bail, with black enameled bail-wood handle. SOLDER HEAVILY FLOWED OVER ALL SEAMS AND RIVETS making it easily cleaned and eliminating the usual cracks and crevices which harbor bacteria. Heavy drawn cover, made in one piece, with well rounded corners and deep crown that insures a tight fit. Rolled edge on wide flange extends well over rolled edge on top of can, preventing dirt and other particles from getting between the cover and body.

Nos.	96	98	912	916	920
Actual Capacity, Qts.	6	8	12	16	18
Height of body, ins.	7	9	13	17	19
Diameter inside, ins.	8⅝	8⅝	8⅝	8⅝	8⅝
Weight, per dozen	29	32	39	46	49

Packed one-half dozen in carton

DAIRY PAILS

Made of bright coke tinplate. Raised dome bottom. Heavy wired top rim. Heavy ears riveted to body. No. 4 sanitary tinned wire bail. All seams neatly soldered. 12 quart capacity. Furnished in both IX (135 lb.) and IC (107 lb.) quality coke tinplate.

LIPPED DAIRY PAILS

Specially designed lip for easy pouring. Holds 12 quarts. All seams soldered. Top rim reinforced with heavy gauge wire. No. 4 sanitary tinned wire bail. Body made of bright coke tinplate. Ears riveted to body. Raised dome bottom. Furnished in both IX (135 lb.) and IC (107 lb.) quality coke tinplate.

IX STRAINERS

SANITARY

IX bright tin. Foot easily removed for cleaning strainer disc, making it thoroughly sanitary. Size of strainer disc gives ready flow to milk assuring far greater straining capacity than ordinary strainers. As the strainer cloth is always the first part of a strainer to give way the Sanitary is in the end the most economical since new discs can be had for a fraction of the price of a new strainer.

No. S50—Diam. top 10 ins.; height 4½ ins.; diam. bottom 3¾ ins.

1 dozen in carton; weight per carton, 8 pounds

EXTRA STRAINER DISCS

No. DS50—For No. S50 sanitary strainers.

STOVE PIPE COLLARS

PLAIN

Made of Bright Tinplate

Nos.	6	7
Pipe, ins.	6	7
Price Each	$........	$........
Wt., per grs.	20	29

12 Dozen in carton

WIDE FLANGE

Made of Bright Tinplate with extra wide flange

Nos.	023	024	025	026
Diameter, ins.	9¼	9¼	9¼	10⅝
For Pipe, ins.	3	4	5	6
Wt., per gross	30	27	25	32

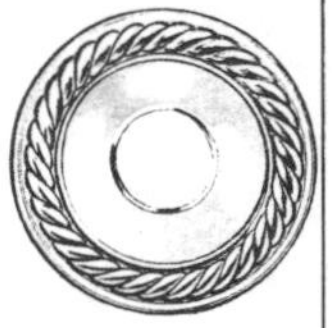

Hand Cultivator

THE DUPLICATE of a 1930s tool found in a New England barn, this garden cultivator has a wooden handle and spring-action steel prongs. Length: 10 inches. Shipping weight: 1 lb.

Price: Vermont Country Store catalog #15617, $4.95.

Delivery charge (based on shipping weight) required in advance.

Seasonal catalogs available from The Vermont Country Store, Catalog Request, Route 100, Weston, VT 05161.

The Vermont Country Store

Mail Order Office
P.O. Box 3000
Manchester Center, VT 05255

Cumberland General Store Farm Implements

Heavy-Duty Milk Cans

THESE 10-gallon milk cans have been used and have worn finishes, so Cumberland sells them "as is." The store requests that you state your preference for either the recessed- or umbrella-lidded can, but must ship what is available nonetheless. Shipping weight: 28 lbs.

    Price: Cumberland catalog #5387, $24.95 each.

Old-Style Weed Cutter

EXACTLY how old is unclear, but the Cumberland General Store's early-twentieth-century weed cutter employs an A-shaped blade for the easy passing of cut grass through the cutter. The removable blade is made of high-carbon steel that has been sharpened to a keen edge, with a hardwood handle shaped to fit the hand. Shipping weight: 4 lbs.

    Price: Cumberland catalog #8566, $11.60, F.O.B. Crossville, Tennessee.

Gem Water Elevator Chain Pump

THE Gem chain pump is made of galvanized steel, painted gray, varnished, lettered, and trimmed in black. It has malleable iron castings, a round iron sprocket, and a wooden handle, black. The Gem measures 8 by 16 inches at its outside base and is 36½ inches high. Shipping weight: 25 lbs.

    Price: Cumberland catalog #5162, $116.38.

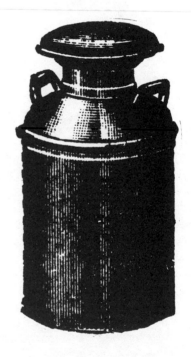

McConnon's Black Ointment

AN OLDTIME universal healing ointment (for man, beast, and poultry) in demand by Cumberland's customers. This external salve is useful for boils, cuts, scratches, open sores, wounds, and some forms of eczema. Livestock uses include galls, harness sores, sore teats, wire cuts, and as an application for contracted hooves. Also good as an antipick salve for chickens, but don't use it on cats! In the original 5-ounce tin. Shipping weight: 1 lb.

    Price: Cumberland catalog #3116, $4.64, F.O.B. Crossville, Tennessee.

"Wish and Want Book" available, $3.75.

Cumberland General Store

Route 3
Crossville, TN 38555
Tel. 615/484-8481

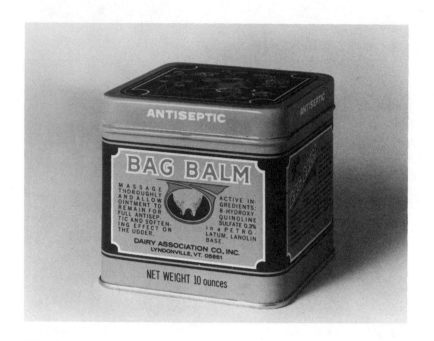

Bag Balm

A SALVE for cows' udders, Bag Balm is still packaged in the same art nouveau tin used when it was first placed on the market. That was in 1909, and rural folk quickly discovered that what Bag Balm could do for a raw dewclaw, it could do for human scrapes, rashes, and cuts as well. But Bag Balm was intended to ease bovine distress before any other, and its value here was appreciated at the end of the Earth.

From the Antarctic to your local mall boutique, Bag Balm transcends attitude as well as latitude. Packaged in little versions of the original can and sold alongside scented candles and drawer sachets, this early-twentieth-century ointment for girth galls and chapped teats is now a suburban favorite too.

Dairy Association Company
Lyndonville, VT 05851

Great Valley New York Box 18
July 30 th. 1936

Dairy Association,Co.Inc.
Dept.S
Lyndonville,Vermont

Dear Sir's;
    Just a line in regards to Bag Balm,
I should have written you a long time ago,but somehow I
misplaced your address,I do not know whether you know it or not
but BAG BALM was used on the Guernsey Cows That I had charge of
for Admiral Byrd on his last Expedition to the Antarctic.

  While I had the Guernsey Cows in a tent for three weeks
before the barn was completed,I had to depend entirely on
(BAG BALM) to keep their teats soft and plyable in sub zero
tempatures ,and when one of our cows did receive a severe frost
bite I healed it up entirely with Bag Balm,the cow that I have
reference too is at present at the Deerfoot Farms in Southboro
Mass. This cow can be examined at any time and you can easily
see that the Bag Balm Healed so perfecly that there is not one
scar left on her udder.
  I know that your company knew that Admiral Byrd took
cattle with him to the Antarctic,but I am sure that you were not
aware that Bag Balm was taken along on the Expedition I chose
Bag Balm because I wanted something that I could depend upon.

  With kind regards I remain;

   Yours Very Truly
   Edgar F Cox
   Edgar F.Cox Box 18
   Great Valley N.Y.

(Herdsman for Admiral Byrd)

Men's and Women's Clothing

It's Easy to Measure for Clothing

Our clothing is carefully made according to correct size standards. You do not need to order larger sizes than we specify. Our descriptions tell you the size range and you can order with the assurance that, if your size is listed, we guarantee the garment will fit you. Our sizes are obtained by securing the average of thousands of men, women and children in each size, and we believe are the most accurate standards in the country.

We Guarantee to Fit and Please You

Men's, Young Men's and Youths' Clothing

How to Take the Measurements

Stand in your natural way, breathe regularly and do not expand chest; also take everything bulky out of your pockets.

Chest. Take measurement over vest. Measure all around body at chest, close up under arms, snug but not tight. Tape measure should be over shoulder blades at the back. See line marked A on Figure 1.

Waist. If you wear a belt, take it off and take your measure over pants all around body at waist. Your waistline is just above hip bones. Feel sides for location of hip bones. See line marked B on Figure 2.

Inseam. This is to show length of pants leg. Stand straight and draw pants well up in crotch. Measure from close up in crotch to bottom of trousers, at length desired. See line marked C on Figure 2. For cuff bottom trousers measure 1 inch shorter than for plain bottom pants.

Figure 1

Figure 2

What Measurements to Give in Your Order

Suits. Give chest and waist measures and length of inseam; also height, weight and age.

Coats of All Kinds, Jackets, Raincoats and Overcoats. State chest measure taken over vest; also height, weight and age.

Vests. Give chest and waist sizes; also height, weight and age.

Pants (Both Dress and Work Pants) and Overalls. Give waist size and length of inseam; also height, weight and age.

WOMEN'S, MISSES' and JUNIORS'

Coats, Dresses, Knickers, Blouses, Raincoats, etc.

HOW TO TAKE MEASUREMENTS:

Always Pull Tape Close but Not Tight.

Do Not Allow. We Will Make All Necessary Allowances.

Give Each Measurement as Stated in Description of Garment You Are Ordering.

Actual Bust Measurement — For any garment, be sure to measure over very largest part of bust with dress or blouse on. Tapeline in back must run on shoulder blades and not below them.

Actual Waist Measurement — This measurement is very important when ordering knickers and skirts. Please do not allow extra. Give actual tape measurement, over dress or blouse.

Actual Lower-Hip Measurement — This means very largest part of figure below waist. Do not "allow." We will make all necessary allowances. Measure over dress or skirt.

Length Garment Desired — For dresses, coats or raincoats, measure down back from neckline to hem, as shown in small diagram, N to L. For skirts measure down front from waist, as shown (W to S).

Height — Knowing your height, we can use the very best judgment in sending you the proper dress, coat, suit or knicker. Give weight, also, if you desire best possible fit.

Tell Us ... garments loose-fitting or close-fitting? See space for answer on order blank.

Use Clothing Order Blank in Back of This Catalog

... Delighted! ... how easily and quickly you can be correctly fitted when above ... given to us. Our years of experience enables us to determine ...

Sweaters

A roomy sweater will give better service. Your proper sweater size is 2 inches larger than actual measure.

Women's Sweaters: Measure all around body at bust over blouse or dress. To your actual bust measure add 2 inches. For example, if your actual bust measure is 38 inches, order size 40 sweater.

Men's Sweaters: Take measure ... over vest and order sweater 2 ... measure. For example, if your ... order size 42.

For children's and misses' sweaters ... age.

Boys' and Girls' Clothing

GIVE AGE SIZE. ... *boy's or girl's chest measure, then consult boys' or girls' scale of sizes below.*

Before ordering a boys' or girls' garment it is necessary to know the chest measure in order ... proper AGE SIZE ... boys of the same age ... and girls of ... measurements of many thousands of boys and girls of each age.

HOW TO MEASURE CHEST. For a boy, see "D" on Figure 5. Measure all around body at chest ... For a girl, see "L" on Figure 6 ...

To Measure for Boys' Long Trousers and Long Trousers Suits

For suits, measure boy's chest, waist and inseam, as shown in figure 7 at N, P and R. For trousers, measure waist and inseam only as in figure 7 at P and R. Our boys' long trousers and long trousers suits are sold according to age, size and measurements. The table below shows you the measurements of the different age sizes. For example: If your boy's chest measure is 27 inches, waist measure 25½ inches and inseam 23 inches, order size 10. If you find that your boy's measurements do not agree with age sizes given in the table, send us the boy's chest, waist and inseam measurements and state his height and weight and we will send a garment that will fit him.

Figure 7

Age Size to Order	5	6	7	8	9	10
Chest Measure, Inches	24	24½	25	26	26½	27
Waist Measure, Inches	23½	24	24	24½	25	25½
Inseam Measure, Inches	18	19	20	21	22	23
Age Size to Order	11	12	13	14	15	16
Chest Measure, Inches	27½	28	29	30¼	32	33
Waist Measure, Inches	26	27	27½	28	29	30
Inseam Measure, Inches	24	25	26	27	28	29

Boys' or Little Fellows'

Knee Pants, Suits, Overcoats, Raincoats, Mackinaw Coats, Blouses and Underwear

How to Use Size Scale

For example: If your boy's chest measure is 24 inches, order age size 5, or if your boy's chest measure is 30½ inches, order age size 14.

In case your boy's chest measure is between two of the measurements given below, order the age size for the next larger chest measure.

For example: If your boy's chest measure is 28½ inches, order age size 13.

Figure 5

BOYS' SIZE SCALE

Boys' Chest Measure, Inches	Age Size to Order
22	3
23	4
24	5
24½	6
25	7
26	8
26½	9
27	10
27½	11
28	12
29	13
30½	14
32	15
33	16
34	17

Girls' or Children's

Dresses, Blouses, Middies, Raincoats and Underwear

How to Use Size Scale

For example: If your girl's chest measure is 22 inches, order age size 3, or if your girl's chest measure is 31 inches, order age size 12.

In case your girl's chest measure is between two of the measurements given below, order the age size for the next larger chest measure.

For example: If your girl's chest measure is 26½ inches, order age size 8.

GIRLS' SIZE SCALE

Girls' Chest Measure, Inches	Age Size to Order	Lgth. of Dress, In.
21	2	20
22	3	22
23	4	23
24	5	24
25	6	26
26	7	27
27	8	28
29	10	32
31	12	36
33	14	40

Figure 6

Men's Underwear

Union Suits and Undershirts. Give chest size. Take off your vest. Measure all around body over your shirt.

Underdrawers. Give waist size.

Men's Dress, Work and Nightshirts. State neck measure.

Gloves

HOLD HAND OUT FLAT WITH FINGERS TOUCHING, THUMB RAISED; draw tape close around hand but not tight, as shown in illustration (do not include thumb). The number of inches shown by this measurement is your correct glove size.

Women's Sizes in Silk Fabric, Knitted Yarn and Fleece Lined Kid Gloves: 6, 6½, 7, 7½, 8, 8½.

Women's Sizes in Unlined Kid Gloves: 5¾, 6, 6¼, 6½, 6¾, 7, 7¼, 7½, 7¾, 8, 8½.

Men's Sizes: 7, 7½, 8, 8½, 9, 9½, 10, 10½.

For gloves for infants and children from 6 months to 14 years of age, give age of child.

Hats and Caps

Men's and Boys' Hats and Caps. Measure all around head, as illustrated; then refer to the table below.

Children's Hat Sizes, 6¼ to 6⅞. **Boys' Hat Sizes,** 6⅝ to 7⅛.
Men's Hat Sizes, 6¾ to 7¾.

If Head Measures, In.	19⅝	19¾	20⅛	20½	20⅞	21¼	21⅝	22	22⅜	22¾	23⅛	23½	23⅞
Order Hat Size	6¼	6⅜	6½	6⅝	6¾	6⅞	7	7⅛	7¼	7⅜	7½	7⅝	7¾

MEN'S AND WOMEN'S HATS

Bill Nader, whose Worthington Street shop is a Springfield, Massachusetts, landmark, was taught his trade by a man he calls "the last true hatter on earth"—his grandfather, Charles J. Nader. Early in the century the elder Nader's shop stood over on Victoria Square.

Using the skills he was taught and the hatter's blocks he inherited, Bill Nader has produced a line of reproduction early-twentieth-century homburgs, cloches, derbys, caps, and other ladies' and gentlemen's headwear. These are fashioned from 100% imported fur felt by the original methods, and, where appropriate, have the hand-formed welt edging and individually fitted satin and oilskin liners no longer to be found on other than the most expensive new hats.

But for all of this, and although Mr. Nader's methods are painstaking ones, he is quick to point out that because materials are now generally inferior, no reproduction hat can be as good as the original it emulates.

Derby

THE DERBY was most commonly worn from 1900 through 1920 and only began to decline after the Armistice brought with it a spirit of greater casualness to men's fashion. Mr. Nader's derby hat is available in black, gray, or brown, and in sizes 6¾ through 7⅝.
   Price: Nader catalog #015, $50.

Eight-Quarter Caps

WORN BY rogues from Ruth to Rockefeller, the eight-quarter cap is probably this century's most democratic (and ubiquitous) topper. They've shown up just about every decade, most recently as "newsboy caps." Bill Nader calls his the St. Andrew's, and it's available in either a brown or gray houndstooth wool blend. Sizes are small, medium, large, and extra-large.
   Price: Nader catalog #084W, $15.

1940s Fedora

NOTED in the May 1940 issue of *Esquire* as suitable for "semi-sports and country," Mr. Nader's Charles fedora comes with a 2¼- or 2⅜-inch snap brim and a 1-inch grosgrain band. It's available in black, gray, navy, taupe, light taupe, or willow, in sizes 6⅞ through 7⅞.

Prices: Nader catalog #005 (2¼-inch brim), $45; Nader catalog #0055 (2⅜-inch brim), also $45.

Snap-Brim Felt Hat

ALTHOUGH Indiana Jones is depicted as living in the 1930s, the soft-felt fedora that he helped to revive in the 1980s was first popularized by the dashing Prince of Wales back in the 1920s. Mr. Nader's reproduction, the Adventurer, has its high crown set on a 2¾-inch-wide brim and wrapped in an extra-wide grosgrain band. The Adventurer is available in black, brown, or taupe in sizes 6¾ through 7¾.

Price: Nader catalog #007, $45.

1930s Women's Hat

THE LIBBY is a Thirties-style ladies' hat trimmed in mink. It's available in black with either a kohinor (a gray, white, and black mix) or black mink trim; or in camel with ranch mink trim. Size 22½ only.

Price: Nader catalog #013, $75.

Homburg

BOTH Bill Nader and the author of a 1919 fashion feature in *Men's Wear* magazine have despaired of finding a real homburg hat anymore, but only the latter went on to wail "Shall we ever return to the magnificent fashions of other days?" The homburg was actually still pretty new in 1919, having only recently become fashionable as the Tyrolean-derived hat that the Prince of Wales had worn on prewar visits to Germany.

With its distinctly tapering crown and moderately narrow, rolled brim, the homburg was an essential part of a well-dressed man's wardrobe. After World War II, however, only Winston Churchill and Dwight Eisenhower ever seemed to want to wear one.

Bill Nader's Churchill Homburg has a grosgrain band, a matching binding, and a 2½- or 2⅜-inch brim. It's available in black, gray, navy, or taupe in sizes 6½ to 7¾.

Prices: Nader catalog #014 (2½-inch brim), $50; Nader catalog #0145 (2⅜-inch brim), $50.

Opera Hat

PRIOR TO 1910 the gibus—or collapsible silk opera hat —was favored for formal evening attire. "Oldsters may retain the high silk topper," one magazine remarked, but "the collapsible opera hat in dull grosgrain is preferred by younger men." Opera hats are usually considered "top hats" now, and that's what Bill Nader calls his. In black silk only, it's available in sizes 6¾ to 7¾.

Price: Nader catalog #016, $95.

To cover the costs of shipping and handling, please add $3 to each order for UPS, or $2.50 for parcel post delivery.

Mr. Nader also sells a large variety of original antique men's and women's hats, and will take orders for custom-made period designs.

Catalog available, $2.

Nader the Hatter, Inc.
340 Worthington St.
Springfield, MA 01103
Tel. 413/736-8081

PAST PATTERNS

The dedication of the Past Patterns company to the preservation and promotion of "American Garment History" is evident in their broad range of design patterns for nineteenth- and early-twentieth-century wearing apparel. Each of these is the result of diligent efforts on the parts of a researcher, designer, and drafter, all devoted to effecting the highest degree of historical accuracy in their work. Following the advice of nationally known scholars and experts in the field of historical costuming, the American Association of State and Local History has selected Past Patterns as its only listed pattern maker. The following is a selection of the company's early-twentieth-century offerings.

Edwardian-Era Corset

THE Edwardian-era "straight-fronted" corset was invented by two Parisians, Dr. Franz Glénhard and Mme Gashes-Sarraute, at the turn of the century. Because it reduced the severe compression of the chest and waist that characterized previous "waspwaist" designs, the corset was considered a healthful as well as a stylish undergarment. Past Pattern's #106 may be worn as a foundation garment to re-create the proper feminine silhouette for the period spanning 1899 to 1908. The Edwardian corset is available in sizes 10 to 20 as a pattern, a kit, or a custom-made garment.

peggy powell

Princess Gown

IT WAS at the turn of the century when stage actresses first assumed the role of arbiters of taste and the theater began to replace high society as a fashion setter. Opening nights provided an occasion to promenade in the latest look—a time when something like Past Pattern's 1900 Princess Gown might have been worn by such highly admired actresses as Lily Langtry or Maxine Elliot. Past Pattern's #112 features a silk taffeta underskirt with a lace overlay, and yards of silk gossamer ribbon, chiffon, and tulle. Available in pattern sizes 10 to 16.

Edwardian Blouses

THE TAILORED jacket led inexorably to the wide variety of Edwardian blouses worn beneath them. These are described in Elizabeth Ewing's *History of 20th-Century Fashions* as "one of the most notable and characteristic items introduced into the wardrobe at this time." Three such available from Past Patterns are the lingerie blouses (#403 and #405), which are distinguished by their tucks, fabrics, and profusion of lace; the mannish blouse (#400), which has a stiff collar and cuffs in the Victorian manner; and the tailored blouses (#404 and #406), softer versions of the mannish blouse that are buttoned at the back or side.

Spectator Jacket

REFLECTING THE VIGOROUS emancipation that women enjoyed during this period, tailored costumes like the 1907 spectator jacket were worn while participating in such popular sports of the day as bicycling, lawn tennis, golf, and croquet. Perhaps thinking it only riflery, Mata Hari insisted on wearing her custom-made spectator jacket to her own execution. Past Pattern's #113 re-creates the exceedingly smart image of the period 1905 to 1911. It is available in pattern sizes 10 to 20.

Boy's Buster Brown Suit

THE **Buster Brown** suit became fashionable in 1908, when artist Richard Foutcault's Buster Brown comic-strip character was at the height of its popularity. The suit was among the first articles of clothing specifically designed for young boys, and reflects the era's growing recognition of childhood as a distinct and separate period of life. Past Patterns #7379 is available in size 7 only.

© 1985 peggy powell

Empire-Style Tea Gown

I wish you girls was married and off my hands. I'd feel easier. I don't trust girls nowadays with these here ankle-length skirts an' all that.
—JOE WILLIAMS, IN JOHN DOS PASSOS' *NINETEEN NINETEEN,* 1930

THE **NATURAL-LINE** and **ankle-length** gown that freed women from corsets were designed in 1912 by the Frenchman Paul Poiret. Poiret, the creator of the Parisian Empire style, once said: "I do not impose my will upon fashion. . . . I am merely the first to perceive women's secret desires and fulfill them."

Past Patterns #8109 Empire tea gown is available in a size 38 bust only.

Tea gown

1926 Slip-On Evening Dress

IN FASHION, as in most everything else, the end of World War I meant the beginning of a celebratory new age. Women's dress styles evolved Poiret's innovations into an even longer silhouette, and skirts seemed to rise by 6 inches overnight. In this, the era of flappers and shebas, womanly curves were hidden by dropping the waist down to the hipline and wearing a bandeau brassiere to flatten the bust. Past Patterns #502 evening slip-on is typical of the period from 1925 to 1927. It is available in sizes 10 to 16.

1920s Step-In and Combination

"**V**ERY DELICATE and lovely undergarments were worn under the straight dresses of the Twenties," writes Past Patterns' Saundra Ros Altman. "Fabrics were silk *crêpe de chine* and satin, and the favorite color, *bois de rose*." Past Patterns #501 combination is a camisole, petticoat, and tap pants attached together at the drop waist. Available in sizes 10 to 16.

1930s Evening Gown

BY 1930 the boyish look was passé, the waist returned to waist height, and natural curves reappeared. The decade's most notable innovation in women's dress was the backless evening gown: high in front, but scooped out almost to the waist in back. Past Patterns #305 evening dress is available in pattern sizes 10 to 16.

The Past Patterns company offers a $5 Victorian Catalog with patterns in multiple sizes of 10 through 20 cut to fit modern *uncorseted* figures; and three Attic Copies Catalogs containing their authentically designed replicas of original period patterns. These are the Select catalog of late-nineteenth- and early-twentieth-century styles for $4.25, and the Teens and Twenties catalogs for $3 each.

Past Patterns

2017 Eastern, S.E.
Grand Rapids, MI 49507
Tel. 616/245-9456

Men's High-Top Shoes

ALTHOUGH the well-dressed Edwardian-era man neither demanded nor expected comfort in his wardrobe, an exception was made for the high-button shoe. In order to be rid of the sharp button-hook necessary to fasten and unfasten these, by 1905 men were indicating a preference for the laced version that had replaced buttons with hooks toward the top of the flaps.

Cumberland General Store's high-top shoes have Vici kid leather uppers, leather soles, rubber heels, and canvas linings. They are available in black and brown, and in D-width sizes 7 through 13 (including half sizes). Shipping weight: 4 lbs.

Price: $63 a pair, F.O.B. Crossville, Tennessee.

"Wish and Want Book," $3.75.

Cumberland General Store

*Route 3
Crossville, TN 38555
Tel. 615/484-8481*

Men's and Women's Footwear

THE English firm of Anello & Davide has been in business for more than sixty years and is the leading theatrical shoemaker in the United Kingdom, if not in all of Europe. The company also supplies footwear for the production of period television dramas in both England and the United States. "We cover most periods and can probably supply the strangest of requests," stated Anello & Davide's Alan Howard, citing his company's work on the films *Star Wars* and *Superman* as examples. Naturally, individual orders are gladly accepted.

The twentieth-century footwear manufactured by Anello & Davide depicted here reflects the wide variety of shoes that have been made available by modern industrialization, as well as the increasing predeliction for low-topped shoes that characterized the period from 1900 to 1950.

Catalog available.

Anello & Davide

*35 Drury Lane
London WC2, England
Tel. 011–44–1/836-1983*

EARLY XX CENTURY

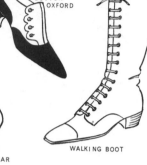

TWO TONE BUTTON OXFORD

WALKING BOOT

TWO BAR SHOE

D'ORSAY COURT SHOE

GIBSON WALKING SHOE

CAN CAN BOOT

TANGO BOOT

XX CENTURY

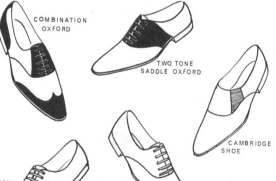

COMBINATION OXFORD

TWO TONE SADDLE OXFORD

CAMBRIDGE SHOE

CROSS BAR SHOE

DERBY SHOE

OXFORD SHOE

GRECIAN SLIPPER

SLING BACK PLATFORM SHOE

INSTEP TIE SHOE

MONK SHOE

FRINGED TONGUE BROGUE

ANKLE STRAP WEDGE SHOE

FROM THE VERMONT COUNTRY STORE

Gentlemen's Romeo Slippers

TO THE early-twentieth-century rule that slippers be plush and ornate, Romeo slippers make a radical exception. Made of brown calfskin and lined with soft leather, they feature a raised heel counter and an elastic gore. The Vermont Country Store claims that other than the addition of crepe soles, these slippers have hardly been changed since their 1906 introduction. Sizes: 7 to 12 in full, half, and medium widths. Shipping weight: 2 lbs.

Price: Vermont Country Store catalog #15345, $36.50.

Gentlemen's Storm Rubbers

IN 1915, when red rubbers were enjoying some limited popularity, the Apsley Rubber Company of Hudson, Massachusetts, advised its retailers "not to buy a big stock of these rubbers" as "people of good judgment steer clear of these fancy things." Because Vermont still has a high incidence of these types, the Vermont Country Store's storm rubbers come in black only. Sizes: small (6½ to 8), medium (8 to 9½), large (9½ to 11), and extra-large (11 to 13). Shipping weight: 2 lbs.

Price: Vermont Country Store catalog #15438, $9.95.

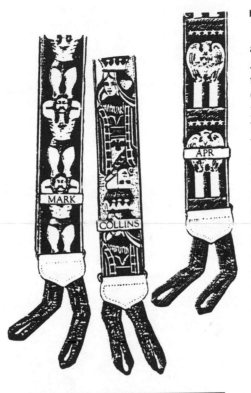

Lady's Cotton Lace Collar

FOR the necks of sweaters and dresses, in 100% cotton. Colors: white and ecru. Shipping weight: ¼ lb.

Price: Vermont Country Store catalog #15496, $8.95.

Delivery charges (based on shipping weight) required in advance.

Seasonal catalogs available from The Vermont Country Store, Catalog Request, Route 100, Weston, VT 05161.

The Vermont Country Store

Mail Order Office
P.O. Box 3000
Manchester Center, VT 05255

Calvin Curtis Braces

THE possession of more money than good sense has always been a sure-fire formula for garishness. And so it was with the "conversation" braces sold by Calvin Curtis, Cravateur, during the Thirties and Forties. Had these outlandish braces not been favored by the New York carriage trade (F. D. R.'s original pair are now on display at his Hyde Park home) they would almost certainly have been considered to be in poor taste. Instead, the braces were positively sought after by wealthy men whom, as the Bernardo brochure characterizes them, "appreciated flair in their dress and style." Give it the proper setting and garishness simply disappears.

Reproduced today by Trafalgar Ltd. under exclusive rights from the International Society of Bracecollectors are three of the Calvin Curtis conversation braces—"Head over Heels," "Card Royalty," and "American Hurrah." All have their designs woven into 100% pure nonelastic silk and are 1½ inches wide. Each pair comes numbered as part of a limited edition, and sports black silk button-ons at the front and light-gray suede button-ons to the rear. An invitation to join the International Society of Bracecollectors accompanies each pair.

Price: $85. Specify style desired.

Bernardo

Suite 108 West
2400 Westheimer Rd.
Houston, TX 77098
Tel. 713/526-2686

Art Deco Jewelry

THE FOLLOWING was supplied by Janice Casali, owner of the Casali company of Springfield, Massachusetts:

The art deco period was a time in which fantasy and that "certain look" reigned. Its influences were partly exotic, and began with the 1910 Paris performance of the Ballets Russes, a company that had stunned all Europe with its lavish Oriental themes. The opening of King Tutankhamen's tomb in 1922 fed the growing popular fascination for things mysterious, sensuous, and exotic; and soon turbans, heavy bangles, large earrings, and yards of pearls in every size and color helped create the look of the sheba and vamp.

A newly affluent working class helped foster the idea that jewelry can create a fashionable look (as against merely being a setting for precious stones) and dramatic changes in its design came about. Now stones were cut asymmetrically, or into pyramids, baguettes, and skyscrapers; glass was deeply carved and pierced; and thick enamels were cast into boldly geometric shapes. Longer and more interesting earrings (sometimes mismatched) and necklaces were called for to go along with the chemise dresses and newly bobbed hairstyles that appeared.

In this setting, such great jewelry designers as Lalique and Cartier flourished. They sold exclusively to the rich, but their designs were successfully translated into the inexpensive new materials then developed—celluloid, bakelite, camphor glass, enamel, and jet—which have since become heirlooms in their own right.

A former textile designer, Ms. Casali has combined her experience with the knowledge she has acquired as an antiques dealer to create a high-quality line of reproduction art deco jewelry. This begins with the purchase of celluloid and glass stones from their original houses in Czechoslovakia, Germany, Italy, and Japan where, in many instances, they've lain dormant for decades. These are then placed into metal settings that have been newly struck from original antique molds. Ms. Casali currently uses solid-brass settings exclusively for her jewelry, but will soon be reproducing earrings, necklaces, and pins in sterling silver as well. Her enamels are hand-painted and baked in the old way, and differ markedly from what is now called enamel, which is produced from a heavy application of epoxy paint. Ms. Casali's glass pieces are available in limited editions only, in prices ranging from $5 to $100.

Send SASE for color brochure to:

Casali
712 Sumner Ave.
Springfield, MA 01108
Tel. 413/734-6100

Edwardian-Era Undergarments

EDWARD VII was ruler of England and Ireland from 1901 until his death in 1910. Although regarded as one of England's most capable monarchs, Edward was a raucous womanizer and bon vivant, notoriously inclined toward the company of "city men, millionaires . . . American heiresses, and pretty women." Edward's hedonism stood in marked contrast to the dour mien of his mother, Victoria, and infused his reign with a certain rogue gaiety. There's no better place to express this than on a young woman's naked back, as do these Edwardian "flimsies" by Folkwear Patterns. Available in pattern sizes 6 to 16.

Literature and price list available.

Folkwear Patterns

P. O. Box 3798
San Rafael, CA 94912
Tel. 415/457-0252

Books and Periodicals

The Best Sellers! $1.69 Each

Have your name and address printed on your writing paper. See page 791.

Usually Retail at $2.00

Here they are! The finest fiction of the year by authors internationally known for the vividness and gripping interest of their novels. Many fascinating hours for you are bound within the covers of the books listed below. Shipping weight, 1¼ pounds.

3K664—God and the Grocery Man. Harold Bell Wright.
3K666—Forlorn River. Zane Grey (Ready November 1st)
3K89—The Mating Call. Rex Beach
3K88—Bellarion, the Fortunate. R. Sabatini
3K90—Under the Tonto Rim. Z. Grey
3K1212—The Understanding Heart. P. B. Kyne
3K1251—The Black Hunter. J. O. Curwood

Any one of the above titles.

3K91—Cherry Square. G. S. Richmond
3K92—Black Pearls. R. W. Alexander
3K99—The Chinese Parrot. E. D. Biggers
3K180—The Incredulity of Father Brown. G. K. Chesterton
3K81—Not Afraid. D. Coolidge
3K89—Preface to a Life. Z. Gale
3K92—The Flame of Courage. G. Gibbs
3K93—Lucky Numbers. M. Glass
3K95—Hand and Ring. A. K. Green
3K32—Confession. C. Hamilton
3K35—The Unearthly. R. Hichens
3K37—The Pope of the Sea. B. V. Ibanez

3K138—Michael Forth. M. Johnston
3K39—St. Michael's Gold. B. H. Jones
3K40—The Blood of Kings. W. R. Kaufman
3K141—The Big Mogul. J. C. Lincoln
3K142—Perella. J. W. Locke
3K143—This Mad World. H. MacGrath
3K144—Kindling and Ashes. G. B. McCutcheon
3K145—The Blue Castle. L. M. Montgomery
3K148—Hearts of Hickory. J. T. Moore
3K153—Harvey Garrard's Crime. E. P. Oppenheim

Intrigue, romance, breath taking adventure, heart stirring love, are portrayed as only master creators can portray them. Look over the titles—notice the authors—every book shown herewill appeal to you and every one is a great value at the low price we ask. Average 300 pages. Bound in cloth. Size, 5¼x7¾ inches.

3K156—The Magic Garden. G. S. Porter
3K163—Pandora. A. B. Reeve
3K171—The Master of the Microbe. R. W. Service
3K173—Folly's Gold. L. Scott
3K176—Far End. M. Sinclair
3K176—Page Mr. Tutt. A. Train
3K178—The Corbin Necklace. H. K. Webster
3K85—The Red-Haired Girl. C. Wells
3K86—Hare and Beyond. E. Wharton
3K87—Beau Sabreur. C. P. Wren.

......$1.69

Biography, Humor, Travel, Drama, Art

Here is published ... the ... of ... fiction books ... quality of white-wove book paper. Bound in cloth. Average 300 pages. Size, in original editions for ... special ... with ...

3K334—Woodrow Wilson As I Know Him. Joseph P. Tumulty
3K335—Science Remaking the World. Otis W. Caldwell and Edwin E. Slosson
3K336—The Autobiography of Benjamin Franklin.

3K344—Jeanne D'Arc. M. O. Oliphant
3K345—Progress and Poverty. Henry George
3K346—Astronomy for Everybody. Prof. Simon Newcomb
3K347—My Life and Work — Henry Ford. Samuel Crowther
3K348—Lincoln's Own Stories. Anthony Gross
3K352—Edge of the Jungle. William Beebe
3K353—Recollections and Letters of General Robert E. Lee. Captain Robert E. Lee
3K354—Second Book of Operas. Henry Edward Krehbiel
3K355—Faery Lands of the South Seas. Hall and Nordhoff
3K364—Shandygaff. Morley.

Any one of the above books. (Shipping weight, 1½ pounds).

......89c

The Famous Readers' Library

Any Two Books, 25c
Any Five Books, 55c

Bound in rich red cloth, beautiful ornamental design stamped in full gilt on side and back. Measures 4½x6½ inches. Average 255 to 350 pages.
Never before has anyone offered such wonderfully well made books at so low a price! Printed from brand new plates, with large, easily read type on a fine quality of white paper. Fancy pictorial end sheets.

Inez. Augusta J. Evans
Ishmael. Mrs. Southworth
Ivanhoe—Vol. I. Scott
Ivanhoe—Vol. II. Scott
Last Days of Pompeii. Bulwer Lytton
Self Raised. Mrs. Southworth
Thelma. Marie Corelli
The Spy. J. Fenimore Cooper
Andersen's Fairy Tales.
Grimms' Fairy Tales.
Hans Brinker. Dodge
Lena Rivers. Mary J. Holmes
Jane Eyre. Charlotte Bronte
Treasure Island. Robert Louis Stevenson
Dr. Jekyll and Mr. Hyde and Kidnapped. Stevenson
Homestead on the Hillside. Mary J. Holmes
Sherlock Holmes Detective Stories. Doyle
Thorns and Orange Blossoms. Bertha M. Clay

3K84—Any two, 25c
Shipping weight, 1 lb.

Alice in Wonderland and Alice Through the Looking Glass. Lewis Carroll
Last of the Mohicans. J. Fenimore Cooper
Black Rock. Ralph Connor
Uncle Tom's Cabin. Harriet Beecher Stowe
Plain Tales From the Hills. Rudyard Kipling
File No. 113. Emile Gaboriau
Murders in the Rue Morgue. Edgar Allan Poe
Little Minister. J. M. Barrie
English Orphans. Holmes
Capitola's Peril. Mrs. E. D. E. N. Southworth
Black Beauty. Anna Sewell
Scarlet Letter. Hawthorne
Under Two Flags. "Ouida"
Marion Grey. Mary J. Holmes
Pilgrim's Progress. John Bunyan
Tom Brown's School Days. Thomas Hughes
Tanglewood Tales. Hawthorne

Any five. Shipping weight, 2½ lbs. 55c
Any ten. Shipping weight, ... lbs. $1.00

American Home Classics 29c each — 2 for 55c

THEIR LOW PRICE ... these good books within the reach of all. Bound in a fine quality of linen weave pattern book cloth. Set off by an ornamental gilt stamping on side and back in a rich dignified design. Printed entirely from new plates in large easily read type on a high grade white book paper. Size, 5x7½ inches. Average 250 pages.

Marble Faun, The. Hawthorne
Merry Men and Other Stories, The. Stevenson
Mill on the Floss, The—Vol. I. Eliot
Mill on the Floss, The—Vol. II. Eliot
New Arabian Nights. Stevenson
Oliver Twist—Vol. I. Dickens
Oliver Twist—Vol. II. Dickens
Pathfinder, The. Cooper
Pere Goriot. Balzac
Phantom 'Rickshaw and Other Stories, The. Kipling
Picture of Dorian Gray, The. Wilde
Pioneers, The. Cooper
Prince Otto. Stevenson
Sappho. Daudet
Soldiers Three and Other Stories. Kipling
Twenty Years After — Vol. I. Dumas
Twenty Years After — Vol. II. Dumas
Vicar of Wakefield, The. Goldsmith
Autocrat of the Breakfast Table. Holmes
Treasure Island. Stevenson
Little Minister, The. Barrie
Scarlet Letter, The. Hawthorne
Tale of Two Cities. Dickens
Three Musketeers, The—Vol. I. Dumas
Three Musketeers, The—Vol. II. Dumas
Lena Rivers. Holmes
Under Two Flags. Ouida
Light That Failed, The. Kipling
Master of Ballantrae, The. Stevenson
Two Orphans, The. D'Ennery
Capitola's Peril. Southworth
Study in Scarlet, A. Doyle
Spy, The. Cooper
Homestead on the Hillside. Holmes

Sherlock Holmes Detective Stories. Doyle
David Copperfield—Vol. I. Dickens
David Copperfield—Vol. II. Dickens
Hunchback of Notre Dame, The—Vol. I. Hugo
Hunchback of Notre Dame, The—Vol. II. Hugo
House of Seven Gables, The. Hawthorne
Christmas Stories. Dickens
Plain Tales From the Hills. Kipling
Jane Eyre. Bronte
Last of the Mohicans, The. Cooper
Ishmael. Southworth
Self Raised. Southworth
Last Days of Pompeii, The. Bulwer Lytton
Tempest and Sunshine. Holmes
Ivanhoe—Vol. I. Scott
Ivanhoe—Vol. II. Scott
Dr. Jekyll and Mr. Hyde and Kidnapped. Stevenson
Marion Grey. Holmes
Uncle Tom's Cabin. Stowe
Thorns and Orange Blossoms. Clay
Old Curiosity Shop — Vol. I. Dickens
Old Curiosity Shop — Vol. II. Dickens
Old Mam'selle's Secret. Marlitt
Courting of Dinah Shadd and Other Stories, The. Kipling
Child's Garden of Verses and Other Poems, A — Stevenson
Vanity Fair—Vol. I. Thackeray
Vanity Fair—Vol. II. Thackeray
Wonder Book. Hawthorne
File No. 113. Gaboriau
Tragedy of the Seas, A. Balzac
Prairie, The. Cooper
Pride and Prejudice. Austen
Lamplighter, The. Cummins

Tales from Shakespeare. Lamb
Pinocchio. Collodi
Thelma. Corelli
Inez. Evans
Murders in the Rue Morgue. Poe
Deerslayer, The. Cooper
Pilgrim's Progress, The. Bunyan
In His Steps. Sheldon
Tanglewood Tales. Hawthorne
Robinson Crusoe. Defoe
Tom Brown's School Days. Hughes
Hans Brinker. Dodge
Black Beauty. Sewell
Alice in Wonderland. Carroll
Grimm's Fairy Tales. Grimm
Andersen's Fairy Tales. Andersen
Swiss Family Robinson. Wyss
Gulliver's Travels. Swift
Barrack Room Ballads, Etc. Kipling
Black Rock. Connor
Bride of the Mist. Holmes
English Orphans, The. Holmes
First Violin, The. Fothergill
Man Who Laughs — Vol. I. Hugo
Man Who Laughs — Vol. II. Hugo

3K199—Any one of the above books. (Shipping weight, each, 1 pound). 29c
Any two for 55c
Any five for $1.35

Lost Horizon

by James Hilton

"We keep ourselves fairly up-to-date, you see," he commented.

"There are people who would hardly agree with you," replied Conway with a smile. *"Quite a lot of things have happened in the world since last year, you know."*

"Nothing of importance, my dear sir, that could not have been foreseen in 1920, or what will not be better understood in 1940."

—THE POSTULANT CHANG, EXPLAINING THE WAYS OF SHANGRI-LA IN JAMES HILTON'S 1933 NOVEL *LOST HORIZON*

As if by subscription to Chang's long view of social history, Pocket Books still publishes the world's first paperback—its 1939 edition of James Hilton's classic tale of the mysterious lamasery hidden in the Mountains of the Blue Moon. Graphically unchanged, the book's front cover shows an airplane that was drawn back when people seemed still a bit unsure of what one should look like, and the back cover contains excerpts from the original reviews. Inside, the Maharajah of Chandapore's personal aeroplane departs Baskul on a Himalayan adventure that unfolds like a literary Saturday matinee.

Price: $3.50, paperback.

In bookstores or through:

Pocket Books

*1230 Avenue of the Americas
New York, NY 10020*

Little Wizard Stories of Oz

by L. Frank Baum

L. FRANK BAUM'S legion of readers are certain to rejoice at this work, a collection of six of his lesser-known stories that were originally published as separate books in 1913, and which have been out of print for nearly half a century.

These are bedtime-length tales for young children, instructive yet adventurous accounts depicting such long-familiar characters as Dorothy, Ozma, Tik-Tok, Jack Pumpkinhead, and the Nome King going about their typically humorous and magical Ozian affairs.

The strongly early-twentieth-century feel of the *Little Wizard Stories of Oz* is greatly enhanced by the typefaces used, and in particular by John R. Neill's original color illustrations. There is also an informative introduction by Michael Patrick Hearn. Hardcover, 147 pages.

Price: $14.95.

In bookstores or through:

Schocken Books

62 Cooper Square
New York, NY 10003
Tel. 212/475-4900

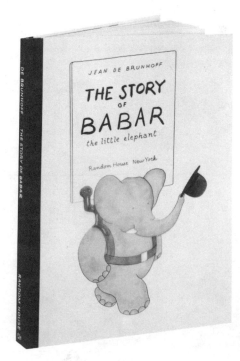

The Story of Babar

by Jean de Brunhoff

IN 1933 the noble elephant who found his way to Paris —where he acquired a smart green suit and a bowler hat—made his debut in Jean de Brunhoff's picturebook classic *The Story of Babar*. This beloved tale, translated into twelve languages and never out of print, was first published in a five-color oversize edition, a beautiful book that fell victim to the paper shortages caused by World War II. But now, and for the first time since, a facsimile of this prewar edition has been produced in Paris from the original plates. These feature the hand-scripted English text that appeared in the first American edition of what rare-book collectors refer to as "the big Babar."

Price: $14.95, hardcover.

In bookstores or through:

Random House, Inc.

201 E. 50th St.
New York, NY 10022
Tel. toll free 800/638-6460 in the continental U.S. except Maryland; in Maryland, toll free 800/492-0782

From Charles Scribner's Sons

Robinson Crusoe

by Daniel Defoe

The outstanding appeal of this fascinating romance . . . is the remarkably sustained sensation one enjoys of Crusoe's contact with the elements—the sea and the sun, the night and the storms, the sand, rocks, vegetation, and animal life. . . . Here is a story that becomes history, history living and moving, carrying with it irresistibly the compelling motive of a lone man's conquest over what seems to be inexorable fate.

FROM THE ILLUSTRATOR'S PREFACE

SCRIBNER'S reprint of this 1929 edition of Defoe's classic shipwreck adventure is illustrated by N. C. Wyeth who, in his preface, goes on to ask: "Do my pictures add a little to the vividness of this story? Do I aid a little in the clearer visualization of Robinson Crusoe as he moves about his sunny island? That is the most I can hope for."

Aiding the artist in the modern edition of his quest, the publisher has printed Wyeth's illustrations from new plates made from his original paintings.

Price: $18.95, hardcover.

At bookstores or through:

Charles Scribner's Sons

597 Fifth Ave.
New York, NY 10017
Tel. 212/486-2888

The Story of King Arthur and His Knights

written and illustrated by Howard Pyle

I believe that King Arthur was the most honorable gentle knight who ever lived in all the world.

—HOWARD PYLE

HOWARD PYLE, who is generally considered the first great American illustrator (at one time N. C. Wyeth, Jessie Willcox, and Maxfield Parrish were his pupils), favored themes that drew the reader into a brilliantly colored vortex of adventure, intrigue, and romance. An illustrator of buccaneers as well as knights, Pyle's four-volume series on the legend of King Arthur and the Knights of the Round Table (of which this is a reprint of the first) remains as one of the works for which the author-illustrator is best remembered. Published in 1903—during a period that has come to be considered the "Golden Age" of children's literature—the book returns "the true spirit of England of [Arthur's] time, when Arthur, son of Uther-Pendragon, was Overlord of Britain and Merlin was a powerful enchanter, when the sword of Excalibur was forged and won, when the Round Table came into being."

Price: $14.95, hardcover.

Rhett and Scarlett Bookends

THREE years before David Selznick's 1939 film version, *Gone With the Wind* by Margaret Mitchell had become the fastest-selling book of all time. Among those products turned out to promote the novel were these 1938 iron bookends, now reproduced in a limited collector's edition from the original molds by Gene Morris of McDonough, Georgia. As they predate the movie, the Rhett and Scarlett bookends do not resemble stars Clark Gable and Vivien Leigh—but they do, asserts Mr. Morris, "portray the self-confidence and hauteur evident in [their] personalities."

Price: $32.50 per pair.

Gene Morris

1555 Chambers Rd.
McDonough, GA 30253

The Outbursts of Everett True

CURMUDGEONLY EVERETT True, whose portliness does not deter him from administering swift battery to every "beetle-brained bat," and "oily-tongued prevaricator" who crosses his path, was a comic-strip character in 1907. True, the milquetoast's champion, the avenging knight hidden in every mollycoddle's breast, will not suffer fools beyond a single cartoon panel. Wielding his umbrella like a cutaway-clad centurion, Everett True anticipated Jimmy Hatlo's "They'll Do It Every Time" with his own "They'll Never Live to Do *That* Again"—and should anyone think True's manner unyielding, they need only wait and see what his wife has in store for *him*. Best of all, cartoonists A. D. Condo and J. W. Raper indirectly provide wonderful insights into the nature of everyday life at the turn of the century. Paperback, 96 pages.

Price: Vestal Press stock #A-55, $4.95 (plus $2 for postage and handling).

Catalog of period industrial book and manual reprints, $2.

The Vestal Press

P.O. Box 97
320 N. Jensen Rd.
Vestal, NY 13850

Frontier Times *Magazine*

IN 1923 J. Marvin Hunter began publishing Frontier Times magazine in Bandera, Texas. Comprised of accounts from early Texas history as told by eyewitnesses, their descendants, and local historians, each issue was avidly collected, even then. Reading a single issue today will soon reveal why this was so, as the magazine's tales of "border tragedy and pioneer achievement" are loaded with lore containing the same authentic charm as stories told at grandpa's knee—or the grisly adventure (such as the scalping of a twelve-year-old white girl related in "Tragedies of the Frontier" in the April 1935 issue) that might've sent shivers up the spines gathered around some hobo jungle's cookfire.

Original copies of *Frontier Times* are now almost impossible to come by, but since 1972 Western Publications of Perkins, Oklahoma, has been reprinting the rarest of issues from the 1920s and 1930s. They do so cover-to-cover, with no extraneous material, and are careful to include all the original ads that appeared for hand-carved steer-heads and the like. Today we are as far away from the years when *Frontier Times* was first published as *they* were from the days of Texas settlement that the magazine recounts. Still, the 150-odd years that separate us from the wildness portrayed in these old stories seem insufficient time for so complete a transformation of man and country as has taken place.

Subscription rates: 1 year (12 issues), $11; 2 years (24 issues), $20.

Hunter's Frontier Times

P.O. Box 665
Perkins, OK 74059

Original Newspaper Editions

He led the way inside, locking the door behind him, through a dining-room where two rocking-chairs stood on either side of a bare table: an oil-lamp, some copies of old American papers, a cupboard.

—GRAHAM GREENE, *THE POWER AND THE GLORY*, 1940

HISTORIC NEWSPAPER Archives of Rahway, New Jersey, has for sale the complete editions—not just the front pages—of original newspapers spanning the period from 1880 through 1974. Their unique archives are not only historical but historic, and at this writing range far beyond the *New York Times* and *Wall Street Journal* to include, in addition to a galaxy of *Suns*, *Stars*, *Worlds*, and *Mondos*, three *Eagles* (the Brooklyn, California, and Berkshire Evening), the euphonious *New Orleans Times Picayune* (1914–1940), the stalwart *Butte-Anaconda Standard* (1913–1940), the alliterative *Fargo Forum* (1898–1955), the redundant *Olympia Olympian* (1956–1958), and the supernal *Shanghai Celestial Empire* (1920–1929).

Catalog available.

Historic Newspaper Archives

1582 Hart St.
Rahway, NJ 07065
Tel. 201/381-2332

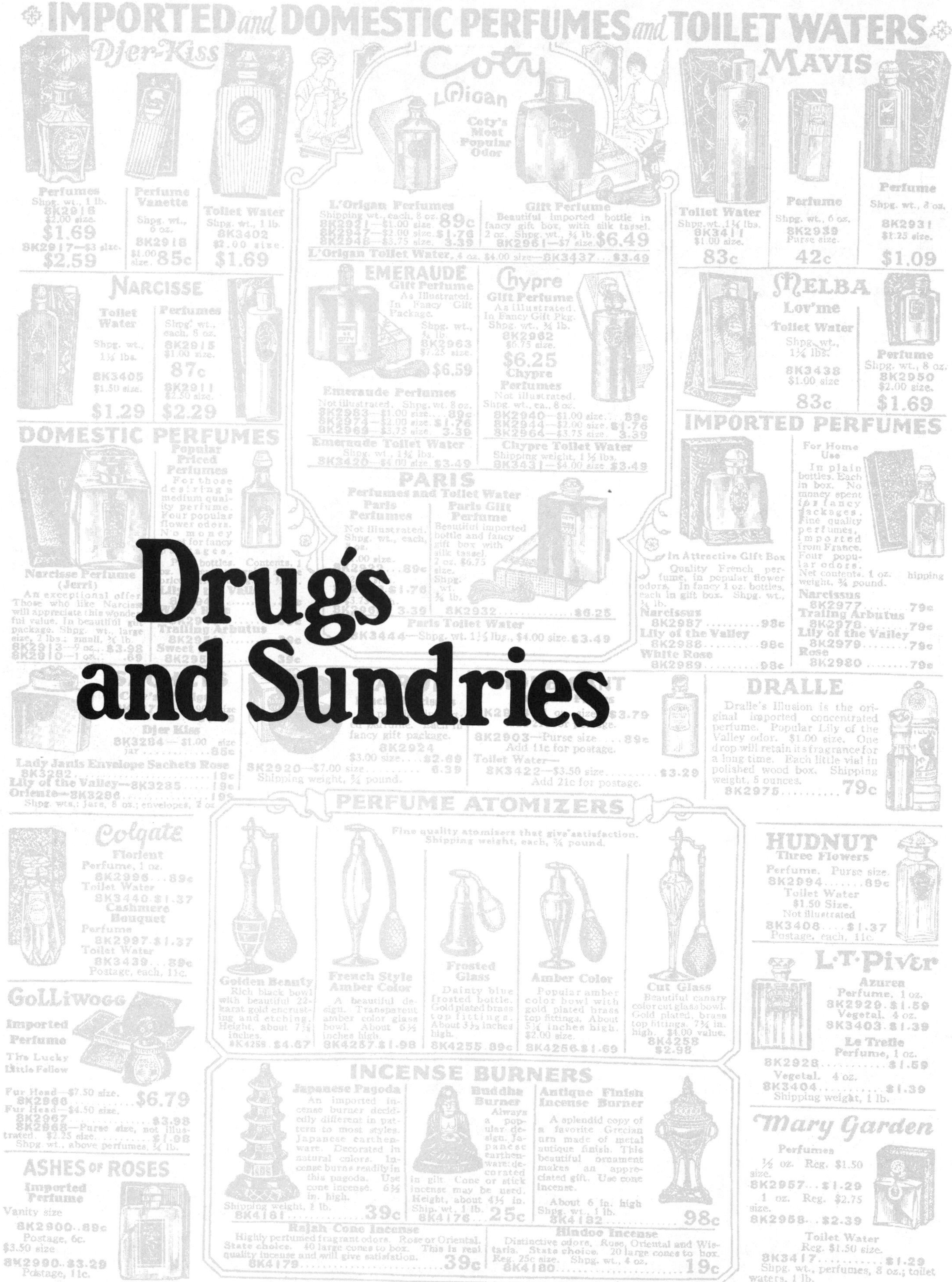

Djer-Kiss

Coty
L'Origan
Coty's Most Popular Odor

MAVIS

Perfumes
Shpg. wt., 1 lb.
8K2916
$1.00 size.
$1.69
8K2917—$3 size.
$2.59

Perfume Vanette
Shpg. wt., 6 oz.
8K2918
$1.00 size. 85c

Toilet Water
Shpg. wt., 1 lb.
8K3402
$2.00 size. $1.69

L'Origan Perfumes
Shipping wt., each, 8 oz. 89c
8K2921—$1.00 size.
8K2947—$2.00 size. $1.76
8K2948—$3.75 size. 3.39
L'Origan Toilet Water, 4 oz. $4.00 size—8K3437 $3.49

Gift Perfume
Beautiful imported bottle in fancy gift box, with silk tassel. 2 oz. Shpg. wt., ¾ lb.
8K2961—$7 size. $6.49

Toilet Water
Shpg. wt., 6 oz.
8K3411
$1.00 size.
83c

Perfume
Shpg. wt., 6 oz.
8K2939
Purse size.
42c

Perfume
Shpg. wt., 8 oz.
8K2931
$1.25 size.
$1.09

NARCISSE

EMERAUDE
Gift Perfume
As illustrated. In Fancy Gift Package.
Shpg. wt., ¼ lb.
8K2963
$7.25 size.
$6.59

Chypre
Gift Perfume
As illustrated. In Fancy Gift Pkg.
Shpg. wt., ¾ lb.
8K2962
$6.75 size.
$6.25

Melba
Lov'me
Toilet Water
Shpg. wt., 1¼ lbs.
8K3438
$1.00 size.
83c

Perfume
Shpg. wt., 8 oz.
8K2950
$2.00 size.
$1.69

Toilet Water
Shpg. wt., 1½ lbs.
8K3405
$1.50 size.
$1.29

Perfumes
Shpg. wt., each 8 oz.
8K2915
$1.00 size.
87c
8K2911
$2.50 size.
$2.29

Emeraude Perfumes
Not illustrated. Shpg. wt. 8 oz.
8K2965—$1.00 size. 89c
8K2973—$2.00 size. $1.76
8K2969—$3.75 size. 3.39
Emeraude Toilet Water
Shpg. wt., 1¼ lbs.
8K2420—$4.00 size. $3.49

Chypre Perfumes
Not illustrated.
Shpg. wt., ea., 8 oz.
8K2940—$1.00 size. 89c
8K2944—$2.00 size. $1.76
8K2968—$3.75 size. 3.39
Chypre Toilet Water
Shipping weight, 1½ lbs.
8K3431—$4.00 size. $3.49

IMPORTED PERFUMES

For Home Use
In plain bottles. Each in box. No money spent for fancy packages. Fine quality perfumes, imported from France. Four popular odors. Net contents. 1 oz. Shipping weight, ¾ pound.

Narcissus
8K2977 .... 79c
Trailing Arbutus
8K2978 .... 79c
Lily of the Valley
8K2979 .... 79c
Rose
8K2980 .... 79c

DOMESTIC PERFUMES

Popular Priced Perfumes
For those desiring a medium quality perfume. Four popular flower odors. No money for fancy packages. Contents, 1 bottles.

PARIS
Perfumes and Toilet Water

Paris Perfumes
Not illustrated. Shpg. wt., each, 8 oz.
$1.00 size. 89c
$2.00 size. $1.76
$3.75 size. 3.39
Paris Toilet Water
8K3444—Shpg. wt. 1½ lbs., $4.00 size. $3.49

Paris Gift Perfume
Beautiful imported bottle and fancy gift box with silk tassel. 2 oz. $6.75 size.
Shpg. wt. ¾ lb.
8K2932 .... $6.25

In Attractive Gift Box
Quality French perfume, in popular flower odors. In fancy 1 oz. bottles, each in gift box. Shpg. wt., ¾ pound.
Narcissus
8K2987 .... 98c
Lily of the Valley
8K2988 .... 98c
White Rose
8K2989 .... 98c

DRALLE
Dralle's Illusion is the original imported concentrated perfume. Popular Lily of the Valley odor. $1.00 size. One drop will retain its fragrance for a long time. Each little vial in polished wood box. Shipping weight, 5 ounces.
8K2975 .... 79c

Narcisse Perfume (Jerri)
An exceptional offer. Those who like Narcisse will appreciate this wonderful value. In beautiful gift package. Shpg. wt. large size, 2 lbs. small, ¾ lb.
8K2913—5 oz., $3.98
8K2910—1 oz., .69

Trailing Arbutus
8K2...
Sweet...
8K2...

$3.79

8K2903—Purse size. 89c
Add 11c for postage.
Toilet Water—
8K3422—$3.50 size. $3.29
Add 21c for postage.

Djer Kiss
8K3294—$1.00 size.
JAY 85c
Lady Janis Envelope Sachets Rose
8K3282 .... 18c
Lily of the Valley—8K3285 19c
Oriente—8K3286 19c
Shpg. wt., ¼ Jars, 8 oz.; envelopes, 2 oz.

8K2924
$3.00 size... $2.69
8K2920—$7.00 size. 6.39
Shipping weight, ¾ pound.

PERFUME ATOMIZERS

Fine quality atomizers that give satisfaction.
Shipping weight, each, ¾ pound.

Golden Beauty
Rich black bowl with beautiful 22-karat gold encrusting and etching. Height, about 7¼ inches.
8K4259. $4.67

French Style Amber Color
A beautiful design. Transparent amber color glass bowl. About 6½ inches high.
8K4257. $1.98

Frosted Glass
Dainty blue frosted bottle. Gold plated brass top fittings. About 3½ inches high.
8K4255. 89c

Amber Color
Popular amber color bowl with gold plated brass top fittings. About 5½ inches high. $2.00 size.
8K4256. $1.69

Cut Glass
Beautiful canary color cut glass bowl. Gold plated, brass top fittings. 7¾ in. high. $4.00 value.
8K4258
$2.98

HUDNUT
Three Flowers
Perfume. Purse size.
8K2994 ...... 89c
Toilet Water
$1.50 Size.
Not illustrated.
8K3408 .... $1.37
Postage, each, 11c.

Colgate
Florient
Perfume, 1 oz.
8K2996 ... 89c
Toilet Water
8K3440. $1.37
Cashmere Bouquet
Perfumes
8K2997. $1.37
Toilet Water
8K3439 ... 89c
Postage, each, 11c.

L·T·Piver
Azurea
Perfume, 1 oz.
8K2929. $1.59
Vegetal. 4 oz.
8K3403. $1.39
Le Trefle
Perfume, 1 oz.
8K2928 ...... $1.59
Vegetal. 4 oz.
8K3404 ... $1.39
Shipping weight, 1 lb.

Golliwogg
Imported Perfume
The Lucky Little Fellow

Fur Head—$7.50 size.
8K2966 .... $6.79
Fur Head—$4.50 size.
8K2967 .... $3.98
8K2968—Purse size, not illustrated. $1.75 size. $1.98
Shpg. wt., above perfumes, ¼ lb.

INCENSE BURNERS

Japanese Pagoda
An imported incense burner decidedly different in pattern to most styles. Japanese earthenware. Decorated in natural colors. Incense burns readily in this pagoda. Use cone incense. 6¾ in. high.
Shipping weight, 1 lb.
8K4181 .... 39c

Buddha Burner
Always a popular design. Japanese earthenware, decorated in gilt. Cone or stick incense may be used. Height, about 4¼ in.
Ship. wt., 1 lb.
8K4176 .... 25c

Antique Finish Incense Burner
A splendid copy of a favorite Grecian urn made of metal antique finish. This beautiful ornament makes an appreciated gift. Use cone incense. About 6 in. high.
Ship. wt., 1 lb.
8K4182 .... 98c

Mary Garden
Perfumes
½ oz. Reg. $1.50 size.
8K2957... $1.29
1 oz. Reg. $2.75 size.
8K2958... $2.39
Toilet Water
Reg. $1.50 size.
8K3417 .... $1.29
Shpg. wt., perfumes, 8 oz.; toilet waters, 1 lb.

ASHES OF ROSES
Imported Perfume
Vanity size.
8K2900. 89c
Postage, 6c.
$3.50 size
8K2990. $3.29
Postage, 11c.

Rajah Cone Incense
Highly perfumed fragrant odors. Rose or Oriental. State choice. 40 large cones to box. This is real quality incense and will give satisfaction.
8K4179 .... 39c

Hindoo Incense
Distinctive odors. Rose, Oriental and Wistaria. State choice. 20 large cones to box. Reg. 25c size. Shpg. wt., 4 oz.
8K4180 .... 19c

Drugs and Sundries

Lofthouse's Original

FISHERMAN'S FRIEND®

EXTRA STRONG

MENTHOLATED LOZENGES

HELPS CLEAR NOSE, THROAT & CHEST

White Cloverine Salve

IT WAS SAID to be "an American Favorite for over 70 years," and folks used to garner premiums through selling Cloverine at home. The salve offers relief for chapped hands, face, and lips, and soothes rough skin, minor burns, sunburn, and windburn. Put up in the original old-style tin and boxed. Shipping weight: 12 ounces.

Price: $2.40, F.O.B. Crossville, Tennessee.

"Wish and Want Book" available, $3.75.

Cumberland General Store

Route 3
Crossville, TN 38555
Tel. 615/484-8481

Fisherman's Friend Extra-Strong Mentholated Lozenges

JUST BEFORE the turn of the century, James Lofthouse sat in his Fleetwood, England, apothecary trying to come up with a proper commercial name for the strong-tasting cough lozenge he had developed. His product had long before become very popular among the men who sailed from Fleetwood to catch the cod that ran in the North Atlantic and Arctic Oceans—so much so that they had come to refer to the lozenges as "fisherman's friends." Well, the century didn't need to turn before Lofthouse had his brand name.

In those days the packaging of an ounce of Fisherman's Friend was done by hand, with exactly 19 lozenges making up the weight. This tradition of 19 lozenges to the package has been upheld by the Lofthouse firm, along with the package's red and black colors, which duplicate those on the founder's first, hand-typed envelopes.

Today, Fisherman's Friend is the largest-selling cough drop in Europe, Australia, and the Far East.

It is imported into the United States by Blazic Associates of Berwyn, Pennsylvania, and has succeeded in part because of its old-fashioned strong flavor.

Available at drug counters throughout the country.

Dealer inquiries welcome.

Blazic & Associates, Inc.

31 Waterloo Ave.
Berwyn, PA 19312
Tel. 215/296-0405

Gold Bond Medicated Powder

GOLD BOND's 1908 can bristles with fleurs-de-lis and contains an original-formula powder "for the relief of bed sores, chafing, sunburn, prickly heat, non-poisonous insect bites, chapped hands, and minor skin irritations."

Gold Bond Sterilizing Powder Company

745 Washington St.
Fairhaven, MA 02719

Perfume from the House of Guerlain

Ne me fait pas rire.
—ANTOINE DE SAINT-EXUPÉRY,
WIND, SAND AND STARS, 1940

THROUGHOUT domestic history the fragrance used has usually been imported. The venerable House of Guerlain began in 1828, when Pierre François Pascal Guerlain arrived in Paris from his native Picardie to open a perfumery shop on the Rue de Rivoli. Fortunately, Guerlain's French perfume has been generally less cloying than the American ad copy used to hawk the stuff. And so it is with the perfumes Guerlain made early in this century that are still available. Concerning these, here is what Guerlain sent:

In 1912, L'Heure Bleue, named for the gentle-hued and all-too-fleeting twilight, came to represent nostalgia and innocence. In the early 1920s, Mitsouko was created for women of an introspective but passionate nature to celebrate the wave of infatuation with the Far East. Guerlain's most famous contribution, Shalimar, was created in 1925 to capture a mid-Eastern romance of legend and history. It was conceived of Shah Jehan's consuming passion for his beloved Indian empress, Mumtaz Mahal—

Chosen One of the Palace—for whom he created the fabled Gardens of Shalimar. It was a tribute to the French novelist Saint-Exupéry that brought about Vol de Nuit in 1933, naming the perfume after Saint-Exupéry's prize-winning novel.

Guerlain products are available at perfume counters in drug and department stores throughout the country.

Aspirin

WITH Germany's invasion of Poland from the west and Soviet Russia's from the east; with Italy's occupation of Albania and with France's and Britain's declaration of war on the Hun; with President Roosevelt's record request to Congress for $552 million in defense expenditures—1939 was an awfully good year for aspirin.

Certified brand is still made and sold as it was then, with the same prewar label.

For further information, contact:

A&S Pharmaceutical Corporation

P.O. Box 2005
Bridgeport, CT 06608

Vinolia Toilet Soap

IN 1912 Vinolia Toilet Soap was eager to promote its association with the R.M.S. *Titanic*, the new White Star liner that, as the largest, fastest, and most luxurious passenger ship ever built, seemed the embodiment of the new century's technological prowess. But the *Titanic*'s name would soon be associated with disaster instead, as shortly before midnight on April 14, while she sped defiantly through a field of icebergs on her maiden voyage from Liverpool to New York, the liner struck a rare black berg that ripped a 300-foot gash along her starboard side and flooded five of her sixteen watertight compartments. Because the blow seemed so slight and the vessel so indomitable, few passengers realized what danger they faced. But at 2:20 on the morning of April 15 the "unsinkable" *Titanic* rose "like a column" and slid beneath the waves off the coast of Newfoundland—the ship's machinery crashing through her bulkheads with a rumble like that of a distant cannonade. While serving as an uncomfortable reminder that British imperial power itself was taking on water, the loss of the *Titanic* seemed to dash the popular hope that the new technology she embodied would bring about an age of peace.

Owing to outdated British Board of Trade regulations, the *Titanic* carried far too few lifeboats for her 2,235 passengers and crew, of whom only 713 survived. Among those who perished were several prominent "money makers" of two continents: John Jacob Astor, Isidor Straus, George Widener, and Benjamin Guggenheim, who, along with his butler, changed into formal attire so as to drown in the manner of a gentleman.

To these first-class passengers, White Star provided Vinolia Otto Soap as an amenity. The same soap (with the name "Otto" since abandoned), a hand-milled moisturizing and cleansing bar, is today available through New York's Caswell-Massey Company. Unlike both the great luxury liner and a humbler brand of soap, Vinolia makes no claim to buoyancy.

Price: $6 for 6 ounces (plus $2 for shipping and handling).

Catalog of grooming products available.

Caswell-Massey Co., Ltd.

Catalogue Division
111 Eighth Ave.
New York, NY 10011

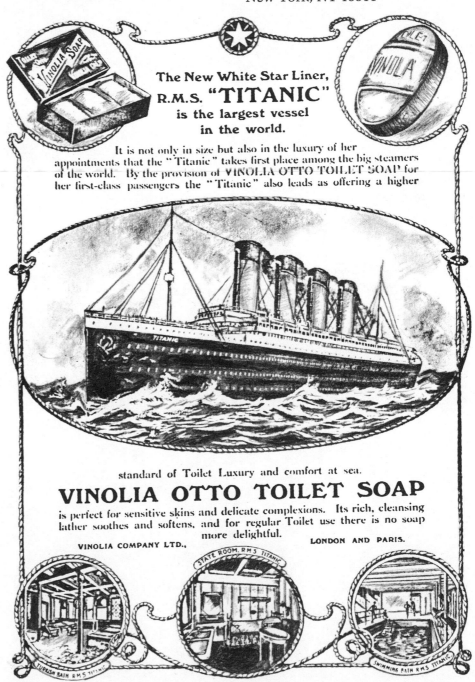

The New White Star Liner, R.M.S. "TITANIC" is the largest vessel in the world.

It is not only in size but also in the luxury of her appointments that the "Titanic" takes first place among the big steamers of the world. By the provision of VINOLIA OTTO TOILET SOAP for her first-class passengers the "Titanic" also leads as offering a higher standard of Toilet Luxury and comfort at sea.

VINOLIA OTTO TOILET SOAP

is perfect for sensitive skins and delicate complexions. Its rich, cleansing lather soothes and softens, and for regular Toilet use there is no soap more delightful.

VINOLIA COMPANY LTD.,   LONDON AND PARIS.

Foods and Beverages

Heinz Tomato Ketchup

FOR ONE who in 1888 built an immense industrial complex in Pittsburgh that included a palatial stable with a Turkish bath for his horses, H. J. Heinz was an uncommonly modest man. For why else— in the age of Buffalo Bill, J. Walter Thompson, the snake-oil circuit, and the ballyhooing broadside— would the purveyor of more than 200 varieties of packaged food lay claim to only 57? Why was this man, who didn't hesitate to euchre (or for that matter, to chow-chow) his beloved pickles, at the same time so respectful of the credibility of a buying public long inured to overstatement? It's as if McDonald's were suddenly to announce: "Many Thousands Sold!"

Some argue that the modesty of Heinz's two-digit boast has long since been swept away by the frequency with which it's been made. But a modest man or not, H. J. was certainly an uncommon one—particularly for a robber-baron (that Pittsburgh plant, incidentally, also included a roof garden, swimming pool, gymnasium, and auditorium for its employees).

The key to his rare character may be found in Heinz's motto: "To do a common thing uncommonly well, brings success." Nowhere has this been more amply demonstrated than with the 1876-recipe ketchup (then, "catsup") that the Heinz company has bottled in essentially the same eight-faceted American icon since 1906. From this, Heinz ketchup emerges like Cleopatra descending from her royal launch, exuding the impassive dignity that comes with tradition-bound excellence. For here in the land where ketchup is Pharaoh, Heinz still reigns.

Campbell's Tomato Soup

She heated up a can of Campbell's soup, as she hadn't taken any time to eat.
—JOHN DOS PASSOS, *NINETEEN NINETEEN,* 1930

DOS PASSOS **didn't say if Anne Elizabeth Trent heated up a can of Campbell's Tomato,** but tomato's the original variety.

Dos Passos didn't say this either, but in 1919 Miss Trent was herself on the verge of becoming a "tomato," which, according to Stuart Berg Flexner's *Listening to America* (New York: Simon & Schuster, 1982), has meant a "good-looking but nice girl" since 1920. So if in your search for soul satisfaction you can't warm up the kind of tomato who'll open a can of Campbell's, then warm up the tomato that's inside one instead. It's easier on the pocket that way too.

Although the Campbell Soup Company was established way back in 1869, condensed soup didn't come along until 1897, when Arthur Dorrance, nephew of founder Joseph Campbell's partner, Dr. J. T. Dorrance, arrived at the idea for it. Tomato was Campbell's first condensed variety and (along with the other Campbell's soups then sold) won the Gold Medal for Excellence at the Paris Exposition of 1900 that has adorned each can ever since.

Underwood Deviled Ham

Throwing the switch

You can see it any day—

A slight shift of the rails, only a few inches one way or the other, yet it makes a difference of hundreds of miles at the end of the road.

You see the same thing all through life. It is one of the big factors in your health. Form the habit of eating good soup every day in the year and you are on the right road to good physical condition.

When you begin your meal with Campbell's appetizing Tomato Soup you not only increase the enjoyment and benefit of that particular meal but the soup strengthens digestion, helps to regulate the entire process of nutrition and is thus a direct means of improved health and condition.

Can you afford to overlook it?

21 kinds   15c a can

Campbell's SOUPS

LOOK FOR THE RED AND WHITE LABEL

White Castle's Flyin' Sliders

White but wrong: Author and friend visit a Greenwich Village White Tower, 1975.

FAST FOOD'S starting gun sounded in 1921 when, with $700 in borrowed cash, entrepreneur Billy Ingram opened his first White Castle restaurant in downtown Wichita. A low cement building that didn't look as if it could hold a dozen burghers and their burgers with any room left for pie, the eatery was modest even by prevailing lunch-counter standards. In fact, the only thing you would've ever noticed about Billy Ingram's place was the crenelated turret that rose from the facade to give it the look of a plucky little white castle.

But that's not enough for the Big Time. Full-blown chain status takes having the right fare. Ingram's answer was to make the lowly hamburger into a delicacy for the *lumpen*—an exquisite square of beef, onion, and bun to be steamed and bought "by the sack." And ever since, White Castle's industrial-belt afficionados (who affectionately call the burgers "sliders" and "belly-bombers") have been doing just that.

While most of the pretending White Towers, Red Beacons, Blue Castles, White Clocks, and White Diamonds have come and gone over the years, White Castle endures. Today, although they've evolved past their long incarnation as simple porcelain night-owls and now flirt with the idea of going suburban with a gang of plasticized mall shoppes, the cheap and tasty slider sells on unaltered.

There are die-hards, I am sure, who cannot enjoy their belly-bombers unless they eat them in a period downtown White Castle (built no later than, say, the 1950s) sitting among a bunch of jamokes who sip their coffee with trembling hands. Others, however, are less particular, and know that their White Castle hamburgers will be tasty even not when contextual. For these, and for those so adrift in far-off market territories as to expect the White Castle chain to have one foot in the National Trust, sliders can now come your way by air. With this new service, White Castle will send its hamburgers skyward, frozen but fully cooked, for the regular Columbus, Ohio, price of 28¢ apiece—plus the cost of special packing, shipping, and handling.

Prices: package of 50 White Castle hamburgers, $57; package of 100, $82.

White Castle's Hamburgers to Fly   *Tel. toll free 800/922-7853*

This Columbus, Ohio, White Castle opened in 1929.

Manhattan Special Coffee Soda

ASIDE from those computer-friendly chicken scratches on the label, the "new twist-off" cap on the Manhattan Special bottle seems the only modern aspect of this soda, brewed in Brooklyn for more than ninety years.

That's right, I said *brewed*—for the primary ingredient of Manhattan Special soda is coffee . . . pure Italian espresso to be exact. Remove the cap and the aroma that emerges lands you smack in the middle of an Italian street *caffè*, where the copper urn with the eagle on top is producing a deluge of espresso for the Feast of St. Anthony or some such. In fact, it was right in Manhattan's Little Italy that this bubbly brown brew got its start.

At the time Manhattan Special was first bottled—three years before the 1898 municipal union—Manhattan *was* someplace special to Brooklyn. By 1905, according to company president Eileen Passaro, about 80,000 cases of coffee soda were being carted by horse into Manhattan's Italian neighborhoods, and in 1918 (about the time when the current label was designed, from the look of it) a merger with an Irish-American bottler brought Manhattan Special beyond its Houston Street pale. Among the notable early-twentieth-century Italian-Americans who savored Manhattan Special Coffee Soda's subtle effervescence, bittersweet taste, and creamy finish have been Enrico Caruso and Fiorello LaGuardia.

Manhattan Special Coffee Soda is available in all five boroughs of New York City as well as in parts of New Jersey and Florida. For those traveling to Brooklyn, it can be purchased at the plant in 24-bottle cases for $10, or about 41¢ per 10-ounce bottle, plus a $1.20 deposit. A 12-bottle case of 28-ounce bottles is also available for $10.25, plus a 60¢ deposit.

Manhattan Special Bottling Company

342 Manhattan Ave.
Brooklyn, NY 11211
Tel. 718/388-4144

Blenheim Extra Pale Ginger Ale

THE SOUTH, known historically for its ornate Claghorn oratory, is careful to keep its warnings terse. A fine example can be found in Blenheim Ginger Ale's unofficial motto which, advising first-time drinkers about the amount of hot Jamaican ginger within each 1920s bottle, cautions: "We'll burn ya."

This is not without its medicinal purpose, as the 1903 formula for Blenheim Extra Pale (mislabeled "mild"—there's also a hotter, albeit far newer, "Old No. 3" formula available) was developed by a doctor who must've been looking for a way to bring back the dead. The high sulfur content of the mineral well water used in Blenheim is partly responsible for its bite, as well as for the ale's sweet aftertaste, so favored in Dixie.

Price and ordering information available from:

Blenheim Bottling Company

Blenheim, SC 29516
Tel. 803/528-3901

Fancifood Wild Rice

Robert tested the wild rice and changed it to a shorter hook for steaming.
—KATHERINE S. PINKERTON, *WILDERNESS WIFE, 1939*

FANCIFOOD'S 1940s package, showing the Minnesota Indians gathering wild rice from a canoe, is tasteful and nearly as pleasing as the product it contains.

Liberty-Ramsey Imports

66 Broad St.
Carlstadt, NJ 07072
Tel. 201/935-4500

Life Savers

. . . O something green,
Beyond all sesames of science
was thy choice
Wherewith to bind us throbbing
with one voice.
—HART CRANE, "CAPE HATTERAS," 1923

LIFE SAVERS were the invention of poet Hart Crane's father Clarence, a Cleveland, Ohio, chocolate-candy manufacturer who sold them as a summertime replacement for chocolates. Today, Life Savers are produced by Nabisco Brands, Inc.

Available at drug and candy counters throughout the country.

Barnum's Animal Crackers

Animal Crackers and cocoa to drink,
That is the finest of suppers, I think;
When I am grown up and can have what I please,
I think I shall always insist upon these.
—CHRISTOPHER MORELY, *THE PHILOSOPHER POET, 1917*

BY THE TIME author-editor Christopher Morely had published this verse, children had been emptying National Biscuit's circus-train boxes of animal crackers for fifteen years. Today, Nabisco attributes the lion's share of animal cracker's success to the 1902 decision to put the name (and a bit of the showmanship) of Phineus T. Barnum on every box.

Available at all leading food and grocery stores.

Hershey's Chocolates

*I observe
That chocolate is an aphrodisiac
Unfortunately
Mild*
— FROM "VARIATION ON A THEME
OF CATULLUS"
BY LOUIS GILMORE, 1927

AMERICAN chocolates don't come with any curlicues on their labels, or at least they shouldn't. The first bite of one won't send you cruising heavenward in a paroxysm of ecstacy as in the case with many of those delicately creamy European varieties. But what of it? American chocolate is supposed to be more practical and direct—more Frank and Jesse than William and Henry—and looks to stoke the stomach without too much of a billowing of the soul. Hershey's came along at a time when it was important in America to get chocolate's job done without inducing the kind of somnambulistic reverie that might interfere with pushing back any frontiers in science and technology. Little wonder then that Hershey's chocolate is the same age as manned flight!

Modern chocolate fanciers—often the kind of people who'd get their *corn* from France if they could—won't provide Hershey's with the kind of recognition that even contempt affords. But for good or ill, the Hershey Bar that was first marketed in 1903 by Milton Snavely Hershey is the essential domestic variety.

Mr. Hershey had already made a million in the caramel business when he developed his chocolate formula in 1895. He did this, as the Hershey's literature disingenuously claims, because chocolate was his first love (isn't it everyone's?) and "because he loved making people happy with his candies."

Mr. Hershey's mother is known to have hand-wrapped the first of his most elegant little confections—the Candy Kiss—in 1907. Although such candies go well back into the nineteenth century (in the 1830s, "kiss verse" referred to love notes written by the enamored on candy kiss wrappers), the Hershey's Kiss was intended as market competition for the Wilbur Chocolate Bud (which, since 1894, has been sold by the Wilbur Chocolate Company of Lititz, Pennsylvania; see *The American Historical Supply Catalogue: A Nineteenth-Century Sourcebook,* page 122). Perhaps it was the Hershey's Kiss's sweetly innocent name and suggestively erotic shape that helped consign the Wilbur Bud to the confectionery gulag where it now labors.

Hershey's Kisses are available from the company in a reproduction period box bearing the legend "A Kiss for You." The label's illustration shows a Twenties moppet teasingly delivering a Candy Kiss to her little boyfriend, whose puckered puss shows him to be expecting something more in the way of a wet smack on the lips. Inside awaits

a pound of the delectable candy morsels.

The "Settlement" Cook Book, *1903*

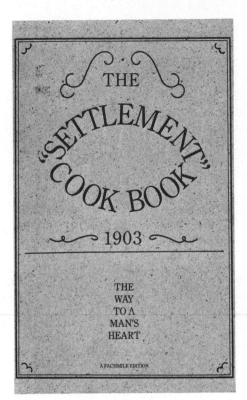

THE MILWAUKEE SETTLEMENT House was established at the turn of the century to aid immigrants in their adjustment to American life. In 1903 Mrs. Simon Kander was the cooking teacher there.

Recognizing that her students spent an inordinate amount of time copying her recipes off the blackboard, Mrs. Kander went to the settlement house board and requested $18 to have her recipes printed. Denied but undeterred, Mrs. Kander figured that she could defray her costs by selling advertising in the publication to local merchants. In this way she soon took in enough money to publish, not the pamphlet that she envisioned, but an elaborate cookbook. Mrs. Kander turned her profits over to the settlement house, which enabled it to move into larger quarters.

Over the years The *"Settlement" Cook Book* has been continually revised to reflect the prevailing culinary fashion. Today, along with *The Fannie Farmer Cookbook* and *The Joy of Cooking*, it's an American kitchen classic.

But thanks to Hugh Lauter Levin Associates of New York, the *un*revised 1903 edition of *The "Settlement" Cook Book* is again obtainable. With it, the soul-satisfying foods that filled the old Milwaukee Settlement House with their aromas can be easily re-created.

Here, in a detailed format, are the original 1903 recipes for such traditional dishes as griddle cakes and roast chicken with chestnut stuffing—as well as for many German-Jewish foods including filled (gefilte) fish, matzo balls, and apple strudel.

Available in bookstores throughout the country.

Imperial Whiskey

Fox's U-Bet

$E = (M + C)s$
(Eggcream equals milk plus chocolate syrup, stirred with seltzer)

THE New York eggcream, which may assume its place alongside the Theory of Relativity as one of the ingenious contributions made to American culture by immigrant twentieth-century European Jews, is a sweet mystery indeed. A soda-fountain drink that originated in the 1920s, the eggcream contains neither egg nor cream, but is delicious beyond either. Its secret ingredient is Fox's U-Bet Chocolate Syrup.

Here is the 40-weight of the Gods, a semi-sweet elixir as baroque as the old Brooklyn from whence it hails. No eggcream lays claim to authenticity without it.

Fox's dates back to 1925, soon after Herman Fox returned from the Texas oilfields (where the phrase "You bet!" was current among those men who staked their fortunes on holes in the ground) to find his black gold waiting for him in Brooklyn. Since then, neither U-Bet's label—with its curly-haired moppet—or formula has ever been changed, except to substitute corn sweetener for sugar. Unchanged as well is the Fox family's ownership and operation of the H. Fox Company, and although grandson David steadfastly ignored my letters and failed to return my telephone calls to him for the purpose of preparing this entry, I find the man easy to forgive. His, after all, is important work.

Fox's U-Bet is available in specialty stores and supermarkets in several of the country's major cities. Write to the company to find the nearest distributor, but if there isn't one close, the company will send a case for $15, plus shipping.

H. Fox & Company

416 Thatford Ave.
Brooklyn, NY 11212
Tel. 718/385-4600

SUPERTONE TENOR BANJOS

"Music Self Played Is Happiness Self Made"

Complete Tenor Banjo Outfit
Everything That's Needed to Play

A splendid instrument. Has 10¾-inch nickel plated wood lined shell with both edges spun over wire. Maple neck. Sixteen nickel plated hexagon brackets. Nickel plated "L" grooved straining hoop. Ebony finish fretboard, inlaid with pearl position dots. Imitation ebony veneered head inlaid with celluloid star. Patent neverslip pegs with celluloid thumbpieces. Nickel plated tailpiece. Fine quality head. Outfit includes a rubberized fabric bag, instruction book, pick, and four-pipe tuner. Shipping wt., 14 lbs.
12K4441½ **$9.95**

Extension Resonator
Metal Filler Ring

Heavy 11-inch maple shell, veneered with birdseye maple and inlaid with a neat stripe. Nickel plated straining hoop. Three-piece maple neck with ebonized head inlaid with pearl ornament. Adjustable dowel brace. Ebonized fretboard bound with celluloid and inlaid with pearl ornaments. Twenty nickel plated hexagon brackets. Selected calf skin head. Patent neverslip pegs. Instruction book, chart and pick included. Shipping weight, 15 pounds.
12K432¼ **$14.95**

Mahogany Finish **$5.95**

Eleven-inch birch veneered shell finished in mahogany. Poplar neck, mahogany finish. Twelve nickel plated hexagon brackets and nickel plated straining hoop. Patent neverslip pegs and nickel tailpiece. Good quality head. With it we include instruction book, chart and fingerboard chart. Shipping wt., 12 lbs.
12K434¼ **$5.95**

Professionals' Tenor Banjo
Metal Filler Ring

Has 11-inch three-ply rim veneered with mahogany. Three piece mahogany neck with veneered head inlaid with pearl ornament. Ebonized fretboard bound with white celluloid and inlaid with pearl position dots. "L" grooved straining hoop. Adjustable dowel brace. Patent professional style neverslip friction pegs. Twenty extension resonator with decorations. Fine calfskin head. Instruction book, chart and pick included.
12K435¼ **$19.45**
12K4012—Side opening keratol (artificial leather) covered flannelette lined case for above. Shipping weight, 6 lbs .. **$7.45**

Artists' Tenor Banjo

Eleven-inch built-up shell. Three-piece walnut neck; ebonized fretboard bound with white celluloid. Head overlaid with pearl amelyth. Nickel plated "U" grooved straining hoop. Twenty brackets. Nickel plated arm rest. Adjustable dowel brace. Ivory finish geared pegs, 2 to 1 ratio. Selected calfskin head. Special nickel plated tone flange and ring. Walnut resonator, convex extension type, artistically inlaid. Filler ring of nickel plated brass. Instruction book, chart and pick included. Shipping weight, 15 pounds.
12K445½ **$28.95**
12K4013—Side opening keratol covered velveteen lined case for above. Shipping weight, 6 pounds ... **$8.95**

Birdseye Maple Shell **$7.45**

Eleven-inch shell, veneered on the outside, with birdseye maple in the natural color. Maple neck. Ebonized fretboard. Nickel plated straining hoop. Sixteen hexagon brackets. Resonator of birdseye maple. Nickel plated tailpiece. Smooth calfskin head. Instruction book, chart and pick included. Shipping weight, 12 lbs.
12K431¼ **$7.45**

Musical Instruments

5-String Banjo **$7.45**
Thirty Brackets

Has 10¾-inch nickel plated wood lined shell with lower edge spun over wire. Maple neck. Nickel plated beveled straining hoop. Thirty hexagon brackets. Ebony finish fretboard (22 frets) with four pearl position dots. Ebony finish pegs. Imitation ebony veneered head with inlaid pearl star. Maple neck. Calfskin head. Patented nickel plated tailpiece. Instruction book and chart included. A real instrument and big value. Shipping weight, 12 pounds.
12K407¼ **$7.45**

Complete 5-String Banjo Outfit **$6.45**

A full size snappy banjo. 10¾-inch nickel plated wood lined shell with lower edge spun over wire, nickel plated straining hoop. Sixteen nickel plated hexagon brackets. Ebony finish fretboard (22 frets) and pegs. Imitation ebony veneered head inlaid with celluloid star. Pearl position dots. Natural finish neck. Good quality head. Outfit includes rubberized cloth bag, instruction book, chart and tuner. Shipping weight, 12 pounds.
12K406¼ **$6.45**

5-String Banjo Inlaid Ornaments **$9.95**

Has 10⅝-inch nickel plated wood lined shell. Maple neck. Nickel plated "L" grooved straining hoop. Thirty hexagon brackets. Ebony finish fretboard and head inlaid with white celluloid ornaments. Celluloid bound fingerboard. Patented nickel plated tailpiece. Calfskin head. Gut strings. A classy looking banjo with a good tone. Instruction book and chart included. Shipping weight, 13 pounds.
12K414¼ **$9.95**

5-String Banjo **$4.45**

Nickel plated wood lined shell. Eight hexagon brackets. Neck in mahogany finish with fretted side in imitation of ebony. Seventeen frets. Ebonized pegs. Goatskin head. As well constructed a banjo as is possible for the money. Instruction book and chart included. Shipping weight, 11 pounds.
12K402¼ **$4.45**

BANJO MANDOLINS

Birdseye Maple Shell **$7.45**

11-inch shell, veneered with birdseye maple. Nickel plated straining hoop. Sixteen hexagon brackets. Screw pattern patent heads. Ebonized fretboard with celluloid dots. Maple neck. Resonator of birdseye maple. Calfskin head. Book, chart and pick included. Shipping weight, 9 lbs.
12K438½ **$7.45**

Nickel Plated Shell **$12.45**

Ten-inch nickel plated wood lined shell, twenty nickel plated shoulder brackets. Head veneered and inlaid with a pearl star and crescent. Nickel plated patent heads. Ebony finish fretboard inlaid with pearl position ornaments. Calfskin head. Nickel plated fancy tailpiece. Book, chart and a pick included. Shipping weight, 9 lbs.
12K446¼ **$12.45**

Dobro Guitars

AUTHENTIC dobro guitars are the product of the Original Music Company, a Huntington Beach, California, concern that is partly owned by Emile "Ed" Dopyera, one of the instrument's original manufacturers and the brother of inventor John Dopyera.

The dobro is distinguished from other guitars by the presence of one or more metal resonator discs inside its body, a device that enabled it to augment conventional guitar sound two decades before the development of electric instruments. Sometimes playing it in the Hawaiian style of Sol Hoopii (across the knees and with a bottleneck) such early hillbilly and country-blues musicians as Bukka White, Leroy Carr, Tampa Red, Blind Boy Fuller, and Buck "Uncle Josh" Graves quickly adopted it for its peculiarly mournful sound. With the exception of Duane Allman, Johnny Winter, and Poco's Rusty Young, most rock artists have completely abandoned the dobro for the electric guitar, but today a revival of interest in the roots of both country and rock music has returned to the dobro some of the veneration generally reserved for those whose names were long ago entered into the "big tally book" in Tex Ritter's Hillbilly Heaven.

Among Original Music's catalog of dobro instruments is the Model 60PS-S depicted here. When first sold in the Twenties, this dobro was known as the Model 45 and went for $45.

Literature available.

Original Music Company

18108 Redondo Circle
Huntington Beach, CA 92648
Tel. 714/848-9823

The Earl Scruggs Gibson Banjo

WITH its go-faster, mountain-holler sound, bluegrass music seems about as old as rifle fire in the Appalachian Mountains. Truth is, though, there are still a few Studebaker pickups around that haven't rotated their tires since DJs like Lee Moore—the "coffee-drinkin' nighthawk" of Wheeling, West Virginia's station WWVA—began sending the first bluegrass out into the ozone back in the 1940s.

The term "bluegrass music" derives from the legendary Bill Monroe and his Blue Grass Boys, the originators of the now-familiar fiddle, guitar, mandolin, and five-string banjo sound. In 1948 guitarist Lester Flatt and banjo-picker Earl Scruggs broke away from Monroe's band to form Flatt and Scruggs, a group that has probably done more than any other to bring bluegrass music into the American mainstream.

That was also the year when Scruggs came across a banjo that had the peculiar tonal quality for

Not a Granada: In 1947 Earl Scruggs was a year away from the banjo for which he searched.

which he had been searching. It was a 1930s Granada five-string, made by Gibson Guitars, a Nashville company that had built banjos since 1918. Today this instrument is revered in bluegrass circles as the one that Scruggs took along on the road back when the Grand Ol' Opry was grander (if newer) than it is now.

Gibson claims that in its tonal quality, as well as its structure and appearance, their new Earl Scruggs model banjo reproduces its namesake's beloved Granada exactly. Scruggs's personal involvement in the instrument's production, as well as his enthusiastic endorsement of it (he signed the first 1,984 produced), appear to verify this.

Available at music retailers, or write:

Gibson

P.O. Box 100087
Nashville, TN 37210

(International Offices: Gibson B. V., Giessemweg 67a, 3044 AK Rotterdam, The Netherlands)

Piano Rolls

JUST 50¢ sent to the Vestal Press of Vestal, New York, buys a complete listing of player-piano roll music covering thousands of titles from the two leading manufacturers, the Play-Rite Company and QRS Music Rolls. Specific information on piano rolls is available for Ampico, Duo-Art, and Welte reproduction pianos.

Catalog of period industrial book and manual reprints, $2.

The Vestal Press

P.O. Box 97
320 N. Jensen Rd.
Vestal, NY 13850

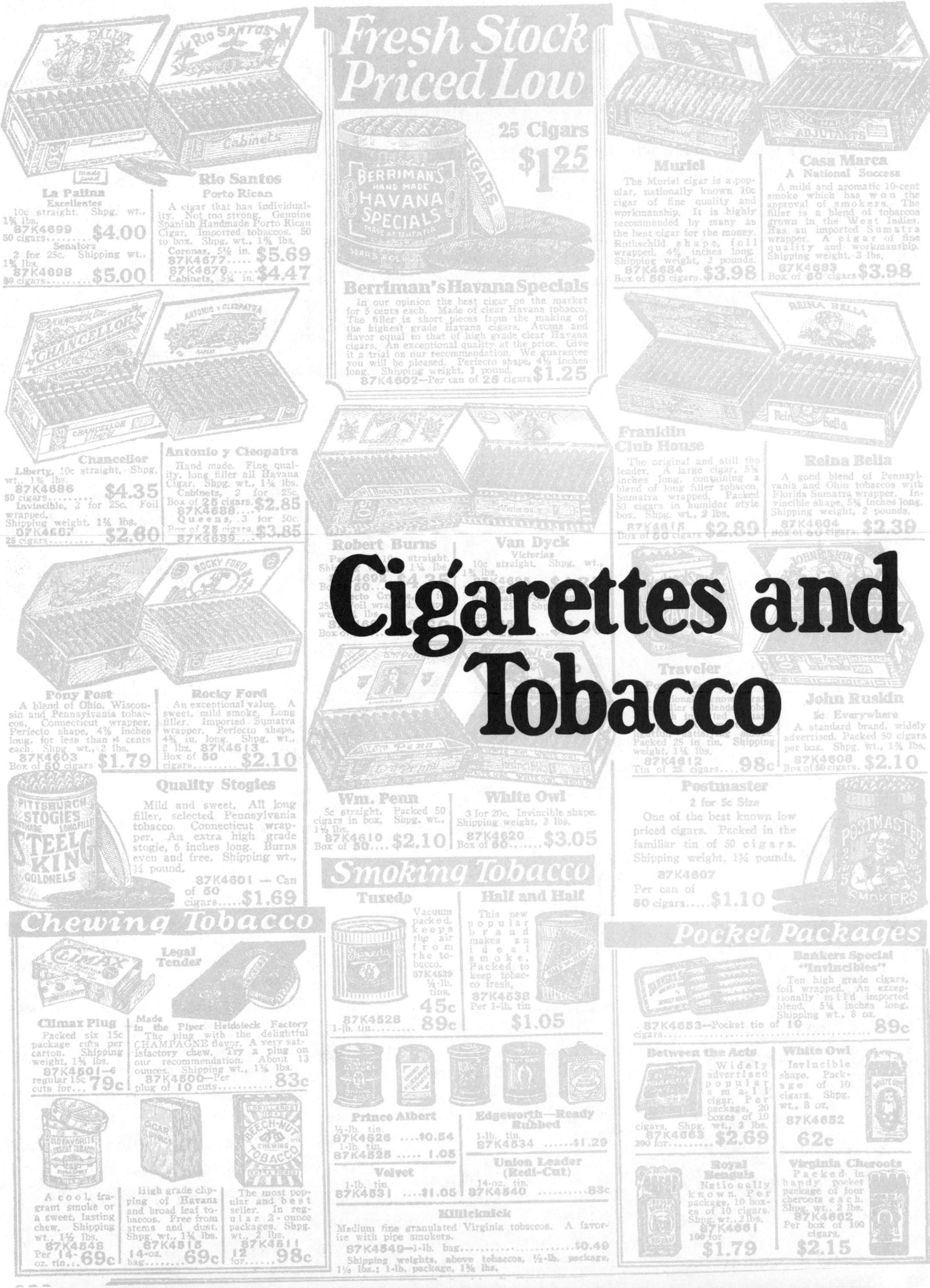

Fresh Stock Priced Low

25 Cigars $1.25

Berriman's Havana Specials
In our opinion the best cigar on the market for 5 cents each. Made of clear Havana tobacco. The filler is short pieces from the highest grade Havana cigars. Aroma and flavor equal to that of high grade clear Havana cigars. An exceptional quality at the price. Give it a trial on our recommendation. We guarantee you will be pleased. Perfecto shape, 4½ inches long. Shipping weight, 1 pound.
87K4602—Per can of 25 cigars......**$1.25**

La Palma
Excellentes
10c straight. Shpg. wt., 1¾ lbs.
87K4699 **$4.00**
Senators
2 for 25c. Shipping wt., 1¾ lbs.
87K4698 **$5.00**
50 cigars.......

Rio Santos
Porto Rican
A cigar that has individuality. Not too strong. Genuine Spanish Handmade Porto Rican Cigar. Imported tobacco. 50 to box. Shpg. wt., 1¾ lbs.
Coronas, 5¼ in. 87K4677 **$5.69**
87K4679, ¾ in. **$4.47**
Cabinets, ¾ in.

Muriel
The Muriel cigar is a popular, nationally known 10c cigar of fine quality and workmanship. It is highly recommended by many as the best cigar for the money. Rothschild shape, foil wrapped, 4½ inches long. Shipping weight, 2 pounds.
87K4684 **$3.98**
Box of 50 cigars

Casa Marca
A National Success
A mild and aromatic 10-cent smoke which has won the approval of smokers. The filler is a blend of tobacco grown in the West Indies. Has an imported Sumatra wrapper. A cigar of fine quality and workmanship. Shipping weight, 3 lbs.
87K4683 **$3.98**
Box of 50 cigars

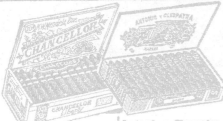

Chancellor
Liberty, 10c straight, Shpg. wt., 1½ lbs.
87K4686 **$4.35**
50 cigars.......
Invincible, 2 for 25c. Foil wrapped. Shipping weight, 1¼ lbs.
87K4607 **$2.60**
25 cigars.......

Antonio y Cleopatra
Hand made. Fine quality, long filler all Havana Cigar. Shpg. wt., 1¾ lbs.
Cabinets, 2 for 25c.
Box of 25 cigars..**$2.85**
87K4688
Queens, 3 for 50c.
Box of 25 cigars **$3.85**
87K4689

Franklin Club House
The original and still the leader. A large cigar, 5¼ inches long, containing a blend of long filler tobacco, Sumatra wrapped. Packed 50 cigars in humidor style box. Shpg. wt., 2 lbs.
87K4615 **$2.89**
Box of 50 cigars

Reina Bella
A good blend of Pennsylvania and Ohio tobaccos with Florida Sumatra wrapper. Invincible shape, 5¼ inches long. Shipping weight, 2 pounds.
87K4604 **$2.39**
Box of 50 cigars,

Cigarettes and Tobacco

Pony Post
A blend of Ohio, Wisconsin and Pennsylvania tobaccos, Connecticut wrapper. Perfecto shape, 4½ inches long, for less than 4 cents each. Shpg. wt., 2 lbs.
87K4603 **$1.79**
Box of 50 cigars

Rocky Ford
An exceptional value. A sweet, mild smoke. Long filler. Imported Sumatra wrapper. Perfecto shape, 4¾ in. long. Shpg. wt., 2 lbs. 87K4613 **$2.10**
Box of 50 cigars.........

Robert Burns
straight, Shpg. wt., 1¾ lbs.
50 cigars.
foil wrapped,

Van Dyck
Victorias
10c straight. Shpg. wt.

Traveler
Packed 25 in tin. Shipping weight, 1¼ lbs.
87K4612 **98c**
Tin of 25 cigars.......

John Ruskin
5c Everywhere
A standard brand, widely advertised. Packed 50 cigars per box. Shpg. wt., 1¾ lbs.
87K4608 **$2.10**
Box of 50 cigars.

Quality Stogies
Mild and sweet. All long filler, selected Pennsylvania tobacco. Connecticut wrapper. An extra high grade stogie, 6 inches long. Burns even and free. Shipping wt., ¾ pound.
87K4601 — Can of 50 cigars.....**$1.69**

Wm. Penn
5c straight. Packed 50 cigars in box. Shpg. wt., 1¾ lbs.
87K4610 **$2.10**
Box of 50.....

White Owl
3 for 20c. Invincible shape. Shipping weight, 2 lbs.
87K4620 **$3.05**
Box of 50.....

Postmaster
2 for 5c Size
One of the best known low priced cigars. Packed in the familiar tin of 50 cigars. Shipping weight, 1¾ pounds.
87K4607
Per can of 50 cigars.....**$1.10**

Chewing Tobacco

Climax Plug
Packed six 15c package cuts per carton. Shipping weight, 1¼ lbs.
87K4501-6 **79c**
regular 15c cuts for....

Legal Tender
Made in the Piper, Heidsieck Factory
The plug with the delightful CHAMPAGNE flavor. A very satisfactory chew. Try a plug on our recommendation. About 13 ounces. Shipping wt., 1¼ lbs.
87K4500—Per plug of 10 cuts..... **83c**

Smoking Tobacco

Tuxedo

Vacuum packed, keeps the air from the tobacco.
87K4529 ½-lb. tins. **45c**
87K4528 1-lb. tin. **89c**

Half and Half

This new popular brand makes an ideal smoke. Packed to keep tobacco fresh.
87K4538 Per 1-lb. tin **$1.05**

Prince Albert
½-lb. tin.
87K4526 ....$0.54
1-lb. tin.
87K4525 ...... 1.05

Edgeworth—Ready Rubbed
1-lb. tin.
87K4534 ......$1.29

Velvet
1-lb. tin.
87K4531 ....$1.05

Union Leader (Redi-Cut)
14-oz. tin.
87K4540 ......83c

Killickinick
Medium fine granulated Virginia tobacco. A favorite with pipe smokers.
87K4549—1-lb. bag........$0.49
Shipping weight, above tobaccos, ½-lb. package, 1¼ lbs.; 1-lb. package, 1¾ lbs.

Pocket Packages

Bankers Special "Invincibles"
Ten high grade cigars, foil wrapped. An exceptionally mild imported blend, 5¼ inches long. Shipping wt., 8 oz.
87K4653—Pocket tin of 10 cigars. **89c**

Between the Acts

Widely advertised popular small cigar. Packed in package of 10, boxes of 10 cigars. Shpg. wt., 3 lbs.
87K4663 **$2.69**
200 for.....

White Owl

Invincible shape. Package of 10 cigars. Shpg. wt., 8 oz.
87K4652 **62c**

Royal Bengals
Nationally known. Packages of 10 boxes of 10 cigars. Shpg. wt., 2 lbs.
87K4661 **$1.79**
100 for.....

Virginia Cheroots
Packed in handy pocket package of four cheroots each. Shpg. wt., 2 lbs.
87K4662 **$2.15**
Per box of 100 cigars.....

A cool, fragrant smoke or a sweet, lasting chew. Shipping wt., 1½ lbs.
87K4548 **69c**
Per 14-oz. tin...

High grade clipping of Havana and broad leaf tobaccos. Free from stems and dust. Shpg. wt., 1¼ lbs.
87K4518 **69c**
14-oz. bag.....

The most popular and best seller. In regular 2-ounce packages. Shpg. wt., 2 lbs.
87K4511 **98c**
12.....

Player's Navy Cut Cigarettes

FEATURING the hale and salty visage of "Hero," Player's Navy Cut Cigarettes were first put on the British market in 1900 at the price of 3d for ten. The man in the Player's lifesaver was, as goes the legend, one Thomas Huntley Wood, a sailor who served during the 1880s on the HMS *Edinburgh*, and who received a pouch of tobacco and a fistful of guineas in exchange for the use of his face. The sturdy Wood is flanked by the HMS *Brittania* (reputed to be one of the largest ships of the line in her day) and her more modern counterpart, the first HMS *Dreadnaught*, which was built in 1875. It's been said that Hero's favoring of the bristling *Dreadnaught* reflected the growing anxiety of the British public to the German naval buildup at the turn of the century.

Player's Navy Cut Cigarettes are today manufactured under license by the Philip Morris Company.

Available at finer tobacco counters throughout the country.

CREDIT: REPRINTED BY PERMISSION OF PHILIP MORRIS, INCORPORATED.

Prince Albert in the Can

You ask me what we need to win the war, I answer tobacco as much as bullets.

—GEN. JOHN J. PERSHING; COMMANDER-IN-CHIEF OF THE AMERICAN EXPEDITIONARY FORCE, 1917

IN 1914, so that there be a war to win, Austrian Archduke Francis Ferdinand, while visiting Yugoslavia, became the victim of an assassin's bullet. When the news broke, Emperor Francis Joseph, vacationing at Bad Ischl, became philosophical; aboard his yacht at Kiel, Kaiser Wilhelm was seen to become pale; and back in Vienna, Foreign Minister Count von Berchtold became, unwisely, militant. Soon Wilhelm, his cousin Czar Nicholas, French Premier Viviani, King George V, and Albert, King of the Belgians, would all become militant as well.

In the U.S., a world away in 1914, Prince Albert became a new cigarette named Camel. But while the rest of the royalty's gone, the crimp-cut, long-burning Prince abides in his crimson tin.

Price: Cumberland catalog # 8069, 89¢.

"Wish and Want Book" available, $3.75.

Cumberland General Store

Route 3
Crossville, TN 38555
Tel. 615/484-8481

Camel Cigarettes

I thought that my name was just about as familiar to everybody as Al Capone's or Camel cigarettes.
    —PRESIDENTIAL CANDIDATE BERZELIUS WINDRIP IN SINCLAIR LEWIS'S 1935 NOVEL, *IT CAN'T HAPPEN HERE*

BUZZ WINDRIP, totalitarian dictator of the United States, swept the country in Sinclair Lewis's fictional account of the 1936 election in much the same way that Camel cigarettes really had done twenty-two years earlier. No matter what you may think of cigarette smoking, if you've read *It Can't Happen Here* you're probably glad that only Windrip's brand of cigarettes is real and his brand of government is not.

Camels, as has been noted, were first produced in 1914 from Prince Albert tobacco—a loose Turkish, Virginia, and burley blend. At the time both the brand's name and its image of "Old Joe" (the Barnum & Bailey dromedary that's appeared on every pack of Camels ever made) were intended to suggest the more expensive all-Turkish blends. That this worked—425 million Camels were sold the first year—can't be argued; but since then a mystique has grown around Joe and his Oriental desert setting. In 1958, when the R. J. Reynolds company tried shifting the pyramid and streamlining the serif on the original Camel label, several tons of protesting consumer mail brought them up straight.

N. W. Ayer & Son's "teaser" campaign for Camel cigarettes began in 1913.

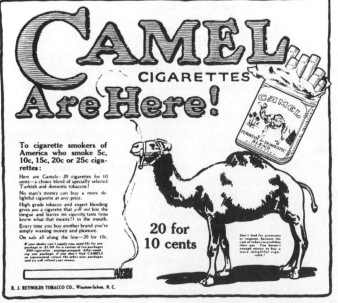

Cigarettes by George Washington Hill

The American Tobacco Company under the leadership of Percival Hill and his able young son, George Washington Hill, introduced two brands of cigarettes that are sold today in much the same form as they were early in this century.

Pall Mall

It seems now like a very simple name to recall and yet on the day in question I thought of every other town in the country, as well as such words and phrases as terra-cotta, Walla-Walla, bill of lading, vice-versa, hoity-toity, Pall Mall, Bodley Head, Schumann-Heink, etc. without even coming close to Perth Amboy.
— JAMES THURBER, *MY LIFE AND HARD TIMES*, 1933

AMERICAN TOBACCO acquired the Pall Mall brand when it purchased the Butler-Butler Company in 1907. By 1916 G. W. Hill's marketing expertise had transformed this relatively unknown cigarette into a contender among the fiercely competitive "Turkish-leaf" brands. Pall Mall's success was bolstered in 1924 when they began to be sold in an elegant red tin box dedicated to HIM (His Imperial Majesty the American Gentleman), but it was in 1939 that Pall Mall scored the greatest marketing coup in the history of cigarettes by introducing the phrase "king size" into the American lexicon. These were sold in the scarlet packages still to be found "Wherever Particular People Congregate."

Lucky Strike

FRESH from his triumph in reviving the moribund Pall Mall name, G. W. Hill applied his considerable talents to Lucky Strike, a brand that American Tobacco had acquired following the 1911 breakup of the Duke tobacco trust. He entered the market sweepstakes then going on between Reynolds's Camel and Liggett & Myer's Chesterfield by pitting Lucky's Gold Rush image against that of the Ship of the Desert and the heraldic aristocrat. In a classic bit of marketing mendacity, Hill created the slogan "It's Toasted" for Luckies, implying that the blend—essentially the same as Camel's—underwent some special process not enjoyed by any other leaf. Despite Camel's 1924 rejoinder "It's Fun to be Fooled," Americans were happy to be anyway. By 1930 Hill's farsightedness had brought "The Lucky Strike Radio Hour" into being and secured a slew of celebrity recommendations for the brand. Hill had now achieved the impossible by outselling both of his competitors.

During these years the Lucky Strike package showed its red bull's eye against a *green* background. As is now well known, Lucky "Green" went to war in 1942 and was later killed at Malmedy.

Bugler Tobacco

"ROLL your own and save your roll" was the advice followed by many cigarette smokers during the Depression. In addition to price reductions on brands such as Wings and the introduction of new, cheap factory-mades like Twenty-Grand (named for 1931's Triple Crown–winning racehorse), life on the skids resulted in the success of several brands of loose tobacco. One such was Bugler, which was offered by the Brown & Williamson company in the fall of 1932. The Bugler "Thrift Kit" contained (in addition to two packages of tobacco) a metal cigarette tin, a hand-operated rolling machine, and a supply of gummed papers.

Bugler still comes with cigarette papers, and both its package and its blend of Turkish and domestic tobaccos remain unchanged.

Available at tobacco counters throughout the country.

Top Smoking Tobacco

IN 1911 when James Buchanan Duke's American Tobacco Company was broken up by the Supreme Court for restraint of trade, it was forced to sell its Top Brand chewing tobacco back to R. J. Reynolds. Reynolds reintroduced Top as loose smoking tobacco in 1939; and when you buy it today, only the price has changed.

Available at tobacco counters throughout the country.

CREDIT: PICTORIAL PARADE

General Douglas MacArthur.

MacArthur Corncob Pipe

MOST will recall this pipe, made to Gen. Douglas MacArthur's specifications, as his personal trademark. But the oversize bowl was also lit in the European Theater of World War II as Lieut.-Gen. John F. Lucas, who commanded the landings at Anzio in January 1944, also smoked one. Lucas, incidentally, was relieved of his command for his failure to accomplish the initial objectives of the assault. Perhaps he should've used some of Mac's tobacco too.

Price: Cumberland catalog #0591, $2.98, F.O.B. Crossville, Tennessee.

"Wish and Want Book" available, $3.75.

Cumberland General Store

Route 3
Crossville, TN 38555
Tel. 615/484-8481

Zippo Cigarette Lighter

IT'S as clean as a microchip and as reliable as a Jeep. It's as eternal as internal combustion and has the utility of the T.V.A. It's so damned democratic that every G.I.—from dogface soldier to Allied commander—carried one into battle. Why, in just lighting up a cigarette, the Zippo expresses more American virtues than does the rear end of a campaign train.

The "lighter that works" was invented in 1932 when hardly anyone else did. It was the brainchild of one George Blaisdell, an oil company executive from Bradford, Pennsylvania, who assembled his first Zippos in a loft over a downtown filling station. These were squared-off affairs, unstreamlined, and even less pretentious than the soft-cornered models with which we're now familiar. Those didn't come along until 1937, and with the exception of the black-finished Zippos that stopped bullets and illuminated cockpit panels during World War II, they've been with us ever since.

In addition to its many other qualities, there's a manly air about a Zippo that begins with the satisfying *ka-clunk* that announces its every flame. If you're a guy and not careful, you may find yourself using your Zippo in a club, showing it to the Bergman-mouthed beauty next to you and saying: "Y'know, this baby saved my life at Riva Ridge." If she's like most modern young women, she won't know what the hell you're talking about.

Toys and Games

Toys to Delight the Kiddies

ALL KIDDIES LOVE ANIMALS 98¢

A Stock Farm Complete With Barn

Here is real sport and lots of play value. Children play for hours putting the animals into the stalls and feeding them imaginary hay. A box of toothpicks makes an ideal rail fence. With old spools, cut in half, and twigs inserted for fence posts and mother's thread a fence can be built. The barn measures 12⅝ inches long; 9 inches high. In it are fourteen wooden farm animals. The barn is made of good grade wood, nicely decorated. Fence materials shown not included. Shipping weight, 6 pounds.
79K9125 .... 98c

35c See the Dog Wiggle

Body is so made up that, as the dog is pulled along the floor, it wiggles and sways back and forth. Strong cardboard, reinforced with cloth and lithographed in natural colors. Length, 23⅜ inches; height, 6¼ inches. Shipping weight, 1 lb.
49K5467 .... 35c

89c The Teddy Speed Racer

Here's a little speed racer made of solid, nicely enameled wood with nickeled and brass engine trimmings. As car is piloted along by the two little speed drivers with little brass caps, you can hear the imitation engine noise. Very strongly made; has cord to pull. Size, over all, 9⅛x3⅜x4 inches. Shipping weight, 1½ lbs.
49K5469 .... 89c

69c A Crackerjack Value for 69c

Happy Ham, who is 9½ in. long, in his gay attire sits back in his bright wood auto like a king. As car is pulled along he bobs back and forth. Giddap Jockey, who is 9 in. long, races his horse along pulling the lines and bobbing back and forth as he goes along with you. Tom Turno, snappy cardboard clown tumbles over his bar and hits the bell on the platform as he is pulled along. Wood platform and wheels in bright colors. 7 in. long, 10⅛ in. high. Shipping wt., 2½ lbs.
49K5480—All 3 for 69c

98¢ 25-Inch Tractor Set

Made of sheet steel, lithographed in natural colors. Consists of tractor with strong spring motor which pulls the harrow, rake and grain wagon. Tractor can be set to run straight or in circle. Shipping weight, 2½ pounds.
49H5748 .... 98c

The Whirling Twins 89c

As toy is pulled along, the enameled wood twins whirl around holding hands; mounted on nicely lithographed metal frame; nothing to go wrong. Size, over all, 8⅝x5⅞x4½ in. Cord for pulling. Shipping wt., 1½ lbs.
49K5460 89c

This Jack Is Some Kicker 79¢

The Peppiest Action Toy of This Year

PEP!

As mule is pulled along. Oh Boy! Just see him kick. Up and out, high and low, bucking, kicking and stamping. Substantially made of wood attractively decorated. Donkey has cord tail and leather ears. Front wheels have rubber tires. Cord for pulling. Size, over all, 9⅝x5⅝x3⅞ inches. Shipping wt., 1⅛ lbs. 79c
49K5463

Hustler Pup This Dog Walks and Barks 89c

Strong hardwood, handsomely finished and enameled in black and white. Imitation leather ears and collar, strong leash about a yard long with rubber bulb on end which, when pressed, imitates dog bark. Mechanism ... causes legs to move ... forward when dog is pulled. ... inches. Length, 8 inches. ... wt., 1½ lbs. 89c

$1.29 14½-In. Long Has Rubber Tires

Doc Hustler—Extra Quality

A beautiful floor toy for those who want something exceptionally nice. See Doc turn his head when his car turns. Made of wood and metal beautifully enameled. All metal parts nickel plated; has bumper, dummy headlight, motometer and running boards. Size, over all, 14½x6½x4½ inches. Shipping wt., 2⅝ pounds.
49K5461 .... $1.29

Schoenhut's Humpty Dumpty Circus

What Fun! Just Like Real Circus

Animals will stand on one leg, sit up or lie down. Clowns can balance on ladder, and figures will do stunts. Figures, made of wood, are full jointed and dressed. Almost unbreakable. Finished in bright enamel colors.

7-Piece Outfit, $1.79 Including 7-in. clown, donkey and elephant; ladder, chair, barrel and tub. Shipping wt., 1⅞ lbs.
69K9135 $1.79

Canvas Tent and Sawdust Ring
Collapsible canvas tent, 30 in. high, decorated with flags and equipped with wire trapeze and rings. Red curtain in back on gilt pole trimmed with gold fiber fringe. Base, 24x18 in., with sawdust glued to it and 16½-inch painted wood ring in center. Shipping weight, 5½ pounds.
79K9145 .... $2.98

12-Piece Outfit, $4.98 6½-in. circus girl and ringmaster. Brown bear, poodle dog, horse and 7 places in 69K9135. Shpg. wt., 2¼ lbs.
69K9144 $4.98

Red Metal Wagon for 29c

Plenty big for the little tot to pull around. Front wheels turn under when turning corner like big wagon. 10¾ x 6¼ in. Twisted wire handle. Shipping weight, 1⅜ pounds.
49K5457 .... 29c

The Kiddie Choo Choo With Bell 89c

Bell rings as choo choo is pulled along floor. Made of wood, nicely enameled with stenciled engine details. Has nickeled boiler rods and nickel plated bell. Has cord for pulling. Size, over all, 10⅞x4⅝x2⅞ inches. Shipping weight, 2 pounds.
49K5465 .... 89c

4 for $1.00

Some Value for Little Tots—Beat This If You Can

1—All Steel Wagon. Front wheels turn under body. Size, 10¼x6¾ inches, 3-inch wheels, wire handle.
2—21-In. Wheelbarrow, red enameled sheet steel body, 8x7x2⅜ inches, round wood handles, 4½-inch double disc steel wheel.
3—Nicely Colored Metal Sand Pail With Handle; shovel 10⅝ inches long.
4—All Steel Sand Crane. Turn crank and scoop will do the rest. Size, 8½x7¾x3⅜ inches.
Shipping weight, 6 pounds.
79K9136—All 4 toys for. $1.00

89c Gray Beauty Pacers

Horses are lifelike, legs moving back and forth when pulled along. This toy is well made and durable. Wheels, legs and all moving parts are made of metal. Red painted slat style hay wagon. Size, over all, 18⅜x6⅛ inches. Shipping wt., 2½ lbs.
79K5454 .... 89c

89c Watch Girl Jump Rope

As she is pulled along the little girl jumps in the most lifelike fashion. Strongly made of wood and metal, nicely enameled in bright colors. Will make any kiddie happy who owns it. Cord for pulling. Size, over all, 7⅝x7⅞x4¾ inches. Shpg. weight, 2 pounds.
49K5464 .... 89c

Pacing Pony 43c

Horse has a lifelike pacing movement when drawn along, legs moving back and forth. Wheels, legs and all moving parts made of metal, balance of wood, nicely decorated. Size, over all, 13½ inches long, 6⅛ inches high. Shpg. wt., 1½ lbs.
49K5455 .... 43c

Fairy Hay Wagon 43c

Painted bright red. Wood, with metal wheels; 24-inch twisted wire handle. Size of wagon, 10¼x5⅛x5⅞ inches. Big enough for blocks and small toys. Shipping wt., 1⅞ pounds.
49K5458 .... 43c

Teddy Jockey 89c

See jockey drive the comical little black wooden horse with heavy cord legs. Gallops with funny motion when pulled along. Beautifully finished. Metal platform with pulling cord. 7⅛ in. high, 6¼ inches long. Shipping weight 1⅞ pounds.
49K5474 .... 89c

Janesville Ball Bearing Coaster Wagon

BEGINNING in the year 1900 and for three decades thereafter, the Janesville Ball Bearing Coaster Wagon was the standard, as the copy line goes, by which all other such toys were judged. The solid-oak Janesville wagon was the model of versatility—it was a racer, a covered wagon (when properly fitted out), a farm wagon, and a bus. When necessary, the durable play-thing could also be pressed into service aiding adults with shopping and laundry—serious tasks that it performed with happy aplomb. The Janesvilles got passed on from one generation to the next, and today they are valuable collector's items.

The Wisconsin Wagon Company began producing the "Series II" Janesville Ball Bearing Wagon in 1979, intent on sacrificing none of the quality of the originals to contemporary standards of workmanship and design. As a result, the Series II precisely replicates their design details, retaining the solid-oak body, the ball-bearing wheels, the unique bracing, the front axle pivot system, as well as all other features.

Dimensions: 16- by 33-inch box with 4-inch sides.

Price: $175 (plus $10 UPS charge, $15 to the West Coast).

Brochure available.

Wisconsin Wagon Company

507 Laurel Ave.
Janesville, WI 53545
Tel. 608/754-0026

Billiard and Pool Tables

TURN-of-the-century Brunswick and English Thurston billiard and pool tables are replicated by the Adler company of Los Angeles. Adler offers a wide range of types, each handcrafted from 1 1/16-inch Pennsylvania slate and kiln-dried hardwoods. Weighing more than 1,600 pounds each, the tables may be ordered with any of several finishes, cloths, friezes, and pocket treatments. Each has been built to meet the commercial specifications of the Billiard Congress of America.

Brochure available.

Pool Tables by Adler

820 S. Hoover St.
Los Angeles, CA 90005
Tel. 213/382-6334

Henry Ford in 1910.

CREDIT: PICTORIAL PARADE

Henry Ford

Henry Ford (1863–1947) seemed about as complex a man as he was a wealthy one. For "the man who put America on wheels" became the twentieth century's greatest (and richest) industrialist without ever discarding the sensibility of a rural, late-nineteenth-century farmer-mechanic. Alongside such peers as Thomas Edison, Warren Harding, and Alfred P. Sloan (of General Motors), Ford seemed a kind of Victorian eccentric—but one significantly in charge of shaping the early "American Century."

He embodied the often checkered quality of greatness—embracing and advocating ideas that were alternatively lofty and earthy, noble and venomous. To those who built his Model Ts, he was the first to introduce profit sharing, the five-day week, and the five-dollar day; in 1916 his "Ford Peace Ship" returned from its European mission scornfully rebuffed; and in the Twenties his anti-Semitism won him a place in Adolph Hitler's thinking as the ideal American *Führer*.

Within Ford's journeyman intellect the elements of an old American conundrum—the reconciliation of the noble agrarian past with the silvery mechanized future—lost and gained ground. And so the builder of the world's largest manufacturing plants dreamed of smaller factories in the fields occupied by men who were still farmers; and the industrialist who scorned history as "the bunk" restored Sudbury, Massachusetts, to its colonial past, and built Greenfield Village in memory of his Michigan boyhood.

Indian Juggler

GREENFIELD VILLAGE has cobbled together a broad range of history with almost 100 historical structures that have been moved there from places as far away as England. These buildings, which include Henry Ford's birthplace and the 1840 Lincoln Courthouse, have been furnished with folk-art decorations and furniture extending back to the early nineteenth century. An early-twentieth-century example of the former presently on sale through the museum store is the Indian Juggler, a toy that rather resembles a clown (or perhaps he's a costumed East Indian). The juggler's arms flail about,

juggling wooden pins. He is approximately 12½ inches high.

Price: Henry Ford Museum Store catalog #92-0094, $14.95 (plus $2 for shipping and handling).

Gift catalog available.

The Edison Institute
Henry Ford Museum and Greenfield Village
Museum Store
P.O. Box 1970
Dearborn, MI 48121

Stuffed Bears

Health to the lions!

—J. P. MORGAN

Rather than as the duly elected representative of the American people, banker Morgan looked on trust-buster Teddy Roosevelt as something of a rival big-time operator. His toast, made on the eve of the president's 1909 African safari, might've been cheered by those wildlife advocates (called "nature fakers" by T. R.) who considered the hunter-president a wanton slaughterer of big game.

But before he was any of these things, Teddy Roosevelt was a sportsman—which is why we have Teddy bears.

As the story goes, a western hunting expedition in 1902 found the president luckless and uncharacteristically solemn. Perhaps fearful that this situation might bring out the bear *in* Roosevelt, a few members of his party presented the president with one to shoot—a 235-pound black bear that they had tied to a tree. T. R. was naturally appalled by the unsportsmanlike proposition and, emphatically turning it down, emancipated the beast.

Soon after this episode was portrayed on the front page of the *Washington Post* by cartoonist Clifford Berryman, one Morris Michtom, a candystore owner in Brook-lyn, had his wife sew a toy bear in the president's honor. After receiving permission from Mr. Roosevelt to name the stuffed bear "Teddy," Mr. Michtom went on to found the Ideal Toy Corporation, now one of the country's largest.

But despite its subsequent fame, Mr. Michtom's stuffed bear wasn't the nation's first. This honor must go to the Gund Company of Edison, New Jersey, which had been producing stuffed bears four years prior to Roosevelt's 1902 hunting trip. Also, the Steiff Company of Giengen, West Germany, had introduced its stuffed bears to the U.S. at a 1903 trade fair and, in 1907, sold close to a million of these in this country.

Clifford Berryman's 1902 Washington Post cartoon that spurred an industry

T.C. Birthday Bear

AMONG **the early-twentieth-century-style bears** that are still available is the T.C. Birthday Bear, which was created by the Gund company to celebrate its eighty-fifth anniversary in 1983. T.C. Birthday is fully jointed and has both leather-like paws and an embroidered nose. According to Gund, he "represents the type of bear which [*sic*] was being made available in the early 1900s."
Price: $25.

Mr. Cinnamon Bear

THEN there's the Steiff company's 1903 Mr. Cinnamon Bear, all hump-backed and snouty, who has movable joints and shoebutton eyes that shine at you like a glad companion's.

1903 Mr. Cinnamon bears

Gold Teddy Bear

MR. Cinnamon's kid brother, the 1909 Gold Teddy Bear has a sibling's humpback and pair of button eyes; but he's also a scrapper, with felt paws that bristle with little claws.

All of these bears are available at gift, toy, and department stores throughout the country.

1909 Gold Teddy Bears

Doll's Straw Hat

THIS HAT, an adaptation of one in the Margaret Woodbury Strong Museum collection that had originally appeared on a 1910 French doll, is hand-woven from natural straw and fitted with a rouge satin ribbon and fabric roses. The doll's straw hat measures approximately 12½ inches in diameter and has a 5-inch brim.

Price: Museum Shop #4176, $40 (plus $3.95 for shipping).

Color gift folder available.

Museum Shop

The Margaret Woodbury Strong Museum
One Manhattan Square
Rochester, NY 14607

Uncle Sam 3-Coin Register Banks

IN 1907 the Durable Toy and Novelty Company started a bank that has weathered boom times and bust with an aplomb that the others may envy. It provides depositers with only an interest-free long-term account, but the 6-inch institution has never known a bank holiday.

The Uncle Sam 3-Coin looks like a little cash register with a mechanical display to show the total amount inside and a drawer that locks after the first 25¢ has been deposited, never to open again until $9.75 in coin has followed it. For an astonishing number of Americans the Uncle Sam 3-Coin provided primary lessons in thrift and larceny both (I was almost ten before I figured a way to use a kitchen knife to make my 3-Coin into a savings and *loan*).

The bank that was invented in Cleveland by a man named Payson looks the same today, its only alterations limited to some improvements in the operating mechanism. And in keeping with the warranty implied by Durable Toy's name, the Uncle Sam is rarely in need of repair. "Once," said Lewis N. Masters, who manufactured the bank from 1957 until 1983 when the DABS company of West Islip, New York, took over, "we had a letter from a lady saying she was enclosing an Uncle Sam 3-Coin Register Bank and hoped we would repair it. The last time it had to be repaired we were good enough to repair it. She enclosed the paperwork. There was an invoice from 1932"—but that was a lousy year for banks generally.

Available in toy stores for $10 to $12 each, or write:

The DABS Company

752 Pine Ave.
West Islip, NY 11795
Tel. 516/422-3222

Cast-Metal Toys from the Cumberland General Store

Toys made of tinplate, cast iron, and aluminum were successors to the wooden toys of the nineteenth century. From 1900 to World War II, cast-metal toys, produced from reusable molds, appeared by the tens of thousands as circus wagons, carriages, fire rigs, walking horses, and farm vehicles.

The following models are made of cast aluminum and are painted in the colors of the original equipment they represent. Designed to a one-twenty-fifth scale, they are highly detailed.

Case Engine

THE CASE TRACTION Engine shown was designed from J. I. Case specifications and blueprints. The original engine was rated at 60 h.p. and sold for $2,350. Its model measures 8 inches long, 4 inches wide, and 5 inches high. The right bull wheel is belted to the belt wheel hub, and when the toy is pushed, the belt wheel, shaft, eccentric, and piston arm all rotate. The boiler is black, the engine and canopy green, and the wheels red. Shipping weight: 2 lbs.
 Price: Cumberland catalog #3872, $49.

Cumberland's Toy Case Engine Water Tank and Separator

Separator

THE CASE Separator has red wheels and a green draw bar and bagger. The belt pulleys do not turn, but the blower pipe swings up into position.
 Dimensions: 12 inches long, 3 inches wide, and 5 inches high with blower and feeder retracted. Shipping weight: 2 lbs.
 Price: Cumberland catalog #3874, $43.75.

Water Tank

THIS is actually a bank, with its wheels painted red, its tank black, and the draw bar green.
 Dimensions: 9 inches long, 4 inches wide, and 3 inches high. Shipping weight: 2 lbs.
 Price: Cumberland catalog #3873, $24.95.

Oil Pull

THE Rumely Oil-Pull is a toy replica of a 1926 25-45 Model R. It is painted green and has red wheels trimmed in gold. The flywheel and belt pulley both turn when the tractor moves.

Dimensions: 6 inches long, 4 inches wide, and 4½ inches high. Shipping weight: 2 lbs.

Price: Cumberland catalog #3876, $43.75.

The following wheeled toys, called "play-purties" in the early-twentieth-century South, are made from cast iron.

Touring Car

ALL BLACK and measuring 6 inches in length. Shipping weight: 4 lbs.

Price: Cumberland catalog #3883, $10.

Patrolman

THE patrolman rides his 6-inch Harley. Both have been painted black.

Price: Cumberland catalog #3886, $7.

All prices are F.O.B. Crossville, Tennessee.

"Wish and Want Book" available, $3.75.

Train

ENGINE AND tender are 11 inches long. Shipping weight: 4 lbs.

Price: Cumberland catalog #3882, $13.

Cumberland General Store

Route 3
Crossville, TN 38555
Tel. 615/484-8481

Balsa-Wood Gliders

PAUL K. GUILLOW, a Wakefield, Massachusetts, aviation enthusiast, sailed his first balsawood glider aloft in 1927, the same year that Charles Lindbergh successfully soloed from New York to Paris.

While Lindbergh's experience ranks among the bravest in the annals of aviation, Guillow's must be about the most universal.

Guillow died in 1951, but the firm he founded still produces more than five million lighter-than-they-look aircraft per year. There are now twenty different models of these, including several from the time you're recalling now.

Prices range from 29¢ to $2.99.

Available at stationery and toy stores throughout the country.

1925 International Truck Toy

THIS replica of a 1925 International Van toy truck is available in a limited edition from Les Paul Collector Trucks of Winamac, Indiana. It is entirely hand-assembled from more than ninety steel parts (with steerable wheels of cast aluminum) and measures 25 inches long, 13 inches high, and 8½ inches wide. The truck's cab is black, its chassis red, and its bed is green.

Price: $300
(plus $10 for shipping and handling).

Les Paul Collector Trucks

R.R. #2, Box 309
Winamac, IN 46996

Parcheesi

Who Plays Club Parcheesi?

This photograph shows Harry Ellerbe, Madge Evans, Dorothy Stickney and Thurston Hall of a popular Broadway stage production enjoying a game of Club Parcheesi.

CLUB PARCHEESI

SOARING HIGHER AND HIGHER IN POPULAR FAVOR

Club Parcheesi holds the spotlight. Newspapers and magazines feature it. Leading stores display it. Smart society plays it, personalities of the stage and screen, statesmen—in fact almost everywhere that you find the kind of people who are a step or two ahead of the crowd, you find Club Parcheesi being played or discussed.

Club Parcheesi is the adult edition of the ever-popular game of Parcheesi with an advanced system of scoring which intrigues and fascinates keen-minded men and women. Stock it and show it. Marvelously attractive sets made to retail at $3.00, $5.00, $10.00 and $25.00 . . . and there's generous profit in each set.

Parcheesi-Backgammon, Backgammon, Checkers, Anagrams, Tidley Winks, Party Games, Racing Games, Archery Sets, American Hero Sets, Puzzle Pictures, Card Games . . . AND . . . SHOOT-A-CAK, the cactus target game.

WRITE FOR LITERATURE FULLY DESCRIBING ALL CLUB PARCHEESI SETS

| SELCHOW & RIGHTER CO. | 200 FIFTH AVE., NEW YORK, N.Y. |

When writing to Selchow & Righter Company, will you please mention PLAYTHINGS?

Radio Flyer Wagon

"**W**HO'S AFRAID of the Big Bad Wolf" was the hit song of 1933, the same year that the Chicago Century of Progress Exposition opened to thumb its nose at the Depression with the same counterfeit bravura. Many of the fair's huge exhibits were grandiose totems that seemed to strive with their size to persuade the gods of economic change to pull the country through. The desire to appease Olympus in adversity is something that even progress by the millennium can't affect.

"Remember?" asks the 1948 Radio Flyer brochure, "back in '33 when Radio Steel Wagons were in their fifteenth year, Chicago sponsored a spectacular exposition amidst a depression.... Radio Steel, with faith in the future, put up a mammoth exhibit ... and became world famous overnight!" As the Radio Flyer Wagon was named by the company's founder to honor the memory of his two great heroes—Guglielmo Marconi (the wireless pioneer he'd met as a boy in Italy) and Charles Lindbergh—you can bet that the huge boy-on-his-wagon exhibit *was* an expression of faith ... the unshakable kind that's harbored by poor immigrants who've done well in America.

Radio Flyer's Model 18 is an improved version of the 1948 "Production-Line Streamliner" and has the semi-pneumatic tires that gave it "the same smooth ride as dad's car." The decal adorning the Model 18's fire-engine-red flanks was introduced at the Chicago fair.

Available at toy and department stores throughout the country, or from

Radio Steel and Manufacturing Company

6515 W. Grand Ave.
Chicago, IL 60635
Tel. 312/637-7100

Monopoly

AMID the gathering clouds of 1935, Germany incorporated the Saarland, Italy invaded Abyssinia, Japan continued seizing territory in northern China, and, with the introduction of Monopoly, Atlantic City began its campaign of world domination.

Like the New Deal, which was also launched in 1935, Monopoly was an antidote to the Depression—only more fun. The game was an exercise in the kind of unbridled capitalism that could make you as rich as a Mellon in about the time that it takes to say "Reconstruction Finance Corporation." But much of Monopoly's early appeal relied on the fact that play money in 1935 seemed only a little less valuable than the real thing anyway.

And Monopoly has been a bestseller ever since: its maker, Parker Brothers, estimates that they've sold more than eighty-five million sets of the game in twenty-eight countries. Of course Monopoly is still considered subversive in the Soviet Union, but as six sets disap-

© 1936 PARKER BROTHERS, INC.

peared from their display at the 1959 American National Exhibition in Moscow (site of the famous Nixon-Khrushchev "Kitchen Debate"), Parker Brothers figures that a few Ruskies still ride the Reading.

In 1985 Parker Brothers celebrated Monopoly's fiftieth anniversary with a special edition that reproduces the original set. This commemorative edition contains the "reissued original tokens and board label, wooden houses, 'Grand Hotels' and ivory-hued dice" that first appeared in 1935.

Available at most major toy and game retailers for $40.

Toys from the Enchanted Doll House

Located on the outskirts of Manchester, Vermont—a town that looks as if it was lifted off a cake— the Enchanted Doll House offers a varied and unique selection of dolls and miniatures, many of which replicate period items. Although when writing the *Nineteenth-Century Sourcebook* I kidded the Enchanted Doll House for not translating their catalog's copy into English from the original Munchkin, they were so nice about it afterward that it's taken all the fun out of being nasty . . . toward *them*, anyway.

Googly and Her Rocking Horse

GOOGLY is a reproduction of a musical doll from the 1930s that plays "Pennies from Heaven." Named for her big, round eyes, Googly represents a black child and is topped with a curly-haired wig. In her flowery dress, Googly sits astride a reproduction 12¼-inch wooden Rocking Horse Pull-Toy with leather stirrups, painted mane, and red velvet bow.

Prices: EDH catalog #8HN901, Googly doll, $45 (plus $4 for shipping and handling); EDH catalog #8Y7K422, rocking horse, $20 (plus $3.50 for shipping and handling).

Wicker carriage with Bisque baby doll

Wicker Carriage and Bisque Baby Doll

FINALLY, the Enchanted Doll House's miniature Wicker Carriage is available upon its undercarriage of solid brass fitted with die-cast wheels. The carriage neatly carries the 1-inch Bisque Baby Doll that may also be purchased. A carriage pad is included.

Prices: EDH catalog #90B23, Wicker Carriage, $60 (plus $4.50 for shipping and handling); EDH catalog #92G2, Bisque Baby Doll, $24 (plus $3.50 for shipping and handling).

Googly mounted atop her rocking horse

Scooties Boy and Girl

THESE are two 16-inch dolls that have been reproduced from original early-twentieth-century molds.

Price: $52 each (plus $4.50 to cover the cost of shipping and handling). Specify EDH catalog #8BH6201 for Scooties Boy, and #8BH6202 for Scooties Girl.

Catalog of dolls, doll accessories, and handcrafted miniatures available, $2.

Enchanted Doll House

Manchester Center, VT 05255
Tel. 802/362-3030

Pouting Bench

THE Enchanted Doll House's Pouting Bench is handcrafted of finished pine by Bee Spears, who will personalize it for any buyer specifying their pouter's name.

Dimensions: 18 inches high, 10 inches deep, and 19 inches wide.

Price: EDH catalog #8EN1, $138.

Breuer Chair

THE Enchanted Doll House's tubular metal Breuer chair, a 1-inch model of the famous chair designed in 1927 by Marcel Breuer, is perfect for the Bauhaus dollhouse.

Price: EDH catalog #9KY16A, $45 (plus 50¢ for shipping and handling).

1920s Kitchen Set

THE SET includes an inch-to-foot-scale Coolidge-era cooler, the monitor-top G.E. refrigerator (1927), a Roper gas range, and a white porcelain kitchen sink—all made of unpainted die-cast metal. It comes unassembled.

Price: EDH catalog #9V18300, $35 (plus $4.50 for shipping and handling).

From FACTORY TO YOU!
Big SAVINGS Guaranteed

OUR FULTON TENT FACTORY
OUR SHOE FACTORY IN THE EAST
OUR CREAM SEPARATOR FACTORY
OUR BRADLEY IMPLEMENT FACTORY
OUR PLUMBING GOODS FACTORY
OUR PAINT FACTORY
OUR MILLWORK FACTORY IN OHIO
OUR STOVE FOUNDRY
ANOTHER OF OUR SHOE FACTORIES
OUR WIRE FENCING FACTORY
OUR OIL STOVE FOUNDRY
OUR WALL PAPER MILL
OUR MILLWORK FACTORY IN NEW JERSEY
OUR LUMBER PLANT IN ILLINOIS

You can tell the ideals of a nation by its advertisements.
—NORMAN DOUGLAS,
SOUTH WIND, 1917

We Manufacture Much of Our Merchandise in Our Own Factories

Naturally, because we supply eleven million families with a [...] enables us to run our business more economically and buy an [...] supply you could possibly have. One of the ways in which we make [...] own manufacturing.

Some of the more important goods we thus produce are:

Shoes — Building Material — Paint
Stoves — Wall Paper — Cream Separator
Plumbing Goods — Tents — Wire Fencing
Farm Implements

An idea of the quantities we manufacture may be gathered from the fact that every yea[r] Paper Mill makes upwards of twenty million 8-yard rolls of wall paper and our Paint Facto[ry] of one million gallons of paint, while our Millwork Factories produce many millions of dolla[rs worth of] building material.

Not only do we cut our costs and handling expenses by this plan, but we are able to insure a higher and more uniform standard of quality.

When you buy merchandise of this class from our catalog, it is equal to buying direct from the factory. You pay only one profit from the time the raw material is received at the factory until the finished merchandise arrives at your home.

In addition to the money saving we make you through our own manufacturing, we make you a large saving on other merchandise by contracting for the entire output or a large share of the output of other large factories, both in the United States and foreign countries. These factories naturally trim their profits to the minimum and enable us to secure high standard merchandise at the lowest prices for which it can be bought.

Whether we do our own manufacturing or buy from other factories we cut out every possible penny of unnecessary profit and expense and give you the full benefit in rock bottom prices.

You can easily see how the World's Largest Store can guarantee to satisfy you and save you money.

Sears, Roebuck and Co.
The World's Largest Store

37,500 OF OUR MODERN HOMES have been built in the U. S. A. This is an illustration of one of them. The millwork and lumber for all these were produced in our own factories. Be sure to see our building material pages in this catalog.

HOUSE PAINT
WALLPAPER
LUMBER

Advertising Items

Advertising Items

125

From the Vestal Press

Advertising Mirrors

UBIQUITOUS now in the gentrified gin mill, the reproduction turn-of-the-century advertising mirror provides upwardly mobile patrons with the names of old companies ripe for leverage takeover along with a handy reflective surface for honing power-staring techniques, correcting tie-knot dimples, and practicing other New Vanity basics.

Gargoyles Limited's replica turn-of-the-century advertising mirrors carry ads for Anheuser-Busch Beer, Fry's Chocolate, Lloyd's 1^D Screws, Chivas Regal Whiskey, the very Edwardian-sounding British Colonial Bicycles, and Harlem Dandy Cigarettes, among others. All have been silkscreened and hand-printed in England.

Literature available.

Gargoyles Ltd.

512 S. 3rd St.
Philadelphia, PA 19147
Tel. 215/629-1700

Nipper Serving Tray

BEFORE he came to be recognized throughout the world, Nipper was the pet fox terrier of the English painter Francis Barraud. His painting *His Master's Voice* was inspired by the late-nineteenth-century sight of Nipper hunched before a talking machine and wearing the same expression that many humans in that situation were wont to wear in those times. In 1901 the Victor Talking Machine Company acquired the rights to the painting, adopting it as their trademark.

The Vestal Press's Nipper serving tray is made of lithographed metal, 14 inches long.

Price: Vestal Press stock #M-49x, $5 (plus $2 for postage and handling).

Advertising and Political Posters

From Nostalgia Decorating Company

To the left it was a half a block to Maginnis's Fancy Groceries, Home and Imported Products. Fainy liked the . . . Cream of Wheat darkey in the window.

—JOHN DOS PASSOS, *THE 42ND PARALLEL*, 1929

THIS poster is still available, along with a $1.50 brochure full of other early-twentieth-century advertising art replicas, from:

Nostalgia Decorating Company

P.O. Box 1312
Kingston, PA 18704
Tel. 717/288-1795

From Buck Hill Associates

MORE than 600 reproductions of nineteenth- and twentieth-century posters, handbills, broadsides, prints, and advertisements are contained in the Buck Hill Associates catalog. Most have been reprinted in the original black-on-white, and appear in such categories as "Turn of the Century," "Automobiles," "The 1900s," and "Movies."

Catalog, $1.

Buck Hill Associates

129 Garnet Lake Rd.
Johnsburg, NY 12843

Herschell-Spillman Company Catalog

THE upstate New York firm was one of America's best-known manufacturers of merry-go-rounds, riding galleries, mountain-valley railways, ferris wheels, and striking machines for amusement park operators. This, their handsome 1911 catalog, features photographs and descriptions of each and the construction details of several.

Price: Vestal Press stock #A-153, $3.

The Herschell-Spillman "Striker," 1911

The Mills Arcade Machine Catalog

A reprint of the Mills Novelty Company's 1918 line of arcade gambling, vending, athletic, and picture machines. Besides the "Jumbo Success" depicted, the 24-page catalog includes illustrations, prices, and descriptions of the Chicago firm's "1918 O.K. Gum Vendor" ("Built like a Typewriter"), "Check Boy," "Umpire Baseball," "New Idea Cigar," "Little Firefly" ("Electricity is Life—One Cent"), "Owl Lifter," "Improved Perfect Peanut," and "20th-Century,"

among many others.

Price: Vestal Press stock #A-121, $3.50.

Include $2 to cover the cost of postage and handling on all orders.

Catalog of period industrial book and manual reprints, $2.

The Vestal Press

P.O. Box 97
320 N. Jensen Rd.
Vestal, NY 13850
Tel. 607/797-4872

Porcelain Enameled Signs

FAITHFUL TO THE originals, these advertising signs have been handmade by an early-twentieth-century process in which each color is applied and fired separately. The blue-and-white "Morton Salt" sign measures 8 by 12 inches; "Old Dutch Cleanser," which is yellow, maroon, blue, and white, is 9 by 13 inches; "Cracker Jack," red and blue on white, is 6 by 12 inches; and "Heinz 57 Varieties," red, white, and green, measures 11½ inches in diameter.

Gift catalog available.

Jenifer House

New Marlboro Stage
Great Barrington, MA 01230
Tel. 413/528-1500

Coca-Cola Glasses and Trays

THE original formula for Coca-Cola, developed in 1886 by Atlanta pharmacist John S. Pemberton, was (until recently) changed only once. That was in 1906 when the newly legislated Pure Food and Drug Act mandated the elimination of the minute amount of cocaine that the formula contained. Despite this, Coke would continue to be called "dope" in the South, and in 1920 the Supreme Court would uphold the soft drink's claim to the name "Coke."

Pepsi-Cola came along during the Thirties to challenge Coke with the offer of twice as much cola for the same money. The jingle created to herald this bargain become one of the most popular in advertising history:

> *Pepsi-Cola hits the spot,*
> *Twelve full ounces, that's a lot.*
> *Twice as much for a nickel too,*
> *Pepsi-Cola is the drink for you.*
> *Nickle, nickle, nickle, nickle,*
> *Trickle, trickle, trickle, trickle. . . .*

While Pepsi has long since established a market niche for the world to envy, it's always been Coke—ancient, fabled Coke—that could lay claim to being "The Real Thing" with everyone instantly knowing what was meant. Then, in 1985, what nickle-nickle-nickle-trickle-trickle-trickle couldn't do, sugar did. Yielding cravenly to a mass-marketed and juvenile preference for the treacle in Pepsi, the venerable Coke formula was, without a by-your-leave, replaced by "New Coke," a fizzy contender. Showing the same absence of character that was their new concoction's only distinction, Coke's blue-suits even tried calling the new flavor "bolder"; but crimes against the language would not avail them, and as everyone knows, a popular cry for good flavor and (invisible to any marketing survey) integrity, brought the old Coke formula back.

Although some scattered bottlers still use the company's graceful 1916 hobbleskirt bottle, the only way left to remember the old Coca-Cola is through some of the facsimiles of its early-twentieth-century advertising that the company has licensed for replication. The early-twentieth-century-style trays and 1919 fountain glasses depicted here are available for sale in retail outlets throughout the United States and Canada.

Kodaks and Eastman Cameras

Brownie Box Cameras

The enviable reputation of Eastman Cameras and Kodaks is world wide. Wherever you go, you find the name Eastman synonymous with high quality, beauty and efficiency. When you purchase an Eastman product you know that you are getting your money's worth—and when you purchase it from Sears, Roebuck and Co. you are doubly sure, because our liberal guarantee, behind everything we sell, makes your satisfaction positive. The Cameras and Kodaks shown on this page are true representatives of Eastman Kodak Company's sterling products.

This is the well known Brownie camera which has satisfied tens of thousands of users. It is well constructed, and simple to operate. Has two shutter speeds—instantaneous and time, and has different diaphragm stops so that you can readily control light conditions. Shpg. wt., 2½ lbs.

3K41050—No. 2 Box Brownie. Takes picture size 2⅛x3¼ inches. **$2.29**

3K41052—No. 2A Box Brownie. Takes picture size 2½x4¼ inches. **$3.19**

3K41053—No. 3 Box Brownie. Takes picture size 3¼x4¼ inches. **$3.98**

3K41054—No. 2C Box Brownie. Takes picture size 2⅞x4⅞ inches. **$4.49**

Vest Pocket Kodak
Picture size 1⅝x2½ inches

Small as a vest pocket. This camera will fit it. No focusing—just set the adjustment for either instantaneous or time, point the lens at the object to be photographed, and "click," the picture is yours. Like all other Kodaks, it is autographic, and the lens and shutters are carefully tested. Will hold an 8-exposure film.

Equipped with Meniscus lens and rotary shutter, four diaphragm stops, two speeds, instantaneous or time. Brilliant reversible finder for vertical or horizontal pictures. Made of metal, covered with durable imitation leather, trimmings finished in nickel and black enamel, one pound shipping weight.

3K41010—Vest Pocket Kodak, Single Lens.

3K41012—Vest Pocket Kodak, Kodar lens.

3K41013—Vest Pocket Kodak, F.6.3. **13.45**

HAWKEYE CAMERAS

3K41025 to 3K41029

3K41024

Made by Eastman Kodak Company

So exact in detail, so true in reproduction, it is readily understood why the Famous Hawkeye Camera has such a large following. With them even a beginner can be sure of obtaining excellent pictures, sure to please immeasurably with their marvelous fidelity to any subject chosen. True to the high standards of the Eastman Company's workmanship, these exceptional cameras are handy, compact and beautiful, as well as remarkably durable and efficient. Here is a camera you will be proud of, both for its appearance and the results it obtains for you.

All load with Kodak roll film, obtainable anywhere.

The reliable Kodex shutter appears on all sizes, with two accurate snapshot speeds in addition to time and bulb settings. Exposures are made either with a lever or with the cable release supplied with each camera. The focus is adjustable. It is aided by an accurate scale and a handy focusing lock. The finder is reversible for horizontal or vertical views, and alternate sockets permit the use of a tripod in either position.

The cameras are covered with fine grain black imitation leather, handsomely embossed. Exposed metal parts are trimmed in durable nickel and brass.

3K41025—No. 2 Vest Pocket. Shpg. wt., 1 lb. Takes picture size 1⅝x2½ inches. **$ 4.25**

3K41026—No. 2 Folding Hawkeye. Shpg. wt., 2 lbs. Takes picture size 2¼x3¼ inches. **6.45**

3K41026—No. 2 Folding Hawkeye. Shpg. wt., 2 lbs. Rapid Rectilinear Lens. Takes picture size 2¼x3¼ inches. **8.45**

3K41027—No. 2A Folding Hawkeye. Shpg. wt., 2½ lbs. Single lens. Takes picture size 2½x4¼ inches. **7.65**

3K41028—No. 2A Folding Hawkeye. Shpg. wt., 2½ lbs. Rapid Rectilinear Lens. Takes picture size 2½x4¼ inches. **9.35**

3K41029—No. 3A Folding Hawkeye. Shpg. wt., 4⅛ lbs. Rapid Rectilinear Lens. Takes picture size 3¼x5½ inches. **12.85**

Eastman Kodaks

Kodak Series I

Automatic focusing arrangement. Brilliant finder, reversible for vertical or horizontal pictures. Two tripod sockets, body is made of aluminum, covered with fine leather, seal grained. Metal parts finished in nickel and black enamel. Rising, falling and sliding front. Black bellows. Has autographic feature which enables you to make a permanent record on each film. Shutters have the following speeds: Kodex shutter, time bulb, 1/25, 1/50 second; the Universal shutter time bulb, 1, 1/2, 1/5, 1/10, 1/25, 1/100 second. Both are equipped with finger and cable release. Shipping weights: No. 1, 2 lbs.; No. 1A, 2½ lbs.; 3A, 4¼ lbs.

3K41000—No. 1, Series I, Single Lens. Takes picture size 2¼x3¼ in. **$ 8.15**

3K41001—No. 1, Series I, Kodar Lens. Takes picture size 2¼x3¼ in. **10.85**

3K41002—No. 1, Series I, F.7.7. Takes picture 2¼x3¼ inches. **13.45**

3K41003—No. 1A, Series I, Single Lens. Takes picture size 2½x4¼ in. **8.95**

3K41004—No. 1A, Series I, Kodar Lens. Takes picture size 2½x4¼ in. **11.65**

3K41005—No. 1A, Series I, F.7.7. Takes picture size 2½x4¼ inches. **14.35**

3K41006—No. 3A, Series I, Kodar Lens. Takes picture size 3¼x5½ in. **16.15**

3K41009—No. 3A, Series I, F.7.7. Takes picture size 3¼x5½ inches. **17.95**

Pocket Kodaks—Series II
Focusing Models

Open the camera and the lens snaps into position. These models offer two equipments. 1. The Diomatic shutter, with four snapshot speeds and timing scale; the famous Kodak Anastigmat F.7.7 lens that makes sharp pictures. 2. Kodex shutter and the semi-anastigmat lens, Kodar F.7.9—adequate equipment for average work.

Both models of the Pocket Kodaks, Series II, are autographic, both fit the pocket.

Capacity—No. 1, 6 exposures; No. 1A, 12 exposures. Focus: Fixed or adjustable. Lenses: Kodar F.7.9, or Kodak Anastigmat F.7.7. Shutters: Kodex speeds 1/25, and 1/50 second; Diomatic speeds 1/10, 1/25, 1/50 and 1/100 second; both with finger release, time and bulb actions. Brilliant finder, reversible for horizontal or vertical pictures. Two tripod sockets. Body: Aluminum. Covering: Leather; metal parts finished in nickel and black enamel. Black bellows. Autographic feature. Shpg. wt., 2 lbs.

3K41014—No. 1 Pocket Kodak, Series II, Single Lens. Takes picture size 2¼x3¼ inches. **$11.25**

3K41015—No. 1 Pocket Kodak, Series II, Kodar Lens. Takes picture size 2¼x3¼ inches. **$14.35**

3K41016—No. 1 Pocket Kodak, Series II, F.7.7. Takes picture size 2¼x3¼ inches. **$18.95**

3K41017—No. 1A Pocket Kodak, Series II, Single Lens. Takes picture size 2½x4¼ inches. **$12.55**

3K41018—No. 1A Pocket Kodak, Series II, Kodar Lens. Takes picture size 2½x4¼ inches. **$16.15**

3K41019—No. 1A Pocket Kodak, Series II, F.7.7. Takes picture size 2½x4¼ inches. **$20.65**

Kodak Series III

For the discriminating user of a Kodak, we recommend the Series III Kodak, as it has all the refinements of the Kodak cameras, together with extra fine lens equipment, diomatic shutter, rising and falling front, autographic feature, reversible brilliant view finder, F.6.3 Anastigmat lens and knurled focusing device which insures absolute accuracy when setting the gauge for distance. Made of aluminum, covered with a fine quality of grained leather. Metal parts highly nickeled. Has handle so that it can be easily carried. Furnished in four sizes. Shipping weight, 3 pounds.

3K41020—No. 1 Pocket Kodak. Takes picture size 2¼x3¼ inches. F.6.3. **$22.50**

3K41021—No. 1A Pocket Kodak. Takes picture size 2½x4¼ inches. F.6.3. **$25.50**

3K41022—No. 2C Pocket Kodak. Takes picture size 2⅞x4⅞ inches. F.6.3. **$28.00**

3K41023—No. 3 Pocket Kodak. Takes picture size 3¼x4¼ inches. F.6.3. **$26.50**

CINE KODAKS

A Moving Picture Camera such as this makes life's happy lights yours forever. Baby's cute gestures, always yours. Mother's gentle smile to be actually recalled long after fleeting years slip by. That boy of yours—exuberant, overflowing—perpetual motion. Preserve those priceless moments, make them living memories with a Cine Moving Picture Camera.

A handy hand camera for personal movies designed for simplicity and economy in operation. Has spring motor which eliminates hand cranking. Ready for instant use, as it requires no tripod.

3K43247—Cine Kodak, Model B, with Kodak Anastigmat Lens, F.3.5. Shpg. wt., 3½ lbs. **$89.00**

3K43248—Kodascope, Model C Projector. Shipping weight, 6 pounds. **54.00**

3K43251—Complete Outfit, Camera and projector. **141.50**

3K41043—Cine Kodak, Model B, F.6.5. Shipping weight, 4 pounds. **$69.00**

3K41046—Screen, 22x30 inches. Shipping weight, 2½ pounds. **9.75**

3K41047—Screen, 30x30 inches. Shipping weight, 3½ pounds. **13.50**

3K41048—Combination Case Holding Cine Kodak and two rolls of film. Shipping weight, 3 pounds. **9.75**

3K43249—Cine Film, including processing, 50 feet. Shipping weight, 4 ounces. **3.60**

3K43250—Cine Film, including processing, 100 feet. Shipping weight, 6 ounces. **5.40**

Carrying Cases

3K42818—Imitation Leather Carrying Case, with shoulder strap, for No. 2 Size Conley Cameras. Shpg. wt., ¾ lb. **$1.80**

3K42822—Imitation Leather Carrying Case, with shoulder strap, for No. 2A Size Conley Cameras. Shpg. wt., 1¼ lbs. **$1.98**

3K42825—Imitation Leather Carrying Case, with shoulder strap, for No. 3 Size Conley Cameras. Shpg. wt., 1½ lbs. **$2.15**

3K42828—Imitation Leather Carrying Case, with shoulder strap, for No. 3A Size Conley Cameras. Shpg. wt., 1¾ lbs. **$2.25**

View Cameras

IN 1920, with their late-nine-teenth-century Premo-View cameras gone from the market, Laban F. Deardorff and his sons began production of the 8- by 10-inch View Cameras. Setting up operations in an old wagon factory, they produced their first ten View Cameras using mahogany salvaged from bars that had been scrapped during Prohibition. A 5- by 7-inch model was brought out in 1923.

L. F. Deardorff & Sons

315 S. Peoria St.
Chicago, IL 60607
Tel. 312/829-5655

Stationery Supplies

Good Service Fountain Pens
Popular Non-Breakable Desk Set. Self filling fountain pen, about 7¾ inches long, 14-karat solid gold iridium tipped point, medium point only. Airtight pen receptacle. Ink will not become dry. Patent device for pen and receptacle to rest on base when not in use. Base measures about 4⅜x6¾ inches, grooved to hold pencils. Comes in three colors. Order by catalog number the color desired. Shipping weight, 1¼ pounds.
4K6500—Black base, pen black jade green $3.98
4K6502—Jade green color base, pen black and jade green $3.98
4K6504—Mahogany (reddish brown) base pen black and mahogany $3.98
Popular Non-Breakable Double Desk Set. Two self filling fountain pens with airtight receptacles, ink will not become dry. Pens, about 7¾ inches long, gold filled levers, solid gold iridium tipped pen points, medium point only. Base has groove for pin bowl and groove for pencil. Calendar attachment. Base measures about 4½x9¾ in.
4K6506—Black base, pens black and jade green combination....$5.98
4K6508—Jade green color base, pens jade green and black combination....$5.98
4K6510—Mahogany (reddish brown color) base, pens black and mahogany combination....$5.98
Single set, with one pen, without calendar. Mention color wanted, black, jade or mahogany. Shpg. wt., 1¼ lbs.
4K6512....$2.75
Shpg. wt., 2 lbs.
Use Fountain Pen Ink in All Our Pens
ALICE
JANE
ETHEL
Ladies' Non-Breakable Fountain Pen and Ribbon Guard to match the color of the pen. Self filler with 14-karat solid gold medium pen point, tipped with iridium. Ribbon guard, about 45 inches long, gold plated slide. Be sure to mention name wanted.
4K6518 Black pen. $1.25
4K6520 Green pen. $1.25
4K6522 Light blue pen. $1.25
Ladies' Chatelaine Self Filling Fountain Pen, complete with ribbon. A very pretty fountain pen of hard black rubber, beautifully chased. 14-karat solid gold medium pen point, tipped with genuine iridium. Has non-leakable screw cap. Red color tips on cap and barrel. Length, with cap over pen, about 4¼ in. Illustration shows reduced size. Black ribbon guard, about 22 in. when doubled, has gold plated slide. Mention name to be stamped.
4K6514—Illustration shows reduced size..$1.48
Your Name Stamped in Gold Letters Without Extra Charge on All Pens or Pencils Showing Name. We cannot accept returned pens and pencils when engraved according to your instructions. Pens and Pencils furnished without name if desired.
Ladies' Black Hard Rubber Fountain Pen, beautifully chased. Self filler, 14-karat solid gold medium pen point, tipped with hard iridium. Gold filled bands, lever and ring attachment. Length of pen, opened, about 5¾ in. Illustration shows reduced size. Mention name to be stamped.
4K6536 $1.25
Same style, but without bands.
4K6540..98c
H.E. DAVIS
Men's Fountain Pen and Pencil Set. Non-breakable, 14-karat solid gold pen point, medium point only. Gold filled lever and safety clips. Length of pen and pencil, about 5⅛ inches. Illustration shows reduced size. Shpg. wt., 5 oz.
$1.98
4K6530—Jade green color with white stripe, black tips....$1.98
4K6532—Terra cotta (light red color), black tips....$1.98
Illustrations are actual size unless otherwise stated.
Shpg. wt. of articles on this page, 3 oz., unless otherwise stated.
Fountain Pens on this page furnished with medium points only.
C. TAYLOR
85c
Men's Hard Black Rubber Fountain Pen. Self filler, 14-karat solid gold iridium tipped medium point, gold filled lever and pocket clip. Mention name to be stamped....85c
A.B. MURRAY
98c
4K6548—Men's Hard Black Rubber Self Filling Fountain Pen. 14-karat solid gold iridium tipped point. Gold filled lever, pocket clip and tip cap. Mention name to be stamped....98c
4K6550—Ladies' size, about 4½ inches long. Ring on cap of pen, can be worn on chain....98c
4K6554—Men's Non-Breakable Nickel Plated Self Filling Fountain Pen. 14-karat solid gold iridium tipped medium point. Pocket clip. This Pen Cannot Be Stamped With Name....98c
4K6556—Ladies' size, about 4 inches long. Ring on cap of pen....98c
P. L. NELSON
GOOD SERVICE FOUNTAIN PEN CO. CHICAGO ILL.
4K6558—Self Filling Writegraph Ink Pencil of chased black rubber. Can be used for carbon copies. The feed wire that comes in contact with ink is made of gold, insuring long service. Gold filled lever and pocket clip. Mention name to be engraved....$1.45
4K6560—Same style, but not self filler....85c
MARIAN
Ladies' Self Filling Non-Breakable Fountain Pen. Furnished in four colors. 14-karat solid gold iridium tipped medium point. Gold filled lever and ring on cap. Mention name to be stamped. Order by catalog number the color of pen wanted.
4K6564—Black....$1.25
4K6566—Light blue....1.25
4K6568—Red....1.25
4K6570—Light green....1.25
W. A. LEWIS
J. THOMAS
Men's Self Filling Fountain Pen of highly polished black rubber. Red color tip on cap. 14-karat solid gold iridium tipped medium pen point. Gold filled lever and pocket clip. Mention name to be stamped.
4K6592. $1.25
Same style, but ladies' size, about 4½ inches long. Ring in cap, can be worn on chain or guard.
4K6594 ..$1.25
4K6572—Men's Gold Plated Pencil. Eraser and extra leads. Propels and repels lead. Pocket clip....50c
4K6574—Ladies' size, with ring on cap, same design, about 4½ inches long....50c
High Grade Pencil. Propels and repels lead. Men's or Ladies' size in gold filled and solid silver. Illustration shows men's size with pocket clip. Eraser and extra leads.
4K6576—Men's solid silver....$1.45
4K6578—Men's gold filled....1.45
4K6580—Ladies' solid silver, about 4½ inches long, ring on cap....$1.45
4K6582—Ladies' size, gold filled....1.45
D. C. ADAMS
Automatic Jumbo Size Pencil. Very well made. Propels and repels the lead. Comes in four colors. Made of non-breakable material. Gold filled tip, cap and safety pocket clip. Eraser and extra leads. Mention name to be stamped.
4K6584—Jade green color....$1.98
4K6586—Terra cotta (light red color)....1.98
4K6588—Mahogany (dark reddish brown color)....$1.98
4K6590—Black....1.98
Combination Self Filling Fountain Pen and Pencil. Fountain Pen and Pencil made of black highly polished rubber. Gold filled lever and safety pocket clip. 14-karat solid gold iridium tipped medium pen point. We furnish an extra box of thin leads to refill pencil. Mention name to be stamped.
4K6596 $1.48

Mongol Pencils

EBERHARD FABER CAME to New York from Bavaria as a sales agent for the European Pencil Company, a circumstance that helped make it apparent to him that America needed a pencil factory of its own. So in 1861 he opened one in New York City at 42nd Street and the East River, where the United Nations building now stands.

The bright-yellow Mongol pencil with which all Americans are now familiar was introduced by Faber in 1900. It is believed by some that the pencil's name was inspired by the fondness that one of Faber's brothers had for a popular dish of the era, purée Mongol; but more likely it was the desire to suggest that the Mongol used Siberian graphite—then the highest-quality—that resulted in the name.

Available at stationery stores throughout the country.

MONGOL ◆ EBERHARD FABER U.S.A. 482 – № 2

Crayola Crayons

ALTHOUGH ITS name carries a certain enchantment, until early in the century a crayon was no more or less magical than any other artist's tool, its useful niche established by its pigment's oily base: "In sketching, use the crayon purchased for that purpose, which, being of an oily nature, will not be washed out by the water-color passing over it," advised the editors of *The New American Encyclopedia of Social and Commercial Information* of 1905. There's surely no magic there, but then in '05 the Crayola crayon had only just been introduced, and it's likely that no one at the encyclopedia had ever had the pleasure of being smartly saluted by a brilliantly colored platoon of Crayolas brand-new in the box.

As we all know from personal experience, Crayola crayons leave a strong impression on the young. From a box's green-and-yellow chevrons to the delicate architec-

ture of a single cone of burnt sienna, they marry purpose with play, their waxy bouquet beckoning.

Crayola crayons were developed by the Binney & Smith Company of Peekskill, New York, which was formed at the turn of the century to produce slate pencils. Alice Stead Binney, a schoolteacher and wife of founder Edwin, prevailed upon her husband to come up with a crayon formula that would offer American schoolchildren the quality of the European crayons that they loved but could not afford. It was Alice who named the new product, combining the words *crayon* and *olea*—the latter from *oleaginous*, or oily.

The original Crayola boxes of 8, 16, and 24 crayons now range up to massively duplexed freighters of 64 and include colors once known only to the most cloistered walls of Egyptian pyramids. Fortunately, size hasn't spoiled the charm of Crayola crayons any, nor has infla-

tion the price.

The name "Crayola" is a registered trademark of Binney & Smith Incorporated.

Fountain Pen

THE Sheaffer "Nostalgia," a 1972 reissue of a fountain pen first produced by the company in 1914, is available in either Vermeil (a 23-karat gold electroplate over solid sterling silver) or in solid sterling silver. Both are fitted with a 14-karat gold nib.

Suggested retail prices: vermeil Nostalgia Fountain pen, $295; sterling-silver Nostalgia pen, $250.

Available at stationery stores, or contact:

Sheaffer-Eaton

75 S. Church St.
Pittsfield, MA 01201

Die-Cut Greeting Cards

WHILE most of the Paper Potpourri's die-cut cards are in the nineteenth-century style, proprietor Francine Kirsch has graciously provided us with her sole twentieth-century example, accompanied by the following lore:

The little girl depicted is representative of the "type" that superseded the sweet, sentimental, and very realistic children shown in late Victorian illustrations. Almost cartoon-like, this cupid look was popularized by scores of now-anonymous artists and some well-known illustrators—Rose O'Neill with her Kewpies, Grace Drayton with the Campbell Soup Kids. As time went on, the big eyes, rosebud lips, and bobbed hair turned

into the 1920s flapper.

As a greeting card this item was typical of the period c. 1915–1930 when fussy, elaborate, *and* cruelly comic valentines had become passé. By the time of the Depression, our modern four-fold card had become the prevailing style.

The Paper Potpourri's Rosy Girl card is manufactured by the Winslow Press of Princeton, New Jersey, and is made of heavy cardboard. The card is 9 inches high and comes with both an envelope and a fold-down easel backing for display.

Price: $2.50 (plus $1 for shipping).

Catalog available, $1.

The Paper Potpourri

P.O. Box 698
Oakland Gardens, NY 11364

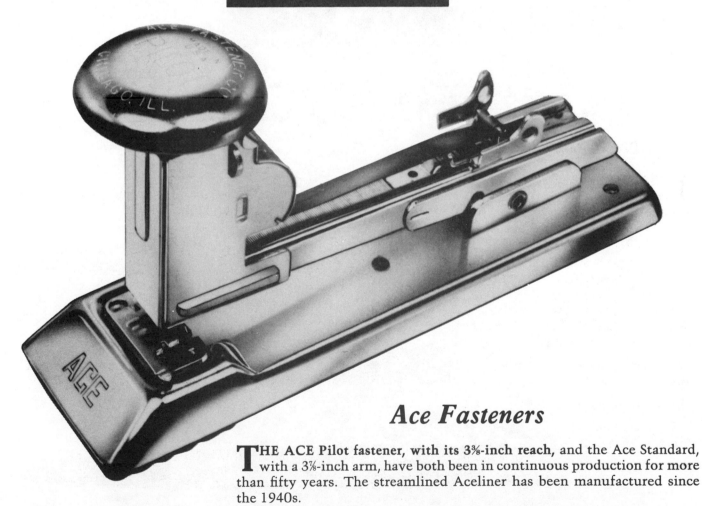

Ace Fasteners

THE ACE Pilot fastener, with its 3⅝-inch reach, and the Ace Standard, with a 3⅞-inch arm, have both been in continuous production for more than fifty years. The streamlined Aceliner has been manufactured since the 1940s.

Available at stationery stores and dealers throughout the country.

Automobiles and Motorcycles

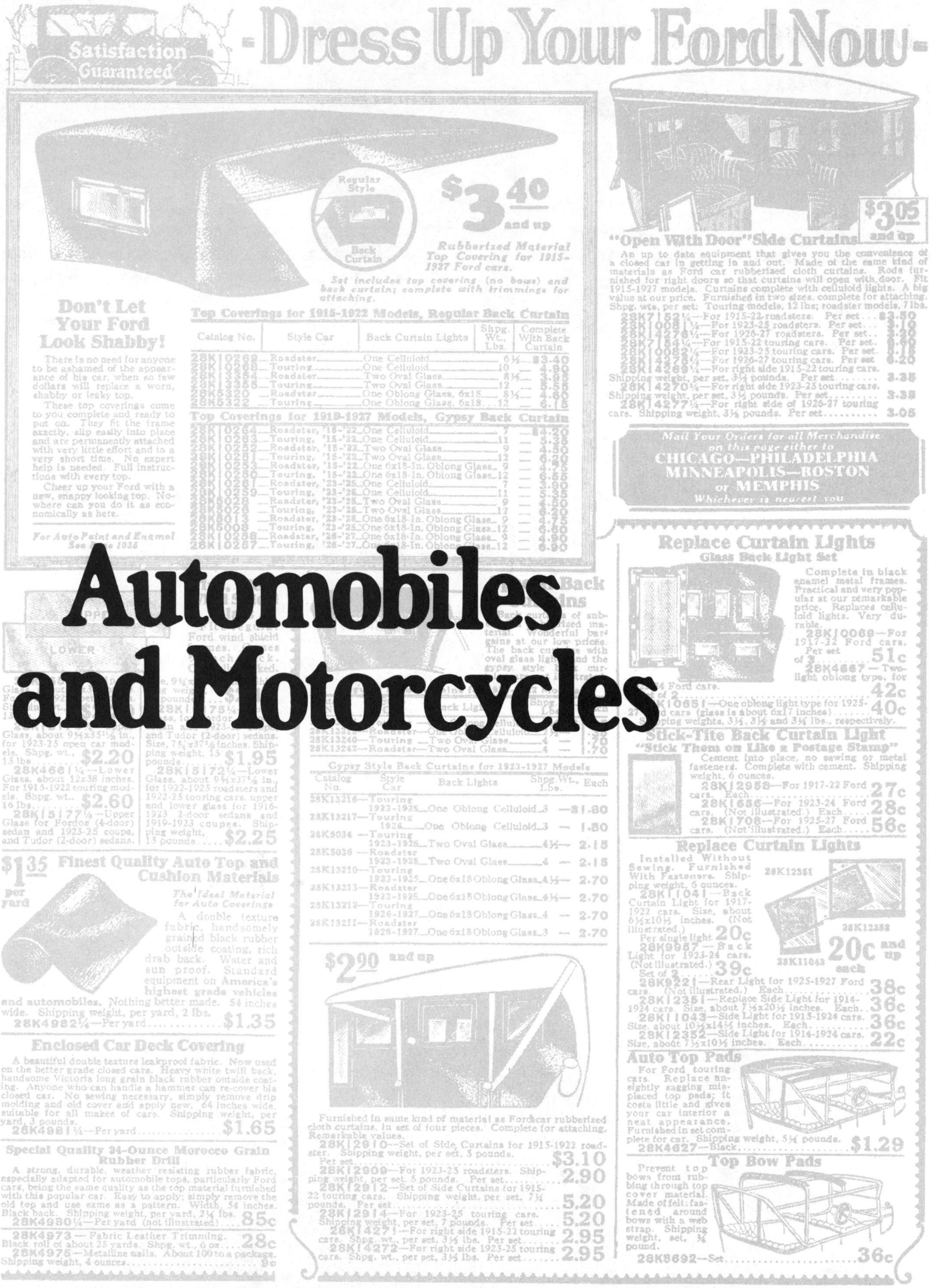

-Dress Up Your Ford Now-

Satisfaction Guaranteed

Regular Style — Back Curtain

$3.40 and up

Rubberized Material Top Covering for 1915-1927 Ford cars.

Set includes top covering (no bows) and back curtain; complete with trimmings for attaching.

Don't Let Your Ford Look Shabby!

There is no need for anyone to be ashamed of the appearance of his car, when so few dollars will replace a worn, shabby or leaky top.

These top coverings come to you complete and ready to put on. They fit the frame exactly, slip easily into place and are permanently attached with very little effort and in a very short time. No expert help is needed. Full instructions with every top.

Cheer up your Ford with a new, snappy looking top. Nowhere can you do it as economically as here.

For Auto Paint and Enamel See Page 1035

Top Coverings for 1915-1922 Models, Regular Back Curtain

Catalog No.	Style Car	Back Curtain Lights	Shpg. Wt., Lbs.	Complete With Back Curtain
28K10269	Roadster	One Celluloid	6½	$3.40
28K10268	Touring	One Celluloid	10	4.90
28K13354	Roadster	Two Oval Glass	8½	3.95
28K13355	Touring	Two Oval Glass	12	5.55
28K5320	Roadster	One Oblong Glass, 6x18	8½	4.60
28K5322	Touring	One Oblong Glass, 6x18	12	6.15

Top Coverings for 1915-1927 Models, Gypsy Back Curtain

Catalog No.	Style Car	Back Curtain Lights	Shpg. Wt., Lbs.	Price
28K10264	Roadster, '15-'22	One Celluloid	7	$4.20
28K10263	Touring, '15-'22	One Celluloid	11	5.35
28K10252	Roadster, '15-'22	Two Oval Glass	9	4.50
28K10251	Touring, '15-'22	Two Oval Glass	12	6.20
28K10253	Roadster, '15-'22	One 6x18-In. Oblong Glass	9	4.75
28K10250	Touring, '15-'22	One 6x18-In. Oblong Glass	12	6.65
28K10261	Roadster, '23-'25	One Celluloid	7	3.90
28K10259	Touring, '23-'25	One Celluloid	11	5.35
28K5028	Roadster, '23-'25	Two Oval Glass	9	4.50
28K5026	Touring, '23-'25	Two Oval Glass	12	6.20
28K5013	Roadster, '23-'25	One 6x18-In. Oblong Glass	9	4.75
28K5008	Touring, '23-'25	One 6x18-In. Oblong Glass	12	6.60
28K10258	Roadster, '26-'27	One 6x18-In. Oblong Glass	9	4.90
28K10257	Touring, '26-'27	One 6x18-In. Oblong Glass	12	6.90

"Open With Door" Side Curtains $3.05 and up

An up to date equipment that gives you the convenience of a closed car in getting in and out. Made of the same kind of materials as Ford car rubberized cloth curtains. Rods furnished for right doors so that curtains will open with door. Fit 1915-1927 models. Curtains complete with celluloid lights. A big value at our price. Furnished in two sizes, complete for attaching. Shpg. wts. per set: Touring models, 12 lbs; roadster models, 7 lbs.

28K7152¼—For 1915-22 roadsters. Per set... $3.50
28K10081¼—For 1923-25 roadsters. Per set... 3.10
28K14276¼—For 1926-27 roadsters. Per set... 3.20
28K7154¼—For 1915-22 touring cars. Per set. 6.60
28K10082¼—For 1923-25 touring cars. Per set. 5.10
28K14278¼—For 1926-27 touring cars. Per set. 6.20
28K14269¼—For right side 1915-22 touring cars. Shipping weight, per set, 3½ pounds. Per set........ 3.35
28K14270¼—For right side 1923-25 touring cars. Shipping weight, per set, 3½ pounds. Per set........ 3.35
28K14277¼—For right side of 1926-27 touring cars. Shipping weight, 3½ pounds. Per set.......... 3.05

Mail Your Orders for all Merchandise on this page either to
CHICAGO—PHILADELPHIA
MINNEAPOLIS—BOSTON
or MEMPHIS
Whichever is nearest you

Replace Curtain Lights
Glass Back Light Set

Complete in black enamel metal frames. Practical and very popular at our remarkable price. Replaces celluloid lights. Very durable.
28K10069—For 1917-22 Ford cars. Per set of 3 .... 51c
28K4667—Two-light oblong type, for ...4 Ford cars. Set of 2 .... 42c
28K10651—One oblong light type for 1925-27 Ford cars (glass is about 6x17 inches) 40c
Shipping weights, 3½, 3½ and 3¼ lbs., respectively.

Stick-Tite Back Curtain Light
"Stick Them on Like a Postage Stamp"

Cement into place, no sewing or metal fasteners. Complete with cement. Shipping weight, 6 ounces.
28K12958—For 1917-22 Ford cars. Each 27c
28K1656—For 1923-24 Ford cars. (Not illustrated.) Each 28c
28K1708—For 1925-27 Ford cars. (Not illustrated.) Each 56c

Replace Curtain Lights

Installed Without Sewing. Furnished With Fasteners. Shipping weight, 6 ounces.
28K11041—Back Curtain Light for 1917-1922 cars. Size, about 6½x10½ inches. (Not illustrated.) Per single light 20c
28K9957—Back Light for 1923-24 cars. (Not illustrated.) Set of 2 .... 39c
28K12351 — 28K12352 — 28K11043 — 20c and up each
28K9221—Rear Light for 1925-1927 Ford cars. (Not illustrated.) Each 38c
28K12351—Replace Side Light for 1914-1924 cars. Size, about 7½x20½ inches. Each 36c
28K11043—Side Light for 1913-1924 cars. Size, about 10½x14½ inches. Each 36c
28K12352—Side Light for 1914-1924 cars. Size, about 7½x10½ inches. Each 22c

Auto Top Pads

For Ford touring cars. Replace unsightly sagging misplaced top pads; it costs little and gives your car interior a neat appearance. Furnished in set complete for car. Shipping weight, 5¼ pounds.
28K4627—Black $1.29

Top Bow Pads

Prevent top bows from rubbing through top cover material. Made of felt; fastened around bows with a web strap. Shipping weight, set, ¾ pound.
28K8692—Set 36c

Ford wind shield frames. ... LOWER

Glass, about 9¾x35½ in., for 1923-25 open car models. Shpg. wt., 13 lbs. $2.20
28K4681¼—Lower Glass, about 12x38 inches. For 1915-1922 touring models. Shpg. wt., 16 lbs. $2.60
28K15177½—Upper Glass for Fordor (4-door) sedan and 1923-25 coupe, and Tudor (2-door) sedans.
and Tudor (2-door) sedans. Size, 7¾x37⅛ inches. Shipping weight, 13 pounds $1.95
28K15172¼—Lower Glass, about 9¾x37⅛ in., for 1922-1925 roadsters and 1922-25 touring cars, upper and lower glass for 1916-1923 2-door sedans and 1919-1923 coupes. Shipping weight, 13 pounds $2.25

Back Curtains

Back curtains of rubberized material. Wonderful bargains at our low prices. The back curtains with oval glass lights and the gypsy style back curtains ...

28K13240—Touring—Two Oval Glass—4 — 1.70
28K13242—Roadster—Two Oval Glass—4 — 1.70

Gypsy Style Back Curtains for 1923-1927 Models

Catalog No.	Style Car	Back Lights	Shpg. Wt., Lbs.	Each
28K13216	Touring 1923-1925	One Oblong Celluloid	3	$1.80
28K13217	Touring 1926	One Oblong Celluloid	3	1.80
28K5034	Touring 1923-1926	Two Oval Glass	4½	2.15
28K5036	Roadster 1923-1925	Two Oval Glass	4	2.15
28K13210	Touring 1923-1925	One 6x18 Oblong Glass	4½	2.70
28K13213	Roadster 1923-1925	One 6x18 Oblong Glass	4½	2.70
28K13212	Touring 1926-1927	One 6x18 Oblong Glass	4	2.70
28K13211	Roadster 1926-1927	One 6x18 Oblong Glass	3	2.70

$1.35 per yard — Finest Quality Auto Top and Cushion Materials

The Ideal Material for Auto Coverings

A double texture fabric, handsomely grained black rubber outside coating, rich drab back. Water and sun proof. Standard equipment on America's highest grade vehicles and automobiles. Nothing better made. 54 inches wide. Shipping weight, per yard, 2 lbs.
28K4982¼—Per yard $1.35

Enclosed Car Deck Covering

A beautiful double texture leakproof fabric. Now used on the better grade closed cars. Heavy white twill back, handsome Victoria long grain black rubber outside coating. Anyone who can handle a hammer can re-cover his closed car. No sewing necessary, simply remove drip molding and old cover and apply new. 64 inches wide, suitable for all makes of cars. Shipping weight, per yard, 3 pounds.
28K4981¼—Per yard $1.65

Special Quality 34-Ounce Morocco Grain Rubber Drill

A strong, durable, weather resisting rubber fabric, especially adapted for automobile tops, particularly Ford cars, being the same quality as the top material furnished with this popular car. Easy to apply; simply remove the old top and use same as a pattern. Width, 54 inches. Black back. Shipping weight, per yard, 2¼ lbs.
28K4980¼—Per yard (not illustrated) 85c
28K4973—Fabric Leather Trimming. Black roll of about 25 yards. Shpg. wt., 6 oz. 28c
28K4975—Metalline nails. About 100 to a package. Shipping weight, 4 ounces 9c

$2.90 and up

Furnished in same kind of material as Ford car rubberized cloth curtains, in set of four pieces. Complete for attaching. Remarkable values.
28K12910—Set of Side Curtains for 1915-1922 roadster. Shipping weight, per set, 5 pounds. Per set $3.10
28K12909—For 1923-25 roadsters. Shipping weight, per set, 5 pounds. Per set 2.90
28K12912—Set of Side Curtains for 1915-22 touring cars. Shipping weight, per set, 7¼ pounds. Per set 5.20
28K12914—For 1923-25 touring cars. Shipping weight, per set, 7 pounds. Per set 5.20
28K14271—For right side 1915-22 touring cars. Shpg. wt., per set, 3½ lbs. Per set 2.95
28K14272—For right side 1923-25 touring cars. Shpg. wt., per set, 3½ lbs. Per set 2.95

DeWitt Horseless Carriage

IF ASKED in 1909 what the "double nickel" was, Andrew Carnegie would probably have figured it to be some kind of dime; and had Teddy Roosevelt heard mention of "rack and pinion" back then, it might have brought images of deer hunting in the Southwest to mind. For while these citizens and their countrymen surely went around in automobiles during this century's first decade, the cars themselves were quite different contraptions then.

With the following exception:

In 1910 there were more than 735* makes of automobiles being manufactured, all a part of the primordial gravy out of which the handful of domestic marques that our dads used to drive later emerged. In North Manchester, Indiana, that year, V. L. DeWitt's enterprise, DeWitt Motor Vehicles, burned to the ground. The fire was suspicious, but as Henry Ford had already been mass-producing his Model Ts for a couple of years, the conflagration might have been considered just a quick, high-carbon harbinger of what was about to happen to flivvers like the DeWitt anyway.

About 200 DeWitts had been built at the time of the factory fire,

*James Flink, *America Adopts the Automobile, 1895–1910* (Boston: MIT Press, 1970).

which seemed to mark the end of the line. But following a schedule roughly synchronous with that of Halley's Comet, three-quarters of a century later DeWitts are again being assembled within the blare of a brass horn of the original plant. This means that today, for about the price of a Camaro Z28, you can buy a brand-new replica of a 1909 DeWitt, and choose from a two-passenger, four-passenger (with either two or four doors), or truck model in the bargain.

The germ of the DeWitt's resurrection was planted in 1973 when Russell Egolf, a successful North Manchester businessman, built a full-scale replica of the highwheeler for a town parade. This version was a rough one, based on some vintage photographs and the recollections of local oldtimers. But it was also good enough to warrant donation to the county historical society and, more important, to set the perfectionist Egolf on a ten-year course leading to production of refined DeWitt replicas.

With the aid of associate Steve Farringer and a pragmatic attitude typical of automotive pioneers,

Egolf is not turning out frail museum pieces, but an actual road car intended for regular use. The 18-h.p. DeWitt will never win a berth at Indy (*Car & Driver* magazine clocked it pegging 40 m.p.h. at the Chrysler Proving Grounds in '84), but it *does* move right along—1910, after all, was the year that Congress felt the need to pass the Mann Act into law.

The DeWitt is also a well-wrought car, thanks in part to the quality work of the Amish craftsmen responsible for its hickory wheels, vinyl top, and side curtains. The car has a solid yellow-poplar body, and uses solid metal for all brass fixtures including clutch lever, steering column, and the removable headlamps. Seats are of top-quality leather.

Price: from $14,500 to $16,500.

DeWitt horseless carriages are backed by a one-year guarantee and full parts availability.

Call or write for further details:

DeWitt Motor Company
*802 W. South St.
North Manchester, IN 46962
Tel. 219/982-2010*

1934 Ford Roadster

EVERYONE who's met him seems to remark about how honest and likeable a fellow Andrew Timmis is. Although my own dealings with the man have been both short-lived and long distance, I do know one thing for certain: Mr. Timmis's claim to having created "the most authentic reproduction automobiles ever built" is shot through with understatement.

The Timmis Ford is a fiberglass-bodied reproduction of a 1934 Ford V-8 roadster—which is about the worst thing that you can say about it. Actually, Mr. Timmis's company doesn't so much reproduce these cars as manufacture them after a hiatus of half a century. In fact, because they're built on original 1934 Ford frames, the Royal Canadian Mounted Police requires that they be registered as 1934 vehicles.

Nor does this use of new old stock end with the frames, as the Timmis Fords are substantially assembled from parts that have been retrieved brand-new from ancient packing crates shipped to British Columbia from as far away as Greece and the Orient. The roadster's drivetrain is only a little less exotic, as it's built from newly made period (1948–1954) Ford parts that have the combined virtues of being precisely the same as original stock in appearance while superseding it in quality and performance (also, the availability of these parts makes the negligible servicing required

My uncle and I got out of the Ford roadster in the middle of his land and began to walk over the dry earth.
—WILLIAM SAROYAN,
MY NAME IS ARAM, 1937

by the Timmis Ford a breeze to perform). And authenticity continues into the engine compartment where a refined version of the famous Ford 239-cubic-inch flathead V-8 has been installed by Ford of Canada's engine remanufacturing facility. The power plant is accompanied by a 12,000-mile guarantee.

To top everything off, the Timmis roadsters are then assembled as few Fords have ever been, by a team of craftsmen who dedicate nearly a full year's effort to the production of every automobile. Little wonder that even the car's fiberglass body has been described by one trade reviewer as a flawlessly honed masterpiece.

In all, the Timmis Ford roadster appears to muster out as a supremely roadworthy vehicle requiring no more kid-glove treatment than does any new car. The only difference here is that *this* new car is a 1934 model. You needn't take my word for it—just ask any Mountie.

Prices, based on the Timmis Ford's limited production runs, are high. As of this writing two roadsters, one yellow, the other maroon, are available for $42,000 (U.S.) each.

Timmis Motor Company
4351 Blenkinsop Rd.
Victoria, BC V8X 2C3 Canada
Tel. 604/388-6229

Auburn Boat-Tailed Speedsters

IN THE realm of replica automobiles—or replicars, as they are often derisively called—fiberglass kits are generally to be avoided, particularly by those for whom authenticity is the ranking concern. There are a couple of exceptions to this rule, however, and (despite its suspiciously presumptive name) Elegant Motors of Indianapolis offers one: its boat-tailed 856 Auburn Speedster convertible.

The Auburn company introduced its renowned Speedster in the late 1920s—its sleek rear distinguished by a resemblance to an overturned boat prow. But it wasn't until the Gordon Buehrig–designed 851s set the 1935 stock car speed records at the Bonneville Salt Flats that the nation's imagination became captured by the marque. This car and the 852 that followed it in 1936 were each guaranteed to do at least 100 miles per hour, and are considered to be among the most powerful sports cars ever produced. Today, original 1935 and 1936 Auburn Speedsters regularly bring around $100,000 at auction.

Although Elegant Motors has replaced the original 850-series' straight-eight Lycoming aircraft engine with a 350-cubic-inch Chevrolet V-8 (rated at 118 miles per hour) and, naturally, its 856 Speedster's fiberglass body and aluminum side panels replace sheet-metal, Elegant president Del Amy has exercised a devotion to quality and authenticity that's won hearty praise from reviewers. It's often

mentioned (albeit with no reference to his age at the time) that designer Buehrig himself once mistook an Elegant 856 for the real thing.

Price: $42,995 assembled.

Free literature available; "Collector's Series" brochure, $5.

Elegant Motors, Inc.
P.O. Box 30188
Indianapolis, IN 46230
Tel. 317/253–9898

A 1936 Auburn advertisement

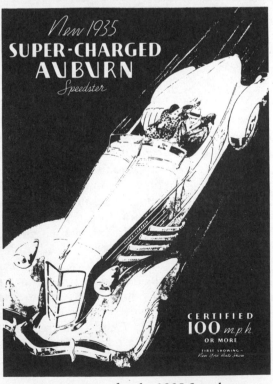

An advertisement for the 1935 Speedster

1937 Cord 812 Sportsman

Motor Classics' two-passenger 1937 Cord Sportsmen replicas

THE sleek "coffin-nosed" Cord 810s were introduced in 1936 as specialty market "baby Dusenbergs" slotted to shore up Errett Lobban Cord's faltering automotive empire, which included both cars. Although too hastily rushed into production to succeed in their mission, both the 810 Cords and the 812s that followed them in 1937 surpassed the landmark Chrysler Airflow as graceful representations of the first streamlined automobiles. These Cords generally play Beauty to the 1958 Edsel's lemon-sucking Beast on the short list of U.S. automotive history's most instantly recognizable cars.

Like the Cord-built Auburn Speedsters described earlier, both the Cord 810s and 812s were designed by Gordon Buehrig and powered by Lycoming V-8 engines. E. L. Cord's desire for the car to strike a low silhouette enabled the tradition of the front-wheel-drive Cord automobile—interrupted in 1932—to continue. Approximately 3,000 Cords were built during 1936 and 1937, selling for between $2,000 and $3,000 apiece.

The Classic Factory of Pomona, California, replicates a fiberglass-bodied 1937 Cord Sportsman convertible using molds that have been cast from the panels of an original in their possession. The replica sits on a custom platform that uses intermediate General Motors components—including frame, running gear, suspension, and a small-block V-8. The engine-turned instrument panel closely replicates Cord's original stainless-steel version, and includes Stewart Warner gauges. Many of the car's metal parts have been reproduced from original Cord castings.

Price: completed car, $45,000; kit, $11,995.

Further information available, $5.

The Classic Factory

1454 E. Ninth St.
Pomona, CA 91766
Tel. 714/629-5968

Indian

Indian Motorcycles

IFIRST heard the Legend one summer afternoon in Stanford. It was 1971 and some hippie auto mechanics and I were opening a few beers after an impromptu Saturday engine-tuning party. "Man," said one, emerging from a long draft of Oly, "I'd sure as hell like to get ahold of one of those Indians." His pronouncement was met with the kind of cowboy enthusiasm that in the movies meant a posse was about to mount up (and which made me wonder if I had fallen in with a nest of redskin-bashing night riders). But suddenly the first kid set me straight: "We're talking about flatheads here, Al," he said, "Indian motorcycle flathead twins."

Now as all our anthro-major girl-friends were off fixing something called Rocky Mountain spaghetti in the kitchen, I should've guessed that this wasn't going to be about the Navajo Creation Myth or anything like that. I did, however, know a couple of things about Indian bikes: namely, that they had been built in Springfield, Massachusetts, for most of the century until 1953, and that they were the ranking American cult machines—bigger than James Dean and about as fast. But as I'd never actually *seen* an Indian, it seemed to me that they had all long since passed down the misty macadam that leads to their Happy Proving Ground. Now, fifthhand, I was going to hear the

Legend of the California Indian Warehouse.

The kid went on to tell of his parts man, whose wife had heard (from someone like a toll collector) that there was, in some arid corner of the state, a boarded-up warehouse. In it, 1940s Indians still in the cosmoline stood in their packing crates; and for floor after floor the crates ran to the rafters.

According to the countercultural standards then obtaining, this story was actually a pretty down-to-earth one. After all, there wasn't any unicorn, black syph, or verse from Uncle Ho to be found in it anywhere. It was nice, and I wanted to believe in it in something like the way one believes in the Navajo Creation Myth. But, unfortunately, too little beer had gone by for this, so I soberly figured that I was witness to the local Ghost Dance religion—the ritual Millertime gathering of a few flathead fanatics waiting for their mythic bikes to return to them in the manner of the buffalo to the plains.

Well, sir, don't believe everything you don't believe.

When Jacob Junkers heard the Legend a decade or so earlier, he believed it right off. First of all, he was only a boy at the time; and second, it was his dad who related it. This time the warehouse was the legacy of an eccentric car dealer who went into the motorcycle business sometime in the 1940s only to give it all up again within a few weeks. Supposedly, his entire Indian stock was still under lock and key just a county over.

Junkers recalled this tale just a few years ago when he—although a highly regarded Lake Elsinore motocross mechanic—was ready for a change. The Indian dealer had long since passed away, but his widow was still around to confirm the story to Junkers, who went out to the warehouse, looked it over, and struck a deal. Suddenly Junkers found himself in the possession of motorcycling's Holy Grail. Inside the warehouse were stored four truckloads of motorcycles (many in

A pre-World War I police chief

their original packing crates), along with a stockroom of frames, engines, parts, saddlebags, literature, and displays. In short, a complete, brand-new 1947 Indian motorcycle dealership about to see the California sun for the first time in some thirty-five years.

For Junkers, a recognized mechanical genius, this was only the beginning. From his large supply of new old stock he began to fabricate replica parts, many superior to the originals in quality. His first offerings were duplicate Indian toolboxes, complete with the distinctively scripted latches of the originals. After Junkers wrote these up in his new publication, *Indian Motorcycle News*, the response he received from antique bike collectors was almost overwhelming. Today Junker's stock of replica Indian parts fills a 65-page catalog—and there are in fact enough of these to enable him to remanufacture Indian motorcycles that, from their fringed saddlebags to their original paint colors, are 60% new.

Or, as Junkers himself puts it, "almost new." "I'll do ten or twelve of them a year," he told *Cycle Guide* magazine, "ground-up handlebar to crank-pin rebuilds."

Needless to say, they've heard of Jacob Junkers back in Springfield. When they utter his name there at the Indian Motorcycle Museum, their eyes narrow like those of jealous priests at the approach of a heretic. For not only is Jacob Junkers the man who revealed one of the Indian's sacred legends, he may also be the one who brings about the bike's resurrection as a brand-new machine. If that's what's upsetting the old Indian motorcycle cult's clergy, Junkers needn't worry—for it's just the sort of heresy that makes saints out of mortals.

Prices for Junkers' almost new Indian Sportsmen, Clubmen, and Chiefs begin at $6,995.

Catalog available, $5.

Indian Motorcycle News

P.O. Box 455
32606 Hartley
Lake Elsinore, CA 92330
Tel. 714/678-1583

"*THE EXPRESS CRUISER*"

Indian Day
February 22

—the biggest annual national event in the world of motorcycles!

THE day on which the wigwams of over 2800 dealers—all over the United States—will be the gathering places of present and future Indian riders, on edge to get their first personal view of the 1916 models of the Indian.

⟨ And what a treat is in store for them when they first see the New Indian Powerplus Motor with new ideals of power, silence, endurance, cleanliness, accessibility, speed! Everybody is talking

POWERPLUS

AND THE NEW INDIAN FEATHERWEIGHT AND NEW INDIAN BICYCLES

⟨ How the old timers will examine the Powerplus makeup and marvel at its completeness, its ability to purr sweetly and silently to the tune of 70 miles an hour right out of the crate it's shipped in!

⟨ How the new riders will enjoy the simple, efficient little Featherweight model!

⟨ How the youngsters will admire the trim, red Indian Bicycles!

⟨ Make an Indian showroom your headquarters on Washington's Birthday.

⟨ Get in touch with the Indian riders of your community. Listen to them swap Indian experiences. Let them tell you how the Indian has stood by them year after year *on the road*—and why they consider it the first choice machine from every performing, mechanical and economical angle.

⟨ See the 1916 Powerplus models yourself—go over them with one of the experts who can tell you its big points, its honest values.

⟨ Don't neglect your Indian education.

⟨ Doors open from the time you get up until you get ready to turn in. Stay as long as you like you'll find something doing every minute.

⟨ Indian Day is always the greatest "get-together" event of the year for motorcycle enthusiasts. It'll be bigger than ever this year. Wholesome fun, instruction, souvenirs.

Remember the Date—February 22

Your local dealer's announcement will appear in the newspapers. Watch for it. He'll probably have something special.

HENDEE MANUFACTURING COMPANY, 701 State Street, Springfield, Mass.
1916 Catalogue Ready. For Canadian Edition, write Canadian Branch, 12-14 Mercer St., Toronto, Ontario

Geronomobile: Indian motorcycles were building their legends as early as 1916.

Limousine Rental

Old Cadillacs never die.
—DIZZY GILLESPIE

Besides the loftily named "Black Pearl," a 1935 Cadillac Fleetwood that's flagship to the Classic Limousine rental fleet, Bostonians (as well as those visiting there) can choose from either a 1948 Chrysler Crown Imperial or a Dodge Custom of the same vintage. Each automobile (even the "Gray Lady," er, Dodge) arrives at its customer's curb sporting a fresh bouquet of flowers and flowing with classical music and, if desired, chilled champagne.

Classical Limousine Service

34 Union Park
Boston, MA 02118
Tel. 617/266-3980

Automotive Items from the Cumberland General Store

Git some water for the radiator.
—ERSKINE CALDWELL,
AMERICAN EARTH, 1931

These items appear as they do in the Cumberland General Store catalog:

"Wish and Want Book" available, $3.75.

Cumberland General Store

Route 3
Crossville, TN 38555
Tel. 615/484-8481

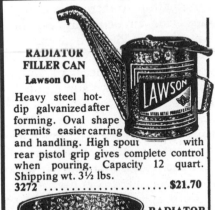

RADIATOR FILLER CAN
Lawson Oval

Heavy steel hot-dip galvanized after forming. Oval shape permits easier carring and handling. High spout with rear pistol grip gives complete control when pouring. Capacity 12 quart. Shipping wt. 3½ lbs.
3272 .... $21.70

RADIATOR DRAIN PANS

Heavy steel hot-dip galvanized with corrugated reinforced bottom and side Pouring lip and flow control baffle plate for easy pouring. Conveniently located rigid handles to aid in carrying and pouring. Large enough to hold contents of any radiator. Will slide under lowest cars. Capacity 6 gallons, diameter 19", height 6". Shipping wt. 4 lb.
3273 .... $11.17

FUNNEL MEASURES

Lawson Approved
Heavy guage black steel, hot-dip galvanized after being formed. Locked seamed & roll welded. New production methods make them practically seamless. Fast-pouring funnel top with convenient pouring handle 1 qt. capacity. Shipping wt. 2 lbs.
3269 .... $7.27
2 quart capacity. Shipping wt. 3 lbs.
3270 .... $8.00
4 quart capacity. Shipping wt. 3 lbs.
3271 .... $9.10

LAWSON FLEXIBLE SPOUT

Heavy approved commercial grade for both oil and anti-freeze. The curved rigid spout permits reaching hard-to-get at openings. Spill-proof top galvanized. 1 quart capacity. Ship. wt. 3 lb.
3266 .... $9.53
2 quart capacity. Shipping wt. 4 lbs.
3267 .... $9.50
4 quart capacity. Shipping wt. 4 lbs.
3268 .... $12.99

HUFFMAN FLEX SPOUT

Heavy gauge black sheet steel, copper plated, then painted industrial red for a lifetime finish. Constructed with spill-proof tops, extra long flexible steel hose with reinforced hooked spout, one-piece valve control, and shaped pouring handle. 2 quart capacity. Shipping wt. 4 lbs.
3264 .... $31.34

4 quart capacity. Shipping wt. 5 lbs.
3265 .... $35.59

Engine, Chassis, Wiring, and Brake Parts

Y'say yer '36 Ford's
got a fuel pump on the fritz?
And yer Kaiser's old camshaft's
been shakin' loose yer wits?
The Nash is N.F.G.?
Yer low on do-re-mi?
Then write to the place
that's got the part that fits.

There's ball-joints for old
Buicks,
and rods to keep Reos alive.
Wiring for the Whippet—
none of the above is jive.
And all this stuff's brand new,
So skip the further adieu—

Catalog (revised in October '85), $1.50.

Egge Machine Company

8403 Allport Ave.
Santa Fe Springs, CA 90607
Tel. 213/945-3419

Tool Bag

AVAILABLE for $1.48 from the 1908 Sears, Roebuck catalog, Cumberland General Store's tool bag is made from a single piece of No. 8 20-ounce white duck that has been tailored to a 12-gauge steel frame. Features leather handles and straps.

Dimensions: length, 22 inches; width, 6 inches; depth, 15 inches. Shipping weight: 1½ lbs.
Price: $34.16, F.O.B. Crossville, Tennessee.

"Wish and Want Book" available, $3.75.

Cumberland General Store

Route 3
Crossville, TN 38555
Tel. 615/484-8481

From the Vestal Press

American Bantam Advertising Literature

WHEN it came to economizing American cars, the sun didn't rise with the Japanese. The American Bantam was a Depression-inspired effort to introduce European ideas for an economy car in an American model. To do this, the British Austin Seven was dragooned into service in 1930 and Americanized with some punched-in hood louvres, fixed-disc wheels, and the like. Still, the Bantam's tommy heritage was betrayed by its neat little bicycle fenders and the fact that, once Stateside, it looked like a renegade Corgi toy.

So, despite a list price of $425, the Bantam barely sold and its U.S. manufacturer went into receivership in 1934. The following year Roy Evans, a board member, bought the firm's assets for $5,000 and set about gearing up for the model he'd introduce in 1938—the smashing little streamliner that we see here. But still too far ahead of its time, the American Bantam was killed for good in 1940 after its manufacturer was awarded the contract to produce the first Jeep.

The Vestal Press reprint of a four-page piece of advertising literature for the 1939 Bantam came about as the result of Sales Director Gill Williams's discovery of the original in an Ithaca, New York, auto dealership.

Price: Vestal Press stock #D-1, $2.

1916 Harley-Davidson Motorcycle Catalog

IF the Indian is America's mythic motorcycle, then the Harley-Davidson is the country's most representative. William S. Harley and Arthur Davidson—sort of the Wright brothers of the shimmering blacktop—turned out their first V-twin in 1903 following a few years of tinkering in a shack out behind Davidson's Milwaukee home. By the time this 1916 catalog appeared, the Harley motorcycle had already begun demonstrating its storied petrosinew in races, endurance runs, and hill-climbs from coast to coast.

This high-quality reprint of the Harley-Davidson company's original 24-page catalog shows nineteen illustrations of the several 1916 models, along with their parts and accessories.

Price: Vestal Press stock #D-31, $5 (plus $2 for shipping and handling).

Cretor's Popcorn Wagons—1913

'THIS is one of the most beautiful catalogs** the Vestal Press has ever had the chance to reproduce," writes the sales director, Gill Williams. "Not only is it jammed with pictures of the colorful popcorn wagons of the turn-of-the-century era, it's also filled with fascinating sales pitches and testimonials designed to make you want to own one so badly you'll be unable to wait to cash in on the big-profit popcorn business!" Paperback, 10 by 13 inches on slick paper, 56 pages.

Vestal Press stock #D-69, $7.

Gasoline Globes

DURING the 1910s gasoline was usually sold from "split-pump stations," filling stations that offered several brands of fuel at the same time. As their products could not be distinguished by their color, odor, or any other characteristic within the ken of most motorists, the oil companies (whose rivalries had been made all the keener by the 1911 breakup of John D. Rockefeller's Standard Oil trust) began designing strongly graphic logotypes to help the consumer in his quest for brand loyalty. In aid of this, globes emblazoned with the new logos were affixed above the new "visible pumps" that were then appearing. These allowed purchased gas to flow into a graduated cylinder atop the pump where the motorist could see it before it drained through a hose into his car's tank.

Vestal Press's gasoline globe replicas are the same size as the originals and have their glass fronts and backs supported by plastic shells. Neither lamps nor wire is included with them.

Styles: Esso, Mobilgas, Flying A, Pennzoil, Sinclair, Cities Service, Fleet Wing, Sinclair Aircraft, White Rose, Shell, Conoco, Texaco, Tydol, Gulf, Signal, Lion, Phillips 66, Purol, and Richfield.

Price: Vestal Press stock #M-50, $73 each (plus $5 for shipping outside the United States).

Catalog of period industrial book
and manual reprints, $2.

The Vestal Press

P.O. Box 97
320 N. Jensen Rd.
Vestal, NY 13850
Tel. 607/797-4872

... this INDEX
Makes It Easy to Find Any of
Our 35,000 Bargains

A

al | **ar** | **au** | **au** | **au** | **au**

"A" Batteries 714
"A" Power Units..712
Abdominal Bands,
 Accouchement ...146
Abdominal Bands,
 Babies' 148, 151
Abdominal Belts..638
Abdominal Sup-
 ports (Corsetry)
 108-112, 116-120, 143
Absorbent Cotton.641
Absorbers, Shock
 ....477, 493
Accelerators 460
Accelerator Foot
 Rests 480
Accordions .678-679
Accordions, Blow..792
Accouchement
 Bands 146
Acids, Photo.......800
Acid Gloves.......640
Acid Measures....974
Acid Recharges,
 Extinguisher ...1016
Adapters
 Cord Tip......717
 Film Pack.....800
 Radio Tube......717
Adding Machines..794
Address Books....794
Address Cards,
 Mailing 535
Adhesive Plasters.641
Adjusters
 Casement 978
 Tire Chain 484
 Violin String...670
Adzes and Handles.985
Aerators, Milk ...974
Aerials and Sup-
 plies, Radio......716

Agricultural
 Boilers 1066
 Foundation 706
 Implements and
  Repairs .1060-1065
 Machinery.1036-
  1044, 1062 - 1063
 Tools 998-1000
 —Also see "Farm."
Air Cleaners,
 Motor....471, 494
Air Cushions.....641
Air Ferns....921-922
Air Filters......W2
Air Gauges, Tire..467
Air Moisteners....962
Air Rifles, Shot..507
Air Valves, Siphon.962
Airizers, Vacuum
 Cleaner 660
Alarm Clocks
 ....767, 769
Alaskas 342-343
Albums 801
Albums, Record...696
Album Leaves.....801
Alcohol, Rubbing..643
Alcohol, Solidi-
 fied 646
Alcohol .Lamps...718
Alcoves, Break-
 fast 1086
Alfalfa Forks....1000
Allover Laces....248
Almonds 606
Almond Cream....631
Almond Lotions..631
Alpacas 214
Altar Candlesticks.766
Altar Services....765
Alto Horns.......681
Alum 642
Aluminum Clean-
 ers 964

Aluminum Letters
 and Figures.....977
Aluminum Paint..1025
Aluminum Pow-
 der 1025
Aluminum Ware
 ....954-965, 967, 969
Aluminum Ware,
 Campers 498
Amber Goggles,
 ....491, 771
Ammeters....468, 715
Ammoniac 997
Ammunition
508-509
Ammunition Belts.510
Amplifier Panels..717
Amplifier Tubes...713
Analgesic Balm....643
Anchors
 Decoy 510
 Embroidered 249
 Guy Wire 716
 Stanchion 1068
Anchor Loops,
 Track 1068
Andirons 1084
Angel Food Cake
 Pans......928, 965
Angelus .Toilet
 Preparations ...631
Angle Valves....1012
Angular Boring
 Attachments 988
Animal Baits.....513
Animal Cookies...606
Animal Scents....513
Animal Smokers...513
Animal Traps.512-513
Ankle Boots
 Horse 1052
Ankle Supports..
 .....516, 519, 636
Announcements,
 Birth......639, 776
Annunciator Wire.716
Ant Killers......646
Antenna Equip-
 ment 716
Anti-Cow Kickers.974
Anti-Rattlers.477, 490
Antiphlogistine ..643
Antiseptics 643
Antonyms 788
Anvils
993
Anvils, Jewelers'..718
Anvil, Vise and
 Drill 992
Anvil Saw Sets...984
Anvil Tools 993
Apple Parers.....968

Aprons
 Babies' Bib....155
 Blacksmiths' ...993
 Clothespin 970
 Girls'.76-83, 141, 158
 Mechanics'..387, 993
 Sanitary 252
 Stamped 245
 Storekeepers' ..387
 Waterproof, Chil-
  dren's.141, 155, 158
 Waterproof,
  Men's...381, 800
 Waterproof,
  Women's 141
 Women's
  ....81-82, 88, 141
Apron Ginghams.
166-168
Aquariums ..922, 927
Arch Supports....636
Arch Support
 Shoes, Men's...
 ....320-321, 333
Arch Support
 Shoes, Women's
 .....307, 313-314
Architects' Instru-
 ments and Sup-
 plies.....797, 986

Arctics 335, 338, 340
Arithmetic Books..788
Arms, Tone, Phon-
 ograph 696
Arm Bags....104-106
Arm Bands......446
Arm Chairs ....
 ....848-849, 852-
 857, 867 - 869, 908
Arm Rests. Banjo.676
Arm Shields....253
Army Goods
 Breeches 385
 Carrying Cases..536
 Coats...385, 402-403
 Jacks 1001
 Leggings 541
 Lockers 536
 Puttees 339, 541
 Shoes..324, 333, 541
 Socks 272
 Vests 385
Arnica, Tincture of.643
Arresters, Light-
 ning......666, 716
Art Linens.......223
Art Needle Work
 See "Fancywork"
Art Ticking......181
Art Toweling.223, 228
Artgum 797
Artificial
 Flowers, Plants.
 239-240, 572, 921-922
 Flowers, Hat....103
 Fruits 921
 Leather...813, 1003
 Silk—See "Rayon"
Artists' Mate-
 rials 795-797
Artists' Smocks...88
Asafetida Pills....643
Asbestos
 Furnace Cement.962
 Gaskets 482
 Joint Runners..1016
 Lighting Rings..955
 Pads, Table...
 ....224, 230-231
 Paper 961
 Pipe Covering
961-962
 Roof Cement...1020
Aseptic Ganze....641
Ash Dumps......1084
Ash Trays, Stands
 238, 615, 618,
 764, 766, 904, 921-923
Asphalt Paint....1021
Asphalt Roofing..
1078-1081
Asphalt Shingles.1080
Aspirin 643
Astrakhans 211
Athletic Goods
516-525
Athletic Supports
 ....519, 637
Athletic Trophies..765
Atlases 784
Atomizers.614, 630, 641
Attic Sash.....1086
Augers, Closet...1016
Augers, Hollow..988
Augers, Post Hole
 ....999, 1014
Augers, Well...1014
Auger Bits 988
Austrian Cloths..815
Autograph Albums
801
Auto Strop Raz-
 ors 527-528
Automatic
 See Name of Ar-
 ticle Wanted.
Automobiles, Chil-
 dren's 605
Automobiles, Toy
 .594, 595, 597, 605

**Automobile
Accessories**
458-497
Accelerators 480
Accelerator Foot
 Rests...........480
Air-Cleaners.471, 494
Anti-Rattlers 477,490
Awnings 458
Axle Parts.....
 ....476, 480, 495
Baby Cribs.....499
Balloon Tires.460-463
Balloon Tire
 Wheels....476, 494
Batteries ..468-469
 Battery Charg-
  ers 714
 Battery Termi-
  nals..469, 473, 494
 Battery Test-
  ers...468-469, 496
 Bearing Caps...474
Bearing Scrapers.486
Beds 499
Bendix Drives...475
Blowout Boots..466
Bodiez, Truck...481
Body Irons,
 Truck 481
Books 785
Brakes 481
 Brake Bands
  and Sundries..
  ....475, 489, 494
 Brushes 493
Brushes, Paint.1029
Bumpers 480
Bushings..474, 480
Bushing Tools...475
Buttons, Horn...472
Camp Equipment
 .498-501, 513, 536
Carbon Remov-
 ers...485, 488, 496
Carburetors and
 Controls 480
Carrying Cases..536
Celluloid 490
Celluloid Cement
 ....469, 490
Chains ...467, 484
Chamois ...493, 646
Cheesecloth 177
Cigar Lighters..482
Circulators.471, 481
Clocks 491
Clutch Facings..486
Clutch Release..474
Coils...472-473, 482
 Coil Parts......473
Connecting Rods
 ....474, 480
Connecting Rod
 Bolts....474, 480
Cotter Pins.....488
Cotter Pin Ex-
 tractors...488, 496
Cotton Waste..1016
Covers (Canvas).501
Crank Holders...476
Crakshafts 474
Creepers 496
Cribs, Babies'..499
Cup Grease.....457
Current Regula-
 tors 472
Curtains
 .478-479, 490, 495

**FORD
OWNERS!**
*See Pages 459-465,
468-491, 1064.*

**CHEVROLET
OWNERS**
See Pages 494-495.

Auto—Cont'd
Curtain Fasten-
 ers 490
Curtain Lights..
 ....478, 490
Cushions
 ...458, 479, 490
Cut-Outs...477, 491
Cut - Out Con-
 trols 491
Cylinder Heads..475
Cylinder Head
 Gaskets 474
Dash Boards...479
Dash Lamps....479
Differential Lu-
 bricants 457
Distributer Parts.482
Door Covers....479
Door Hand Pads.479
Door Handles...479
Drive Shafts....480
Dusters...646, 973
Piston Parts...474
Emblems
 471, ...787
Enamels....1035
Fan Belts..
 ...471, 481,
Fenders ......
Fender Braces..
Fender ......
Flashlights 667
Floor Boards...494
Foot Boards....47
Foot Rests....
Gas Savers....480
Gaskets...474, 482
Gasoline Cans..
 ....484, 941
Gasoline Filters.
 ....480, 486
Gasoline Gauges.480
Gear Pullers....496
Gears 473-
 474, 476, 489, 494
Gloves 126,
 415, 420, 432-433
Goggles...491, 771
Greases 457
Grease Guns.475, 493
Grease Retainers.474
Guide Signals...472
Hammers 985
Headlights 472
Heaters....494, 497
Hoists 1000
Hoods, Women's 127
Hood Covers....497
Horns.472, 474, 484
Hub Parts.476, 495
Hydrometers ...
 ...468-469, 496
Ignition...473, 482
Inner Casings..466
Inner Tubes
459-464
 Inner Tube Re-
  pairs 466-467
 Iron Cement....474
Jacks 487, 496,1001
 Lacquer 1035
Lamps and Ac-
 cessories ....
 ..472, 482-483, 496
Lathes, Valve
 Refacing..488, 496
Luggage Car-
 riers 495
Magneto Files..990
Magneto Parts..482
Main Bearing
 Caps 474
Manifold Heat-
 ers 494
Maps 491

Auto—Cont'd
Mats .....
 ...479, 490-491, 497
Mirrors....479, 484
Mittens 419-420
Motometers.471, 486
Mufflers 487
Neutral Control.480
Nuts 488
Oils and Greases
 ...455-457, 492-493
Oil Cans......996
Oil Gauges.....480
Oil Guns...475, 493
Oiler Cans......493
Oiling Systems.
 ...475, 480, 493
Packing, Sheet..995
Packing, Valve..474
Paints 1035
Pedal, Pads.....479
Pistons.474, 481, 494
Piston Parts...474
Piston Rings...
 474, 481, 486, 494
Pliers 989
Pumps ....
493
Radiator Acces-
 sories 470-
 471, 481, 495, 497
Reamers ....
Repair Supplies
Rotary Engine
 Pump 471
Rim Tools.....
 ....467, 475, 487
Robes 455
Robe Rails......479
Running Boards
 and Sundries
476-
 477, 487, 490-491
Running Board
 Coops 1074
Running Board
 Trunks 536
Saws 984
Scales, Truck..1076
Scarfs 243
Screwdrivers.488,988
Seat Covers
 ....458, 479, 490
Seat Cover Ma-
 terials....181, 478
Seat Cushions..
 ...458, 479, 490
Seat Dressing..1035
Seat Pads......490
Shades 479
Shafts.480, 489, 495
Shim Stock.....486
Shock Absorbers
 ....477, 493
Shoes, Men's...330
Silicate of Soda.491
Sockets, Lamp..472
Sockets, Steel..488
Socket Wrenches
 ...475, 488, 496
Spark Plugs and
 Sundries.473, 482
Speedometers and
 Parts 489
Sponges ..493, 646
Spotlights 483
Springs .....
 ...476-477, 492-493
Spring Covers..476
Spring Parts...476
Steering Attach-
 ments 477
Steering Column
 Braces 477

Auto—Cont'd
Steering Wheels,
 Locks and
 Covers....473, 491
Step Plates.....490
Stoplights..472, 483
Sun Shields.479, 485
Switches....472, 482
Tail Lamps.....
 ...472, 483, 491
Tents 501
Tuners 473, 481
Tuner Wire Sets.473
Tires, Repairs,
 Sundries..460-467
Tires, Inner.....466
Tire Chains 484
Tire Covers....491
Tire Pumps.....487
Tire Reliners....466
Tire Tools..467, 487
Tool Boxes.....491
Tool Kits..482, 489
Top Coverings
 ...476-479, 494
Top Dressing...1035
Tops ....
1003
467
Lubricants.456-457
Transmission
 Parts 475
Truck Bodies...481
Tires, Spares and
 Tubes ....
 ....464, 465
465
536
 ....480, 487
Underslung
 Parts 477
Upholstery 479
Valves 474,
 14/1, 481, 487, 491
Valve Covers...494
Valve Tools
 ...474, 486, 488, 496
 Valve Tools,
  Electric 496
Varnish 1035
Vases 479, 491
Vibrator Points 473
Vises 992
Visors 485
Vulcanizers ...467
Washers.474, 476, 488
Water Pumps..
 ....471, 481
Wax 493
Wheels....476, 494
Wheel Pulls.476, 488
Whistles...472, 484
Windshield Sun-
 dries ....
 ...478-479, 485, 495
Wiring Sets.....473
Wraps 127
Wrenches....475,
 482, 488, 496, 989
Awls, Harness..1054
Awls, Sewing..1057
Awl Blades.....1054
Awl Handles...1054
Awl Needles...1057
Awl Thread....1057
Awnings, Auto..458
Awning Cloth...177
Awning Pulleys.1000
Axes 510, 982
Ax Handles .....
Axles 1001, 1003
Axle Grease....457
Axle Parts.....
 ...476, 480, 495
Axminster Rugs..
 831-832, 834-837, 839

General Aviation

Great Lakes Sport Biplane

Leen-bearg! Leen-bearg!
—ABOUT 100,000 FRENCHMEN
ON MAY 20, 1927

Lindbergh (third from right) and the Spirit of St. Louis.

MORE THAN just its size, it's sometimes rather the setting and scale of an event that makes it important. This may be why many who were born before the age of flight and lived past the first walk on the moon often said that the most memorable day of their lives was the one that Charles Lindbergh's *Spirit of St. Louis* crossed the coast of France to complete the first nonstop transatlantic flight.

Lindbergh's landing punctuated a quarter century of undiminished exhilaration at the notion of manned flight, and seemed to confirm the popular wish, just before the Depression, that men finally had a grip on the controls directing their social destiny. On Wall Street, however, the effects of Lindbergh's New York–Paris puddle-jump were far more prosaic—for the flight had pulled back the stick on all aeronautical stocks, sending them skyrocketing and luring more motor companies and automotive trusts into airplane manufacture. Among these, in the fall of 1928, was the Great Lakes Aircraft Corporation of Cleveland, Ohio.

Although primarily engaged in the design and construction of military aircraft, Great Lakes introduced the first of its 2T-series Sports Trainers at the 1929 All-American Aeronautical Exposition in Detroit. The biplane was the show's leading attraction, and with the aid of such famous barnstormers as Mary Heath, Charlie Meyers, and Tex Rankin (who in January of 1930 became a national hero when he flew a ski-mounted Great Lakes 2T-1 through a blizzard to an isolated Puget Sound community and saved the life of a small girl stricken with pneumonia) the Sports Trainers quickly demonstrated their value as nimble and airworthy aerobatic performers. Even so, after some briefly booming commerce, Great Lakes Aircraft was unable to recover from the Crash of '29 and filed for bankruptcy in 1936, never having earned a profit.

Today's Great Lakes Aircraft was incorporated in 1984 after the purchase of the original designs for the 2T-1A-2 from Dean Franklin, an enthusiastic Great Lakes owner. Their version of this aircraft, the Super 'Lakes, has preserved much of the classic configuration and other attributes of the original 1929 Sports Trainer through the use of these plans in the airplane's design and manufacture. Now powered by a 180-h.p. Lycoming engine, the new 2T-1A-2 also offers an inverted oil and fuel system (for air show performing) and an increase from two to four ailerons.

Base Price: $83,900.

Literature available.

Great Lakes Aircraft Company

Box 1038
Claremont, NH 03743
Tel. 603/542-4520

Charter DC-3s

IT MIGHT BE said that Knute Rockne died so that the DC-3 could live. In Kansas City on March 31, 1931, Rockne boarded a TWA Fokker F-10 en route to California, where he was to provide technical advice to a Hollywood film production. The Fokker, a fabric-and-veneer trimotor typical of those used in the early days of commercial flight, tragically never made it past Kansas. Just a short while after takeoff, a rotted wooden spar in one of the Fokker's wings gave out over a wheatfield and seven aboard—including Rockne—were killed.

The massive notoriety resulting from Rockne's death made TWA realize that their "honeymoon in the Lindbergh cottage" was over. If commercial transportation was to grow, they reasoned, then passengers had to be afforded greater comfort, safety, and speed than their crop of Fords and Fokkers could deliver. In August of 1932 TWA issued a call to airplane manufacturers for a newer, more powerful, all-metal airliner.

One of the first to respond with a company-wide effort was Douglas Aircraft of California. Ten months later when they rolled the first DC-1 out of her Santa Monica hangar, everything else flying suddenly looked ready for the Smithsonian.

The low-winged DC-1 sure appeared to be flight's future, but with only two engines she was not quite what TWA had in mind. Yet once the DC-1 started showing her superior prowess aloft this was quickly forgotten—and tooling for a production model, the DC-2, began almost immediately. The success of this aircraft was demonstrated by the need for a bigger version in quick order, and so, stretched and upgraded, the DC-2 became the DC-3 in 1935.

The DC-3 has altered a lot more history than just aviation's. It has in fact been called "the plane that changed the world," with plenty of justification.

During the first four decades following her introduction the DC-3 flew hundreds of millions of passengers over hundreds of billions of miles in peacetime alone. She was the first aircraft to reach both poles, and she wore the insignia and flew under the flag of nearly every carrier of every country in the world (at one time hauling 90% of the planet's air cargo). Although never designed for war, the C-47s (DC-3s in battle dress) were the only cargo aircraft capable of flying the Himalayan "hump" in 1942 after the Japanese closed the Burma Road; and stories of shell-riddled C-47s

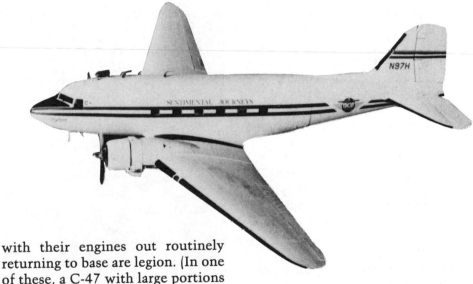

with their engines out routinely returning to base are legion. (In one of these, a C-47 with large portions of its fuselage missing and an engine shot *away* refused to ditch despite her army air force pilot's best efforts. She simply "bounced" off the surface of the North Atlantic, so he flew her back to base!) Small wonder that allied soldiers and airmen showered so much affection on their "Gooney Birds"; that the Russians dubbed their C-47s "Lissunovs" and claimed to have built them all along; that General Eisenhower ranked them as one of the most effective weapons of World War II; and that former Air Force Secretary Harold Talbot lauded them as "quite simply the best single airplane ever built."

Of the 13,641 DC-3s manufactured by Douglas, it's been estimated that some 2,500 are still in service. One of these is N97H, the Douglas "Skytrain" flown by Sentimental Journeys of Bluefield, West Virginia. Refitted and attended by stewardesses in period dress to provide passengers with the sensation of flying a DC-3 of the late 1930s, the aircraft also provides inflight screenings of two DC-3 classics, *The Flying Leathernecks* and *Casablanca* (yup, that was a DC-3 calling Bergman away with its throttling props). All Sentimental Journeys' fares are competitive—when the plane's booked full—with those of commercial flights to

the same destination. So if, as time goes by, you find yourself in Bluefield, don't Bogart that tarmac.

For further information, contact:

Sentimental Journeys

Route 5, Box 202B
Bluefield, WV 24701
Tel. 304/327-8430

FROM THE COCKPIT

New York's Cockpit began operations in 1975 as a mail-order outlet for newly manufactured period flight clothing and accouterments. Their list of products ranges right across this century's history of aviation, and focuses primarily on World War II. For additional Cockpit items, see the section on "Military Goods and Firearms."

Vintage "Raider" Jacket

CARY GRANT AND Thomas Mitchell wore them while piloting their Ford Tri-Motors across Central America in 1937's *Only Angels Have Wings*; two years later Clark Gable wore one in *Test Pilot* while flying Spencer Tracy's race-equipped P-35; in our own time Harrison Ford has resurrected this jacket as part of the uniform of derring-do among the cruelly handsome when he wore it in 1982's *Raiders of the Lost Ark*, itself a revival of the type of twin-prop adventure-romance movie popular between the wars.

The Cockpit's version of this jacket increases a man's sense of invincibility like a pint of rye. Put one on for a run over to the Store 24 for (unfiltered) cigarettes and see if the opportunity for a side trip down Samarkand's Street of the Monkeys to break up a white-slave ring doesn't present itself.

The Raider jacket features double-entry pockets with concealed zippers, an inside stash pocket, bi-swing "work" shoulders, and underarm gussets to provide the maneuvering room necessary when your engine's out and the action in the cockpit resembles that in the bed of a chicken-hauler taking the Baja Road wide open. The jacket's one big drawback is its phony "worn-look" distressed leather that even the most sequestered Tibetan monk could spot right off as a violation of the fashion doctrine of the Noble Eightfold Path.

Price: Cockpit catalog #2129-A, even sizes 36 regular to 46 regular, $199; 38 long to 48 long, $225.

St. Louis Leather Vest

THIS is the Cockpit's update of the type of vest worn by barnstormers during the Twenties and Thirties. It features a lining of light insulation, a heavy-duty waistband, a zipper-and-snap front closure, an inside snap pocket, two hand-warmer pockets, and a zippered cigarette pocket. Artificial "rugged-lifestyle" leather is also part of the package for those who normally come no closer to the cockpit than when they make a special trip forward to ask a stewardess the choice of vegetables on the in-flight meal.

Price: Cockpit catalog #2129-V, small, medium, or large, $125; extra-large, $135.

Color brochure available, $2.

The Cockpit
627 Broadway
New York, NY 10012
Tel. 212/420-1600

Ford Tri-Motor Book of Instruction

Now Henry is in Clover
For he had some tin left over
He will use for making Air
    Plains big and small
All the world is in a hurry
But the people does not worry
For they know that he will make
    an
Air Plain for them all.
          —ETHEL BENNETT,
    IRONWOOD (MICHIGAN) GLOBE,
         JULY 7, 1926

IT was both expected of and by Henry Ford that he would bring airplanes within the reach of the average American family in just the same way that he did the automobile. After the crash of Ford's 1928 "flying flivver" prototype, hopes again soared with the appearance of the Ford Tri-Motor airplane.

But although the Tri-Motor was "tin," it was by no means a mere lizzie. Based on the design of the large German Junkers transport, the Tri-Motor's high-wing configuration and corrugated-metal skin made it ideal for the short takeoff and landing requirements of suburban life, but a crew of mom, dad, and the kids were just out of the question. While the Fords saw a great deal of service as early commercial passenger aircraft, the din set up by all its corrugated metal severely limited its tenure in this role. The Ford company abandoned manufacture of the Tri-Motor in 1932, the year before commercial aviation would be revolutionized by the appearance of the Douglas DC-1.

The Vestal Press has reprinted the Ford Tri-Motor's original *Book of Instruction*, a well-illustrated, 114-page hardcover volume.

Price: Vestal Press stock #A-218X, $12 (plus $2 for handling).

Catalog of period industrial book and manual reprints, $2.

The Vestal Press

P.O. Box 91
320 N. Jensen Rd.
Vestal, NY 13850

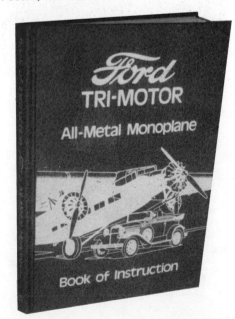

Horton's "Luckie" Casting Rod
Steel with genuine agate guides and agate offset tip, set in German silver mountings. Cork double grip handle with detachable finger hook. Shpg. wt., 1¾ lbs.
6K4343—5 feet...... **$3.98**
6K4344—5½ feet...... **$3.98**

Heddon's Split Bamboo Rod
Genuine agate guides and tip, double solid cork grip. German silver reel seat. Nicely finished in silk windings in two colors. Weight, 5¾ ounces. Shpg. wt., 1½ lbs.
6K4268+5 feet........ **$6.95**
6K4269—5½ feet........ **$6.95**

Heddon's Favorite Split Bamboo Rod No. 6
Brown tone color. Solid double cork grip. Genuine agate mountings. German silver reel seat with locking reel band and ferrules. Closely wound with three colors of silk. In aluminum case. Weight, 5 oz. Shpg. wt., 1 lb.
6K4288—4½ feet...... **$12.95**
6K4289—5 feet...... **$12.95**

Homaco Double Grip Steel Casting Rods
Garnix guides and tip. It has a double cork grip handle with locking band and detachable finger hook. Shipping weight, 1½ pounds.
6K4322—5 feet...... **$1.98**
6K4323—5½ feet...... **$1.98**

Kayo Steel Casting Rod
Three-joint steel casting rod with corrugated wood handle attached to first joint. Nickel plated reel bands. Metal frictionless guide and tip.
6K4319—5 ft. Shpg. wt., 1 lb...... 58c
6K4320—8 ft. Shpg. wt., 1½ lbs. 58c

"Luckie" Telescope Fly Rod with Reversible Handle
Solid cork handle with nickel plated reel seat and band; 28 inches long when telescoped. Shpg. wt., 1½ lbs.
6K4329—9 feet...... **$1.79**
8½-ft. bait casting rod. Same as above, but with three-ring casting guides.
6K4327—Shpg. wt., 1½ lbs. **$1.79**

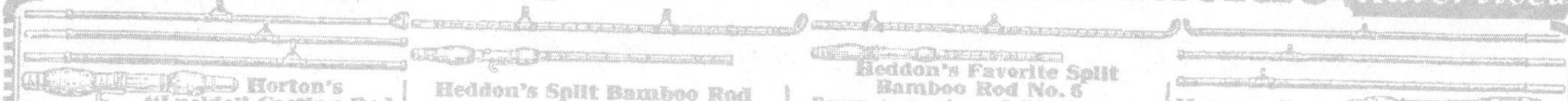

One-piece Chrome Vanadium Steel Rod
Detachable double grip handle of solid cork and wood tip. Nickel plated brass reel seat with finger hook. Reel is black enameled and has two large agatine guides and large agatine tip. Shpg. wt., 2½ lbs.
6K4340—5 feet long...... **$2.89**
6K4341—4 feet long...... **$2.89**

Genuine Bristol No. 27
Steel casting rod with locking reel band. Three genuine agate guides and offset tip. German silver mountings. Cork handle; detachable finger hook. Weight, 9¾ ounces. Shipping weight, 1½ pounds.
6K4304—4½ feet...... **$8.98**
6K4307—5 feet...... **$8.98**

Famous Reels at Low Prices

Shakespeare Criterion Level Winding
Shpg. wt. 1¼ lbs.
100-yard capacity, full quadruple multiplying, correct, level winding, all nickel plated, double white celluloid handles, bronze bearings. Has click and adjustable drag.
6K4154...... **$4.37**

Meisselbach's Okeh Level Winding Reel No. 600
Level winding attachment, fixed spool and closed line guide. Full 80-yard capacity. Seamless nickel brass tubing, full quadruple multiplying. Shpg. wt. ⅓ lb.
6K4120...... **$3.98**

South Bend Level Winding Anti-Backlash
No thumbing required. Full quadruple gear ratio 4 to 1. Nickel silver, satin finish. Will hold 100 yards No. 5 standard size silk line. Shpg. wt. 1 lb.
6K4185 **$14.85**

South Bend Oreno Level Winding Anti-Backlash
Same as above, but not as highly polished; plain bearings and one-piece set plate and supporting pillars. Shpg. wt., 1 lb.
6K4114...... **$7.65**

Heddon's No. 3-25 Level Winding Reel
Non-rusting nickel silver finish. Capacity, 100 yards of 15-lb. test line. Has double steady bar which takes the strain of the level winding attachment entirely off of the reel. Shpg. wt. 1 lb.
6K4103...... **$22.50**

Union Hardware Level Winding Reel
Full quadruple multiplying with positive level winding feature; nickel plated, white double handle, 80-yard capacity. Has adjustable drag click. Shpg. wt., ¾ lb.
6K4100...... **$2.69**

Monarch Automatic Spring Hook
Bait is placed on small hook. When fish nibbles the gaff-like hooks snap shut and hold fish. Shipping weight, 3 ounces.
6K3611—For small fish like croppies, perch and sunfish. 19c
6K3612—For large fish (½ to 1 lb.) 24c

Heddon Basser
A near surface bait which gives an extreme limit of erratic side darting, dipping and sudden swerving action. Glass eyes. Shpg. wt., 4 oz.
6K3326—White body, red head...... 87c

The Heddon Vamp
Resembles a baby pike. Especially beautiful and deceptive in finish. Attractive diving and swimming movements. Shipping weight, 4 oz.
6K3320—White body, red head...... 87c

Heddon's Luny Frog
Travels through the water in a natural frog position. When retrieved, it dives and has a natural swimming movement. Length of body, 4¼ in. Shipping wt., 4 oz.
6K3235 Green Frog...... **$1.10**

Outing's Cantilever Tackle Box
Electrically welded seams; rainproof. With the opening of the lid, trays automatically shift to position outside of box. Of heavy steel, enameled in a rich brown green color. Hinges, locks, snaps and handle loops are heavily brass plated. All 6½ inches wide, 7 inches high. Shipping weights, 7¼, 9¼ and 12 pounds, respectively.

6K3552—12 in. long...... **$5.98**
6K3553—16 in. long...... **6.79**
6K3554—21 in. long...... **8.49**

Boats

South Bend
Pra... single... ner, ... rind snap. Shpg. wt., 4 oz.
6K3352—Red head, white body. 87c

South Bend Fish Oreno
Nickel plated head. Can be used for either surf or deep fishing. Shipping weight 3 ounces.
6K3394—Copper head...... 87c

South Bend
bright ... buck-... weed-... Shipping
6K3390—White body, red head...... **$1.07**

South Bend Bass Oreno Wabbler
Body of red cedar wood, 3½ inches long, enameled finish. Shipping wt., 4 oz.
6K3400—Hollow body spotted...... 87c

Fishing Facts

It tells of fly fishing, bait casting and still fishing; "where" and how to fish. Fully illustrated. Over 200 pages and bound in cloth. Shpg. wt., 1 lb.
6K3508...... 79c

100 Assorted Hooks
Made up of all popular patterns and assorted sizes of each pattern. These hooks are all made from the best spring steel, sharpened to a very fine point and properly tempered.
6K3605—Box of 100 21c

Al. Foss Shimmy Wiggler
Nickel plated brass body and spinner with size 3-0 hook. Can use bucktail or pork rind. Rides upright. Shipping wt., 3 oz.
6K3250...... 79c

Al. Foss Jazz Wiggler
Size 3-0 hook, tied with natural bucktail streamer. Used with or without pork rind. Shipping wt., 3 oz.
6K3339 White...... 59c

Genuine Skinner's Spoon Bait for Game Fish. Hollow point hooks. State size. Shpg. wt., 3 oz.
6K3245 Nos. 4½ and 4¾ Ea. 24c

Natural Preserved Minnows
6K3436—Medium Shiners, about 3 inches long. About 24 to the bottle. Shipping weight 1¼ pounds. Per jar...... 24c

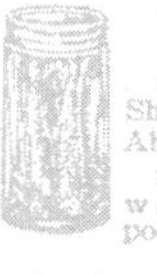

Linen Gill Nets
Can be set where it would be impossible to use a Seine, Hoop or Trap net. As a rule, Gill nets are fished on the bottom, floats hold them up like a fence, but they may be floated near the top with good results. Be sure to order mesh large enough for head of fish to be caught to enter. All our Gill Nets are hung on a one-half basis, that is, 200 yards of netting hung to make a net 100 yards long. All sizes carried in stock.

Catalog No.	Depth. Feet	Sq. Mesh. Inches	Size Twine No.	5 Yds Long	10 Yds Long	20 Yds Long	30 Yds Long	6K2996 Linen Gill Netting Only Per Yard
6K3039	3½	1¾	30-3	0.93	1.89	3.68	$5.55	14c
6K3040	3½	1½	30-3	.72	1.43	2.85	4.35	9c
6K3041	4	1	40-3	1.20	2.35	4.65	6.85	19c
6K3042	4	1¼	30-3	1.28	2.55	5.13	7.85	25c
6K3043	4	1½	30-3	.97	1.95	3.85	5.65	13c
6K3044	4	1¾	30-3	.55	1.65	3.25	4.98	13c
6K3045	4	2	30-3	.77	1.54	3.08	4.75	11c
6K3046	5	1	40-3	1.35	2.68	5.45	8.10	27c
6K3047	5	1¼	30-3	1.43	2.85	5.70	8.75	22c
6K3048	5	1½	30-3	1.17	2.34	4.67	6.95	21c
6K3049	5	1¾	30-3	1.00	1.98	3.95	5.95	17c
6K3050	5	2	30-3	.95	1.85	3.64	5.65	13c
6K3051	5	2¼	30-3	.89	1.75	3.50	5.25	13c
6K3052	6	1	40-3	1.65	3.25	6.40	9.60	33c
6K3053	6	1¼	30-3	1.76	3.50	7.05	10.80	27c
6K3054	6	1½	30-3	1.19	2.15	4.30	6.50	25c
6K3055	6	1¾	30-3	1.01	2.00	4.00	6.15	19c
6K3056	6	2	30-3	.97	1.90	3.75	5.65	15c
6K3057	6	2¼	30-3	.97	1.90	3.75	5.65	15c

We carry only sizes listed. If longer nets are wanted, tie two together. Shpg. wt., per yd., 6 oz.

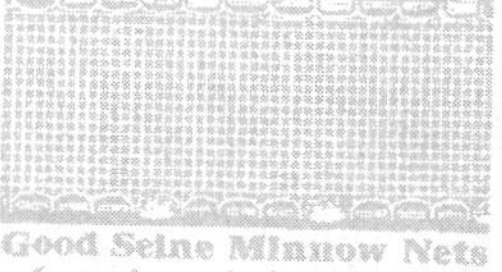

Good Seine Minnow Nets
6 mesh to inch. Medium twine. Complete set. Shpg. wts., 1¼, 2¼, 3¼ and 5¼ lbs.

Catalog No.	Lgh. Ft.	Dpth. Feet	Each
6K2334	6	4	$0.49
6K2335	10	4	.79
6K2336	15	4	1.19
6K2337	25	4	2.05

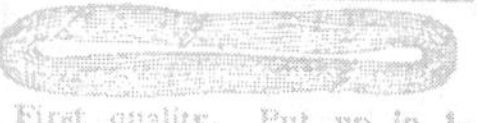

First quality. Put up in 1-pound skeins. We do not sell less than 1 round of a size. State size wanted.
6K2814—Soft Laid Seine Twine. Sizes, 6, 9, 12. Per pound...... 59c
6K2815—Seine Twine. Sizes, 16, 20, 24, 28, 32. Per pound...... 59c
6K2816—Medium Laid Seine Twine. Sizes, 6, 9, 12. Per pound...... 64c
6K2817—Medium Laid Seine Twine. Sizes, 15, 18, 21, 24, 30, 36, 42. Per pound...... 56c

Black Beauty Silk Waterproof Casting Line

Constructed of No. 1 Japan silk. Not affected by the action of alkali or salt waters. Two spools connected if desired. Shpg. wt., 6 oz.

Catalog No.	Breaking Strength	50-Yard Spool
6K3904	14 lbs.	$0.83
6K3905	18 lbs.	.98
6K3906	24 lbs.	1.19

South Bend Silk Casting Line
Color: White and black, striped lengthwise. Fifty-yard spool. Two spools connected if desired. Shpg. wt. 3 oz.

Catalog No.	Breaking Strength	50 Yards
6K3955	12 lbs.	$1.25
6K3956	19 lbs.	1.57
6K3957	25 lbs.	1.95

Brown Mottled Beauty Silk Casting Line
Japan silk. Two spools connected if desired. Shpg. wt., 3 oz.

Catalog No.	Breaking Strength	50-Yard Spool
6K3911	14 lbs.	69c
6K3912	17 lbs.	79c
6K3913	20 lbs.	89c

Highest Quality Genuine Beaver

Twisted Cuttyhunk Linen Line 
The world's best grades of imported linen are used in the building of this sturdy line. Have the greatest possible strength and, at the same time, are absolutely free from any imperfection. 50-yard spools. Six spools connected if desired. Shipping weight, 4 ounces.

Catalog No.	No. of Strands	Breaking Strength	50-Yard Spool
6K3975	9	18 lbs.	33c
6K3976	12	24 lbs.	39c
6K3977	15	30 lbs.	43c
6K3978	18	36 lbs.	49c
6K3979	21	42 lbs.	55c
6K3980	24	48 lbs.	63c
6K3981	27	54 lbs.	69c
6K3982	30	60 lbs.	79c
6K3983	36	72 lbs.	89c

Special Kingfisher Bait Casting Line
Grayish white with black check. Two spools connected if desired. Shpg. wt. 3 oz.

Catalog No.	Breaking Strength	50-Yard Spool
6K3935	12 lbs.	$0.89
6K3936	16 lbs.	1.15
6K3937	23 lbs.	1.27

Steam, Gasoline, and Electric Launches

Nancy 20 Steam Launch

TURN-OF-THE-CENTURY steam launches, with their exposed boilers and tall funnels, were generally used on rivers and as yacht tenders. Walter Beckmann's replica steam launch, the Nancy 20, features the Townsend hull—a design combining the finer points of several antique hulls—which measures 20 feet in length, 4 feet 3 inches in width, and 1 foot 10 inches in depth.

The boat's power plant, assembled from currently available off-the-shelf components, includes a double-acting one-cylinder Semple engine with reverse valving, and a propane-fired Royal 3-h.p. Scotch boiler. The Semple engine is capable of generating 5 h.p., an amount deemed more than necessary due to the Townsend hull's low-drag configuration.

The Nancy 20 is available in either one of two kits and a completed "Steamaway" version. The Standard kit includes everything an amateur builder requires to complete the launch except the wood; and the Deluxe kit includes "the necessary woods for hull and boiler," plus a bilge system, all deck hardware, and an insulated brass boiler stack.

Prices: Nancy 20 "Steamaway," $12,850; kit prices unavailable.

Condor 23 Electric Launch

THIS replica turn-of-the-century electric launch can provide noiseless propulsion through both water and time. The Condor 23 Electric uses the same Standard Doreen 23 hull as the Nimbus 23—only broadened slightly below the waterline to improve the launch's stability.

Price: complete with all propulsion, steering, deck hardware, navigation lights, deep-charge marine batteries, varnished mahogany deck, seats, and floorboards, and electric motor with switch control and charging circuits, $17,950, installed and tested.

The Salome 23 Gasoline Launch

THE Salome 23 also utilizes the Standard Doreen 23 hull, but this time with an antique Easthope 4-6 gasoline engine.

Price: complete with all propulsion, steering, deck hardware, electric bilge pumping, and varnished mahogany deck, seats, and floorboards, $19,450, installed and tested.

Detailed specifications and literature available. Boatyard visits welcomed.

Walter C. Beckmann, Ltd.

P.O. Box 97
Point Judith
Wakefield, RI 02880

(West Coast distributor: Peter Carlick, Reliable Steam Engine Company, P.O. Box 233, Seal Rock, OR 97376)

Nimbus 23 Steam Launch

THE success of steam launches was dampened by the fact that their best deck space was invariably taken up by the engine and boiler. On the Nimbus 23, these are the "well-known and often-envied" Beaumaris Mills engine and Semple vertical-firetube boiler that are together capable of developing 7 h.p. The Nimbus 23's hull is Mr. Beckmann's Standard Doreen 23 type, designed both to have the appearance and to replicate the performance of a turn-of-the-century power launch. It measures 22 feet 9 inches in length, 6 feet 4 inches in width, and 2 feet in depth.

Price: complete with all propulsion, steering, deck hardware, hand-bilge pumping, and varnished mahogany deck, seats, and floorboards, $19,850.

Walter C. Beckmann, Ltd.

P.O. Box 97
Point Judith
Wakefield, RI 02880

(West Coast distributor: Peter Carlick, Reliable Steam Engine Company, P.O. Box 233, Seal Rock, OR 97376)

Nimbus 23 steam launch

26-Foot Sloop

THE Sanford Boat Company, the self-avowed purpose of which is to create "high-performance, seakindly sailboats engineered and built to become heirlooms," sent the following regarding their replica 1912 26-foot sloop:

Rather than develop a new design for our 26' sloop we felt it more sensible to choose a boat that had already proven its ability and desirability. In the past, as today, most designs were strongly influenced by the current fashions or ratings rules that distorted their shapes away from the fastest and most seakindly ones. From time to time, though, boats have been designed with only the sea as a rule and pleasure of movement as a goal. Such was N. G. Herreshoff's *Alerion*, a boat that gave him and her subsequent owners a satisfaction that we seek to reproduce.

Herreshoff built *Alerion* in 1912 for his personal use, and used her for seventeen years until, at the age of eighty-one, he had to give up sailing for reasons of his health. Today *Alerion* belongs to Connecticut's Mystic Seaport, which has restored her to her 1924 rig. While Sanford Boat's replica of the 1912 *Alerion* sloop retains the hull lines, cockpit, and deck layout of the original 26-foot boat exactly, the first *Alerion*'s plank-on-hull frame has been replaced with a modern one of one-piece cold-molded mahogany, which will neither leak nor rot.

Specifications: overall length, 26 feet; beam, 7 feet 7 inches; draft, 2 feet 5 inches (minimum), 5 feet 9 inches (maximum); displacement, 6050 lbs.

For further information, contact:

Sanford Boat Company, Inc.

Lower Pleasant Street
Nantucket, MA 02554
Tel. 617/228-4108

Mahogany-Planked Runabouts

THE CLASSIC wooden speed-boats of the 1920s and 1930s known as mahogany runabouts represent not only the golden age of all such lake-rending motorcraft but also much of the monied elegance evoked by thoughts of the Fitzgerald era.

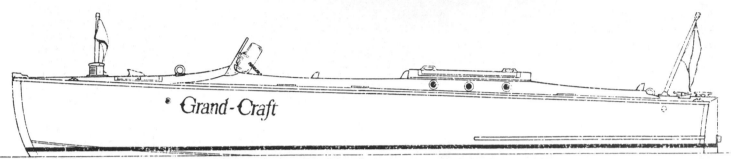

The Chris-Craft company, founded in 1922 by Christopher Columbus Smith, began with the production of a 24-foot runabout that was sold as a "second car" to those for whom commuting might begin with a kiss good-bye at their private dock. The Chris-Crafts were worthy of being called speedboats, and it wasn't long before bootleggers were making good use of their 35-m.p.h. top end to score the surface of one of the Great Lakes on moonless runs down from Canada.

When mahogany began to be replaced by plywood and then fiberglass after the war, it must've been taken as yet another sacrifice to proletarian values among some of the water-borne and filthy rich. Although the burnished-bodied Chris-Craft seemed forever gone, their passing likely went unmourned except at the most exclusive moorings.

Then, in 1981, thirty-two-year-old Steve Northius began thinking that there might again be a market for a luxurious wooden speedboat, and with the aid of Chris Smith (the grandson of Christopher Columbus Smith) he founded what is today the Grand Craft Corporation of Holland, Michigan.

Grand Craft's first runabout, the 24-foot Classic, replicates in its dimensions, design, detail, and handling a 1930 Chris-Craft model. "It's like a big old Packard," said Northius of the forebearer, "a good-handling boat, seaworthy and fast." With the 1983 addition of a 27-footer that replicates a 1932 Chris-Craft runabout, the Grand Craft line of Classic Runabouts was created.

Both speedboats are enhanced replicas that have been updated cautiously and in the direction of increased performance, stability, and structural strength. Grand Craft's devotion to authenticity and period elegance appears evident throughout, and is maintained both by the firm's employment of several former Chris-Craft artisans and its use of original fittings and dies.

Prices begin at $25,000.

For further information, contact:

Grand Craft Corporation
448 W. 21st St.
Holland, MI 49423
Tel. 616/396-5450

From the Vestal Press

Brooks Boats, 1917

BROOKS BOATS WAS a Saginaw, Michigan, firm that sold its customers kits for every kind of vessel from canoes to small cruisers. This reprint of one of their best-illustrated catalogs, according to Harvey Roehl of the Vestal Press, shows "all manner of details and interesting facets of home boat-building, as well as all the parts with which to work."

Price: Vestal Press stock #W-7, $5.50.

Canoe Catalogs

THE Wooden Canoe Heritage Association Ltd. is a nonprofit membership association devoted to the preservation, study, construction, restoration, and use of wooden and birch-bark canoes, and to the dissemination of information about America's canoe heritage. As a part of this, the WCHA offers a "Four-in-One Special" package of reprints of catalogs from early-twentieth-century canoe builders. Included are the 1910 *Rushton Canvas-Covered Canoes*, the 1910 *Old Town Canoes*, the 1908 *Morris Canoes*, and the 1914 *Kennebec Canoes, Boats, & Accessories*. Among the craft illustrated in this set are such noted canoes as the J. H. Rushton "Indian Girl" and "American Beauty," the Old Town "H.W." and "Charles River," the Kennebec "O.G. Special" and "K Special," and four models built by B. N. Morris.

Price: $13.95 ppd.

Wooden Canoe Heritage Association, Ltd.
P.O. Box 5634
Madison, WI 53705

Truscott Wooden Boat Catalog, 1905

A 24-PAGE glossy reprint of the catalog of one of America's most famous boatbuilders, it presents all sizes of wooden boats from rowboats to yachts, with interior and exterior pictures and, where appropriate, engine details.

Price: Vestal Press stock #W-1, $4. Add $2 for shipping and handling for each order.

Catalog available, $2.

The Vestal Press
P.O. Box 97
320 N. Jensen Rd.
Vestal, NY 13850
Tel. 607/797-4872

Military Goods and Firearms

Military Uniforms and Accouterments from James & Son

LOCATED in the city of Philadelphia for more than thirty years, James & Son has supplied armed forces, private collectors, and major museums throughout the world with replica historical military costumes. The company employs, by its own reckoning, some of the nation's finest cutters and tailors; and all finished pieces are personally inspected by the proprietor, Cornelios James. These uniforms are manufactured of top-quality materials, sewn to official period regulations.

Although James & Son can replicate the military costumes of any period, they have a stock catalog of American issue from the eighteenth, nineteenth, and twentieth centuries. Among the last are Spanish-American War field service uniforms, stable fatigues, khaki campaign hats, and canvas gaitors that were authorized in 1898 to replace the dark-blue tunic, shirt, and light-blue trousers that had previously been in use; the World War I service coat and trousers, overseas cap (so named because it was issued after U.S. troops arrived in France in 1917 where their standard brimmed campaign hats proved impractical), leggings, web belt, and ammo pouches for the 30.03 caliber Springfield rifle; and World War II trousers, brown ties, overseas caps, chevrons, and the olive-drab "Ike" jacket that was issued in 1944 as an American version of the British battledress blouse.

Catalog, $1.

James & Son Military Clothiers

1230 Arch St.
Philadelphia, PA 19107
Tel. 215/963-9937

The Burberry Model #21 Trench-Warm

In the covered woodshed to which she had led him, she sat cross-legged upon her golf shoes, his burberry wound about her and her cheeks stung alive by the night air.

—F. SCOTT FITZGERALD, *TENDER IS THE NIGHT*, 1934

ON THAT isle so ancient that traditions take many centuries to mature, the Burberry trenchcoat has been on a fast track. Available now for just seventy-five years, the Burberry's distinguished bearing results from long service as part of the uniform for our age's rich history of exploration, foreign intrigue, correspondence, and above all, military dash. For if the Burberry has advanced rapidly through the ranks of British tradition, it's been mostly due to battlefield promotions.

The coat that Bogart wore to the Casablanca airport got its start with a nineteenth-century country doctor's remark to the young Thomas Burberry that it was better to be wet through than to steam in a macintosh, as the ideal waterproof garment would allow air to reach the wearer's person (Charles MacIntosh's patented process cemented layers of cloth to India rubber, preventing this). So informed, in 1856 Burberry opened a small shop and began the production of his waterproof garments—coats, jackets, shooter's capes, and, some years later, dusters for automobile excursions. These were made from a fabric called "gabardine" by Burberry—a rugged cotton that was doubly proofed and closely woven into a twill finish.

COAT NAMED BY A KING.

HOW "BURBERRYS" WERE CHRISTENED.

"DRY" INVENTOR OF WATERPROOF.

The romance of an English firm built up by the personality and courage of a man with an idea is recalled by the death of Mr. Thomas Burberry, the inventor of the Burberry waterproof coat. He died on Easter Sunday at his residence at Hook, near Basingstoke, in his 91st year.

The origin of the invention of the "Burberry" was a conversation which Mr. Burberry, when a young man, had with a doctor. Stating that it was better for a man to get wet through than to be kept dry in a mackintosh, the doctor expressed the opinion that the ideal waterproof was one which would withstand wind and rain in a reasonable degree and yet allow air to reach the body.

Mr. Burberry christened his invention "Gaberdinee," and it was not known as "Burberry" until King Edward got into the habit of saying, "Give me my Burberry." The name stuck.

Born in 1835 in a Sussex village Mr. Burberry was apprenticed to a draper, and in 1856 started a little draper's shop of his own at Basingstoke.

"He was very fond of sport," said Mr. W. Roller, a director of the firm yesterday. "The firm of Burberrys was

MR. BURBERRY.

built up as a result of his indomitable courage and perseverance. Up to a week ago he took a great interest in the firm, which is now of international standing and has capital of over two millions."

Mr. Burberry cared for little outside his business except temperance, religion and agriculture, and he never read novels. He was a teetotaler and a non-smoker. He had a house at Weymouth, and in that town he carried on a temperance campaign, mainly directed to Sunday closing.

The illness which caused his death is believed to have originated through his preaching a sermon at a Salvation Army gathering about a fortnight ago.

By the century's turn, Burberry had a central warehouse in London set up to supply the chain of agencies that had sprung up all over England. Soon after, these were followed by international branch offices in New York, Buenos Aires, Paris, and Montevideo—and the famous Haymarket, London, premises was prepared to receive customers by 1912. Now all the firm had to do was to await the moment when King Edward would issue the command to "Give me my Burberry" before their name could take its place alongside those of MacIntosh, Wellington, and Cardigan in the popular lexicon.

By the end of the first decade Burberrys had become established as the standard outerwear for explorers and big-game hunters alike. In the 1890s they had been lifted into the outer reaches by intrepid gabardined balloonists, and later they would go along on the first organized ascent of Mount Everest. The fabled Amundsen and the ill-fated Scott expeditions of 1911 were both outfitted with windproof gear and special tents from Burberrys, and it was one of the latter that Amundsen left at the South Pole to inform Scott that he had arrived there first. The Burberry military tradition began with the Boer War (1899–1902) after the British army ordered a quantity of dress uniforms based on one of Mr. Burberry's "Sporting Suits"—a four-pocket affair that is still used by the British army. The first belted overcoat was, at the suggestion of so eminent a soldier as Lord Kitchener, sanctioned for use by the British War Office in 1906.

By this time the British were reflexively turning to Burberrys whenever difficult conditions required rugged clothing. This was never more the case than in the trenches that traversed the ruined landscape of World War I from the Channel to the Alps. It was, according to a 1916 Burberrys advertisment, "to enable the soldier to face the rigorous conditions inevitable in campaigning"—an elegantly understated description of the trench soldier's fetid lot—that the Trench-Warm (or Model #21) was adopted. Between 1914 and 1918 an estimated 500,000 Trench-Warms were issued to combat officers.

Among the many who went down in their Burberrys was Kitchener himself, who drowned in 1916 after a ship taking him to Russia at the invitation of Grand Duke Nicholas struck a mine and sank. Luckier by far was the Royal Flying Corps officer who was shot down over the English Channel. Although he survived the donnybrook, once in the drink he was regrettably forced to abandon his burberry to save his life. After spending five days in the water it was returned to him "none the worse for wear," as he later wrote Burberrys.

Save for the fact that its overall cut varies with annual fashion dictates for fullness and length, with its epaulettes, D-rings, deep yoke, button-down storm flap, and storm pockets, the same Trench-Warm is still a part of the Burberrys catalog.

Price: $450.

Military Goods from the Cockpit

World War I Items

U.S.N. Chief Petty Officer's Shirt

IN THE opening days of America's involvement in World War I, Rear Adm. William S. Sims, defiantly outspoken and nonconforming in the tradition continued by Adm. Hyman Rickover, reviewed the havoc that German U-boats had been wreaking on Allied shipping. During April of 1917 alone some 800,000 tons of food and matériel was expected to be lost to torpedo attacks, so the story that confronted him was a disheartening one. Overall, the Germans had been able to wipe out a third of the margin of shipping that the Allies relied on to both feed Britain and supply their armies in the field.* "Looks as if the Germans are winning the war," the rear admiral laconically observed to First Sea Lord Sir John Jellicoe. "They will unless we stop these losses," rang the reply.

After some bureaucratic maneuvering, thirty-six U.S. destroyers and an armada of support vessels were deployed to accomplish this. By midsummer this "convoy system" ensured that the once-dreaded U-boats would be incapable of interfering with the transport of American soldiers to France.

*S. L. A. Marshall, Brigadier General, U.S.A.R. (ret.), *The American Heritage History of World War I* (New York: The American Heritage Publishing Company, 1964).

U.S. naval deck officers on these Atlantic shipping convoys were issued C.P.O. shirts the same as those now sold by the Cockpit. Designed during the war for this rigorous duty, these shirts are made of 100% melton wool, their yarn dyed to original specifications for colorfastness.

Price: Cockpit catalog #258, sizes small, medium, and large, $39; extra-large, $45.

Trench Lighter

IT WAS one of the many paradoxes of World War I that the beauty and adventure of the European countryside lay so close to the abject misery of life in the trenches. In the damp dugouts where a soldier's time was spent awaiting either death or vermin to pounce from the dark, the cigarette lighter became among the most highly valued of personal possessions. The Cockpit's replica World War I trench lighter authentically features the sliding brass windscreen of the originals.

Price: Cockpit catalog #9547, $10.50.

The Flying Tigers

From the Cockpit catalog:

The Flying Tigers, also known as the American Volunteer Group, were recruited from the ranks of active-duty pilots serving in the U.S. Army, Navy, and Marine Air Corps. They went to China as civilians with the tacit approval of the U.S. government. Starting in the summer of 1941, in defense of China and the Burma Road against the Japanese, the Tigers' shark-mouthed-Curtiss P-40 fighters flew day-in and day-out against overwhelming odds. The number of enemy planes they destroyed made them legend.

Having arrived in China discharged from U.S. military service, they bore no U.S. uniforms and were outfitted by the Chinese. During 1939 the Chinese government had special-ordered quantities of Type G-1 flight jackets, shirts, and trousers. These garments, originally intended for the Chinese military elite, were made of the finest materials available. As a footnote, after the U.S. entered the war in Asia in July 1942, the Tigers were incorporated into the U.S. 14th Air Force and issued Type A-2 leather jackets.

G-I Leather Flight Jacket

FOR the most part the Tigers used the U.S. Navy goatskin jacket that was supplied to them by the Chinese. This prewar jacket was a bit longer than the navy's wartime model, and its moulton collar was slightly thicker. With naturally oiled mahogany-brown goatskins and matched lining, cuffs, and waistband, the Cockpit's replica Flying Tigers G-1 is crafted to duplicate the finest features of the original.

Prices: Cockpit catalog #2250, even sizes 36 to 46, $235; sizes 48 and 50, $255.

The Flying Tigers Commemorative "Crush" Cap

CLAIRE L. CHENNAULT (1890–1958), a pioneer of army aviation, set up the American Volunteer Group (A.V.G.) for Chiang Kai-shek. Chennault taught his fighter pilots what at the time were considered radical tactics, but ones that would eventually become commonplace after 1942. It is believed that Chennault shot down more than forty Japanese aircraft in the period prior to the official U.S. entry into the war.

The Tigers who volunteered to fight with Chennault came from every branch of the U.S. military, bringing with them the few personal possessions that professional soldiers accumulate. For the A.V.G. pilots, this frequently included a "Fifty-Mission Crush" that had been worn either Stateside or in Europe. Upon its arrival in China, the crush's U.S. insignia was replaced with the Nationalist Chinese Wings-and-Star. The Cockpit's commemorative crush cap is made of olive melton wool with a leather beak, and is available in ⅛-inch sizes from 6½ to 7½.

Price: Cockpit catalog #8507, $45.

Type 1930s Cotton Summer Flight Jacket

This jacket is also available.

Price: Cockpit catalog #2237, even sizes 36 to 46, $45; sizes 48 and 50, $55.

Flying Tiger Khakis

THE FLYING TIGER pilots and ground crew frequently wore khakis as their "uniform of the day." These were sturdy twills and poplins similar to the 100% cotton twills that the A.V.G. flyers had worn in the U.S. Army Air Force or the U.S. Navy. The Cockpit's version is a preshrunk 100% cotton twill shirt and trousers. Shirts are available in sizes small, medium, large, and extra-large; trousers all have 36-inch inseams and are available in sizes 28 to 36.

Prices: Cockpit catalog #3408, shirts, $23.50; Cockpit catalog #7409, trousers, $24.50.

Flying Tigers Insignia

THE COCKPIT offers several varieties.

Prices: Cockpit catalog #9380, brass-and-enamel pilot's wings (approximately 3 inches wide), $22.50; catalog #9381, Flying Tigers squadron pin, $13.95; catalog #9382, Flying Tigers bullion on velvet wings, $12.95; catalog #9383, Flying Tigers bullion on velvet tunic jacket emblem, $13.95; catalog #9384, Flying Tigers official cap insignia, $16.95.

Type B-2 Genuine Horsehide Gloves

A REPLICATION of 1935-style open-cockpit fighter pilot's gloves in tanned seal-brown horsehide. Available only in limited quantity in even sizes 8 to 12. **Price:** Cockpit catalog #8144-H, $24.

U.S.N. World War II–Type Goatskin Leather NAF-1092 Flight Helmet

A REPLICATION of the 1938–1943 U.S. Navy-issue helmet. Made to military specifications with a molded leather chin cup, the helmet features earphones compatible with general aviation systems. Sizes small, medium, large, and extra-large.

Price: Cockpit catalog #8115A, $57.50.

1941 Type "50-Mission Crush" Cap

A REPLICATION of the famous service cap popular among B-17 bomber and C-47 transport pilots and crew. Its name is derived from the way it looked after airmen removed the cap's inside grommet to accommodate their earphones. The Cockpit's 1941 crush is made from olive-dyed melton wool and has a reinforced leather visor, its leather strap secured by brass U.S. Army Air Corps buttons. Complete with a nylon satin headliner and perforated leather sweatband, the cap features the regulation coat-of-arms of the United States. Available in ⅛-inch sizes from 6½ to 7½.

Price: Cockpit catalog #8508, $39.

Type B-3 U.S.A.A.F. Sheepskin Flying Jacket

T HIS IS the regulation name for the famous sheepskin jackets worn by American fighter and bomber crews during the war. The Cockpit replica is handcrafted to original specifications from selected leather-tanned nappa sheepskin and has welted-leather seams for extra durability. It features a full-size, double-strapped sheep-fur collar.

Prices: Cockpit catalog #2102, even sizes 36 regular to 46 regular, $370; sizes 48 and 50 regular, $396; sizes 38 long to 48 long, $410.

Aviator's Scarf

M ADE OF pure silk, the Cockpit's classic aviator's scarves are 6 feet in length and 1 foot wide. They are available with or without the U.S. Army Air Force insignia.

Prices: Cockpit catalog #9146 (without insignia), $22.50; catalog #9145 (with insignia), $29.95.

A-2 U.S.A.A.F. Flight Jacket

TO THE best of their knowledge, the Cockpit's A-2 is the first genuine horsehide A-2 to be available since 1945. Army Air Corps Specifications DWG 30-1415 of September 29, 1930, called for a seal-brown jacket to be made of horsehide because of the skin's comfort, durability, and (at the time) availability. Throughout the war horsehide remained the required material for this jacket.

Due to wartime shortages, however, a small number of contractors obtained limited-supply waivers to produce A-2s from goatskin, establishing a popular misconception that *it* was the material that the Army had actually intended for the jackets. As the Cockpit claims the military documentation will support, this is simply not so—although goatskin *was* regulation for U.S. Navy flight jackets (see below).

The Cockpit's horsehide A-2 replicates the seal-brown 1941-issue jacket. As they are limited in number to the company's supply of horsehide, they are a "first-come" limited-edition item.

Prices: Cockpit catalog #2107-H, even sizes 36 to 46, $285; sizes 48 and 50, $325.

1943-Issue Dark-Brown A-2 Jacket

THE COCKPIT also has a cowhide version of the 1943 A-2.
Prices: Cockpit catalog #2107, even sizes 36 regular to 46 regular, $195; sizes 48 and 50 regular, $215; even sizes 38 long to 48 long, $210.

Type G-1 Intermediate Goatskin Leather Flight Jacket

THE COCKPIT's replica World War II Type G-1 Intermediate Goatskin Leather Flight Jacket has a genuine moulton sheepskin fur collar as was used on the original 1944-issue jackets. The contoured pocket flaps, underarm gussets, eyelets, and military-specification zipper and snap fasteners for the interior map pocket (frequently used by combat pilots as a holster) together support the Cockpit's claim to an absolutely authentic replica.

Prices: Cockpit catalog #2108, even sizes 36 regular to 46 regular, $185; sizes 48 and 50 regular, $210; sizes 38 long to 48 long, $210.

Flight Jackets with Bomber Nose Art

THE COCKPIT will provide A-2s with authentically hand-painted bomber nose art like that that adorned the bodies of World War II aircraft and the jackets of the men who flew them. Only the original techniques and patterns are used to produce these, using full-color leather dyes exclusively. Ordered jackets will be sent to the customer for approval before painting, and will require four to six weeks for redelivery completed.

Styles: Cockpit catalog #180, Tantalizing Takeoff; catalog #182, U.S.A.A.F. shoulder insignia; catalog #184, Flying Tigers (1941); catalog #2185-M, Glenn Miller (shown here); catalog #186, Mighty Eighth; catalog #2187-S, I'll Be Seeing You (features a portrait of Frank Sinatra); catalog #188, Man O'War; catalog #189, Sack Time; catalog #190, Wabash Cannonball.

Prices: for Cockpit catalog #2182 (U.S.A.A.F. shoulder insignia), sizes 36 to 46, $230; sizes 48 and 50, $255. For other styles, sizes 36 to 46, $370; sizes 48 and 50, $400.

World War II International Aircraft Recognition Manual

ORIGINALLY printed during the war to assist Allied troops and civilians in the identification of airborne friend and foe. Its absence in the early days of the conflict sometimes resulted in damage to our own planes by antiaircraft gunners who, conversely, also sometimes allowed enemy aircraft in too close before opening fire.

The Cockpit's 150-page reprint includes silhouettes and pictures of all prominent Allied and Axis aircraft, plus data on armaments, their usage, and specifications.

Price: Cockpit catalog #435, $12.96.

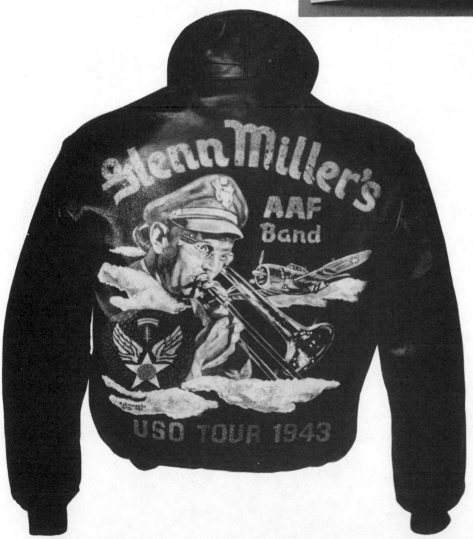

Hand-Painted Leather Squadron Patches

THESE **World War II patches** have been re-created by the original technique using full-color leather dyes.

Styles: Cockpit catalog #740, Eighth Army Air Force; catalog #750, Flying Tigers A.V.G. (1941); catalog #751, Hells Angels, 3rd Squadron A.V.G. (1941); catalog #752, Adam and Eve, 1st Squadron A.V.G. (1941); catalog #753, China Air Task Force (spring 1942); catalog #754, 23rd Fighter Group; catalog #757, 14th Air Force (China, 1942–1945); catalog #762, American Eagle Squadron (England, 1941); catalog #765, P-61 Night Fighter insignia; catalog #769, 4th Bombardment Squadron (B-25s); catalog #770, Dolittle's Tokyo Raiders; catalog #772, 17th Bombardment Squadron; catalog #774, VMF-214, Pappy Boyington's Corsairs; catalog #775, VF 6F-4F Wildcats (U.S.S. *Enterprise*); catalog #776, U.S.N. Dive Bomber Squadron; catalog #779, WASP pilots; catalog #781, U.S. Army Air Force.

Prices: Cockpit catalog #740 and #781, $22.50 each; other styles, $28.95 each.

Color catalog available, $2.

The Cockpit

627 Broadway
New York, NY 10012
Tel. 212/420-1600

World War II Fighter Aircraft

Not a bomber or a Mustang was lost and 21 Nazi interceptors kayoed.
—THE CLARKE COUNTY (ALABAMA) *DEMOCRAT*, NOVEMBER 1, 1944

THE P-51D Mustang—successor to the P-51B that was the first U.S. Army Air Force fighter with the range to escort Allied bomber formations to their German targets and back—was generally considered the best fighter to come out of World War II. Together, both Mustangs virtually eliminated the Luftwaffe as a contending air force. Piloted replicas of these fighters are available today in a 62½% scale from the Historical Aircraft Corporation of Durango, Colorado.

"Historical Aircraft was established to provide serious warbird enthusiasts with authentic replicas of the world's great single-engine fighter and attack aircraft," reports Warren Eberspacher, a professional aeronautical engineer and recognized aviation historian, who incorporated the firm in 1981. "These aircraft will be derived from both U.S. and foreign designs representing the period from 1920 to 1950, and will be available both in kit

form and as custom-built models. The completed fighters will be sized at a scale either 60% or 70% of those of the original aircraft."

These kits, which further depart from the original fighters in their use of a "composite covering" to skin their fuselages, are, as this listing is written, being developed along with their prototypes and should be available as you read it.

In addition to the P-51B and P-51D Mustangs, among the first kits available will be one for the F4U Corsair—the cunning-looking warbird that was called the "Whispering Death" by the Japanese (although, as designer Alan Rose notes, this sounds more like a story that was put out by the U.S. Army War Office). The Corsair, which was the first U.S. fighter capable of checking the vaunted Japanese Zero, is remembered as the bent-wing bird flown by Gregory "Pappy" Boyington and his "Black Sheep" squadron in the South Pacific theater of operations.

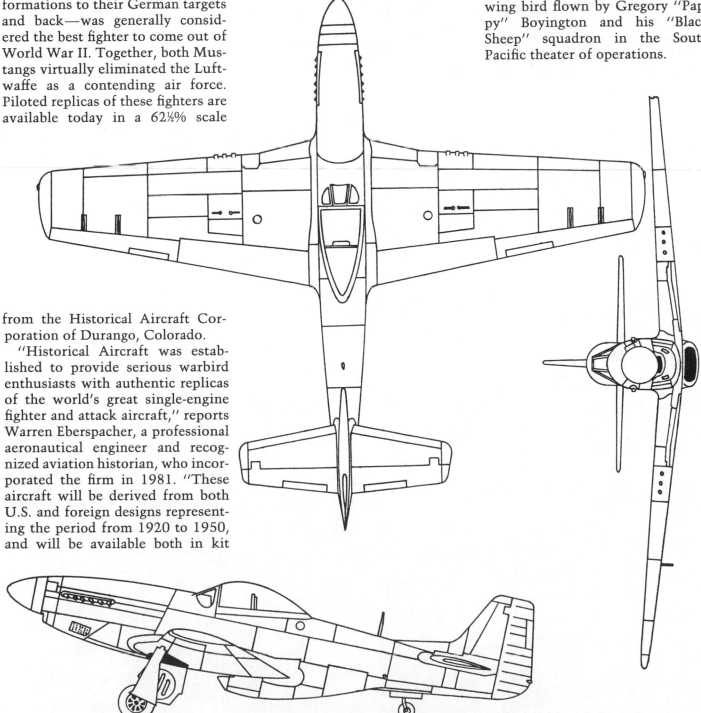

The Corsair is a 60% replica and is (as are the Mustangs) supported by an airframe of welded steel that is capable of withstanding load factors that were typically generated by the combat maneuvers of the fighters they replicate. The replicas are powered by liquid-cooled Ford V-6 engines that have been adapted for aircraft use and have been designed to swing either fixed-blade or constant-speed (variable-pitch) propellors. Each aircraft is equipped with engine, flight, and navigational instrumentation suitable for VFR (visual flight rules, fair-weather) flying; and their cockpit and external details have been taken from pilot and maintenance manuals to ensure authenticity. This interest in realism extends to their use of replica gun-charging handles, optical gunsights, and thick, "armored" windscreens.

The cost of the completed kits is projected to be in the range of $40,000, with final prices likely to have been established as you read this. The kits have been designed to provide builders with complete, authentically scaled VFR fighters, and, in addition to those features already mentioned, will include (but will not necessarily be limited to) the following items: wing spars, engine mount, hydraulically braked landing-gear system, coolant system, basic navcom unit for radio communication and navigation, safety harness, and surface finish material and paint.

Additional equipment (added instrumentation, constant-speed prop, detachable luggage container, etc.) will be available as added-cost options.

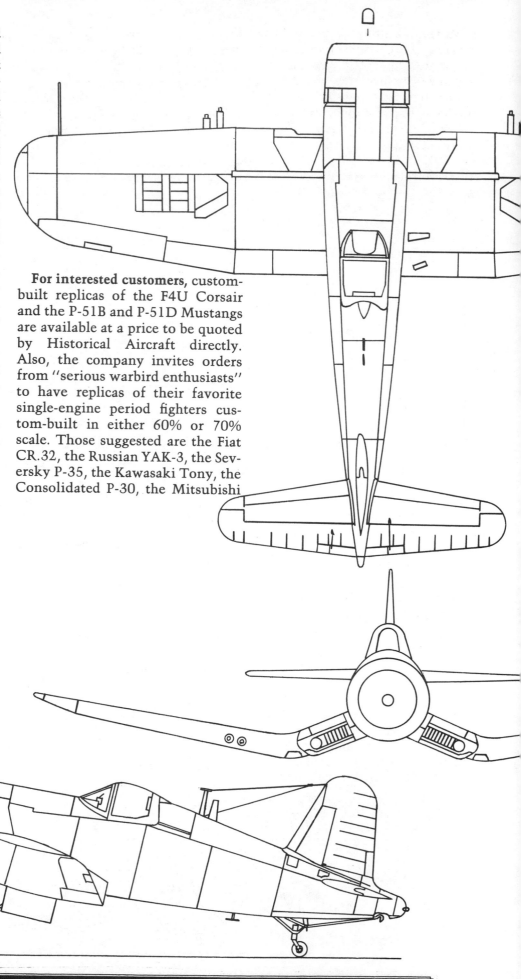

For interested customers, custom-built replicas of the F4U Corsair and the P-51B and P-51D Mustangs are available at a price to be quoted by Historical Aircraft directly. Also, the company invites orders from "serious warbird enthusiasts" to have replicas of their favorite single-engine period fighters custom-built in either 60% or 70% scale. Those suggested are the Fiat CR.32, the Russian YAK-3, the Seversky P-35, the Kawasaki Tony, the Consolidated P-30, the Mitsubishi

A5M, the Blackburn Skua, and the Fokker D.21. Custom-built replicas are painted in carefully researched marking schemes that depict the period and theater of operations sought by the customer.

As the Historical Aircraft Corporation intends its fighters to become the "Rolls-Royces" of warbird replicas, the company has been

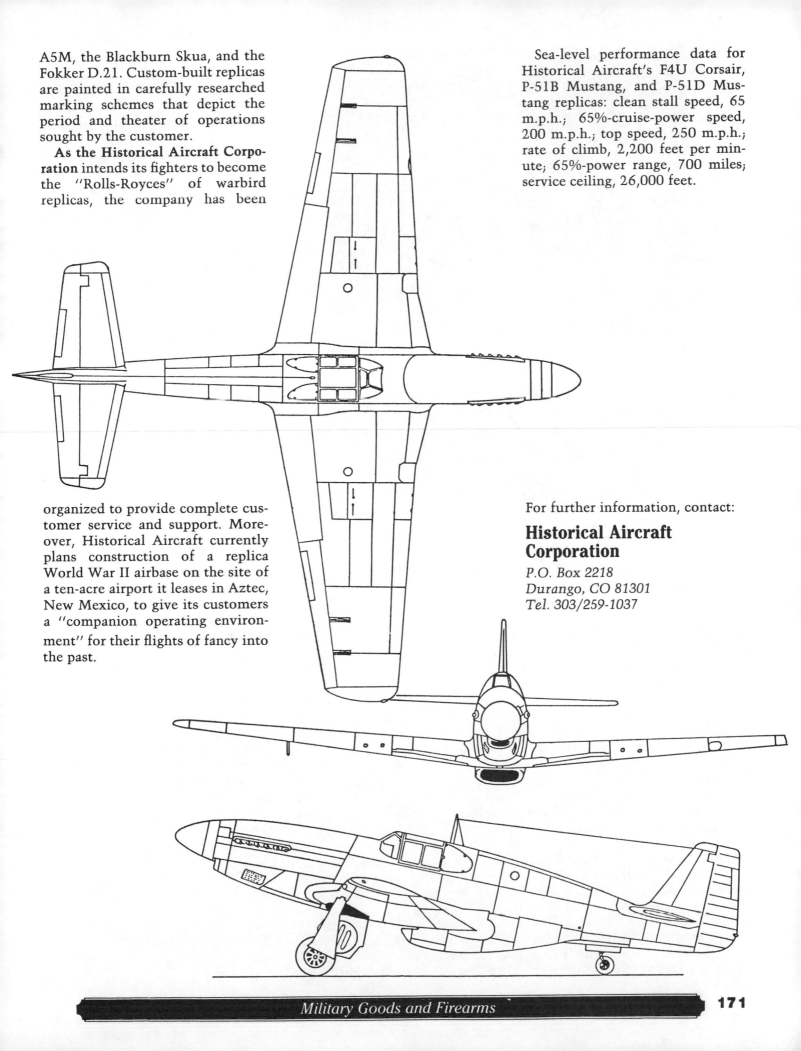

Sea-level performance data for Historical Aircraft's F4U Corsair, P-51B Mustang, and P-51D Mustang replicas: clean stall speed, 65 m.p.h.; 65%-cruise-power speed, 200 m.p.h.; top speed, 250 m.p.h.; rate of climb, 2,200 feet per minute; 65%-power range, 700 miles; service ceiling, 26,000 feet.

organized to provide complete customer service and support. Moreover, Historical Aircraft currently plans construction of a replica World War II airbase on the site of a ten-acre airport it leases in Aztec, New Mexico, to give its customers a "companion operating environment" for their flights of fancy into the past.

For further information, contact:

Historical Aircraft Corporation

P.O. Box 2218
Durango, CO 81301
Tel. 303/259-1037

The Hamilton Marine Chronometer,
quartz movement shown.

World War II Naval Marine Chronometer

THE BATTLE of Leyte Gulf—a successful retaking of the Philippines by forces under Gen. Douglas MacArthur in October 1944—was no cruise in the sun. In fact, the battle today remembered as the one that ended the Japanese navy's offense in the Pacific nearly ended the American campaign instead—with a bloody rout of MacArthur's invaders. With Vice-Adm. Takeo Kurita and his flotilla steaming back toward Japan early in the Leyte campaign, the U.S. Navy brass firmly believed that they had the Imperial Navy on the run. It was without fear of attack, then, that Adm. William F. "Bull" Halsey exposed the entrance to Leyte Gulf on the morning of October 25 by pulling out his Third Fleet to intercept part of the Japanese fleet (under the command of Vice-Adm. Jisaburo Ozawa) that lay to the north. Ozawa's decoy left the gulf's defense in the hands of the U.S. Seventh Fleet's "Taffy 3" force—a puny line of baby flattops and "small boy" destroyers.

When the U.S. spotter pilot first radioed Taffy 3 commander Adm. Clifton Sprague that a large Japanese force was bearing down on him from the southwest, his report was dismissed: "Now there's some young screwball reporting our own forces," Sprague barked. "We've got the whole damn Philippines between us and the Japs now." But Kurita, who had turned his armada around the previous night, was closing fast. Sprague's face slackened when he saw through his long glass the rapidly approaching 18-inch guns and pagoda towers of the *Yamato* and the *Musashi*, then the largest

and most powerful combat ships afloat. In the silence that befell the bridge of Sprague's flagship, its men digested the fact that their cobbled-together group was all that stood between MacArthur's landing and Kurita's four columns of dreadnaught.

Through the checkered light left by rain squalls and the concealing smoke that the U.S. ships trailed at flank speed, a lopsided but sustained battle raged. The Taffy group's annihilation was inevitable, but they inflicted damage far beyond their size and it gave Kurita pause. Although he could easily have plunged on into Leyte Gulf and wreaked havoc with the U.S. forces gathered there, Kurita broke off the battle and wheeled his fleet's hulls in retreat. In commemoration of the American victory at Leyte Gulf, the Hamilton Watch Company has reproduced its historic marine chronometer, which, according to Adm. Arleigh Burke (chief of staff to Vice-Adm. Marc A. Mitscher during Leyte) "was essential to the battle's naval, sea, and air operations." In all of its specifications and materials—from the hand-finished case of FAS (first as selected) mahogany to its solid-brass inlay—the reproduction is essentially the same as those issued during the war to the U.S. Navy Bureau of Ships. The gimbal system is also the same as that used on the World War II model.

Price: available in a limited quantity with either quartz or mechanical movements, $1,595.

Brochure obtainable.

Collector's Classic Edition Society, Ltd.

P.O. Box 7343
1817 William Penn Way
Lancaster, PA 17604
Tel. toll free 800/233-0283
(in Pennsylvania, 717/394-7161,
*   ext. 2175)*

Model 1902 Officer's Saber

Firearms

Colt .45 Pistol

THE PHILIPPINE Insurrection (1899–1913), an expression of Muslim resistance to Christian rule on the islands, pitted the fierce Moros against Filipino Christians, government forces, and the United States Army (the U.S. became a dominant influence in the Philippines after it fell under our control following the Spanish-American War). Here, the U.S. Army was introduced to jungle warfare, a hostile Stateside press, and a local population's elusive hearts and minds fifty years before Vietnam.

It was jungle fighting and the ferociousness of the Moro charges that pointed up the army's need for a lighter and more powerful sidearm than the .38-caliber revolver it had been using. An answer was found in the Browning-designed .45-caliber Colt automatic pistol, which so impressed army brass that the weapon was formally adopted in 1911.

This pistol remained unaltered until the M1911A1—with its decreased trigger width and arched mainspring housing—was introduced in 1923. Here finally was "Old Ugly," the famous Colt .45 which, with other minor refinements, would accompany U.S. fighting men into World War II, Korea, Lebanon, the Dominican Republic, Vietnam, Grenada, and Lebanon again. In January of 1985, just when the Colt .45 seemed as integral a part of army life as drill, the Pentagon suddenly announced a switch to the Italian-made Beretta pistol for all armed forces. Suggested retail prices range from $491.75 to $1,116.90.

Available at firearms dealers throughout the country.

Thompson Submachine Guns

I'm sorry it happened. It was just a piece of hot-headed foolishness.
—DION O'BANNION

ON FEBRUARY 14, 1929, the most renowned rubout in mob history punctuated the struggle taking place for control of Chicago's North Side. George "Bugs" Moran and his gang—which had been built out of Dion O'Bannion's organization—were lured to a garage by Al Capone's men dressed as police. There, they were stood up against a wall and shot with tommy guns, their executioners pouring lines of bullets across their heads, chests, and stomachs.

Moran missed his appointment for the St. Valentine's Day Massacre, but his torpedo, "Machine Gun" McGurn, was there, as was Frank Gusenberg, who, with fourteen bullet holes in his body, when asked who shot him, answered with his last words: "Nobody shot me."

The tommy gun—or, as he called it, the "trench broom"—was developed in 1919 by Gen. John T. Thompson as a weapon to be used in the close-quarter combat of trench warfare and as a foot soldier's defense against machine-gun fire. But, as with the Gatling gun before it, the war ended before the Thompson could be put to use and, after some mostly unsuccessful efforts during the early Twenties to develop home and municipal mar-kets, the weapon fell into the hands of Chicago gangsters.

Although Capone had ordered his first three Thompsons in February of 1926, it was "Hymie" Weiss (Capone's competitor then, and the inventor of "murder by motor") who gave him his first graphic demonstration of the submachine gun's firepower. Weiss, not a man to shrink from taking out any innocent burghers who happened to get in the way of his notorious method of operation, used to like to lay out lead in flying carpets. And so it was on September 20, 1926, when Weiss's Thompson-brandishing gang sent a thousand rounds into Capone's Cicero headquarters during the course of a single tire-squealing flyby of the place. Unhurt, Capone was not unimpressed: "That's the gun!" he shouted, more awed than angered by the attack. "It's got it over a sawed-off shotgun like a shotgun has it over an automatic."

From Chicago, use of the Thompson spread throughout the broad national underground. In the 1920s it became an essential artillery piece for Florida's alcohol smugglers who defied Prohibition with fast, black-hulled boats loaded to the gunnels with elegant booze. In the Middle West of the 1930s such bank robbers as John Dillinger, Bonnie Parker, Clyde Barrow, "Baby Face" Nelson, "Pretty Boy" Floyd, "Machine Gun" Kelly, and "Ma" Barker used Thompsons the way their predecessors did hogleg Colts a generation before. With

their tommy guns barking farewell from fast automobiles, these bandits foiled attempts by state-line-bound police to capture them, and their exploits against the banks won them a place in the hearts of many made silent desperadoes by the Depression's grinding poverty.

But like the American economy itself, the tommy gun's reputation would finally be saved by World War II. Only, as the accompanying picture of Winston Churchill shows, not quite as well. For it's the Thompson's legacy that anyone who ever holds one, even for a moment, can expect to feel far more like a Dillinger than a Disraeli.

Violin carrying case available.

Price-on-request from your local firearms dealer or the Thompson Submachine Gun's original manufacturer:

Auto-Ordnance Corporation
West Hurley, NY 12491
Tel. 914/679-7225

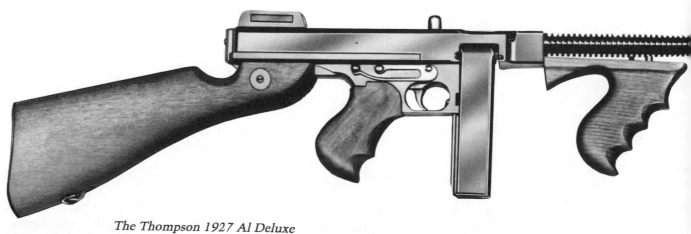

The Thompson 1927 A1 Deluxe

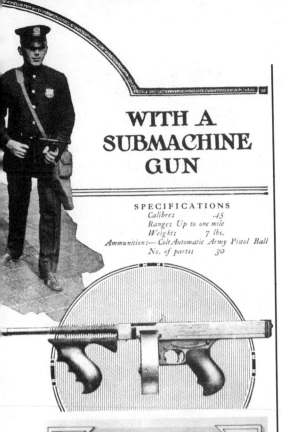

WITH A SUBMACHINE GUN

SPECIFICATIONS
Calibre: .45
Range: Up to one mile
Weight: 7 lbs.
Ammunition:—Colt Automatic Army Pistol Ball
No. of parts: 30

Colt 1927 Detective Special—.38 Caliber

I knew one thing: as soon as anyone said you didn't need a gun, you'd better take along one that worked.
— DETECTIVE NOVELIST
RAYMOND CHANDLER

SAM COLT introduced his first snubnosed pocket revolver, the "Baby Patterson," back in 1837—but it took until the late 1920s for his firm to turn out a double-action snub with a swing-out barrel like the Detective Special. Although Chandler's famous character Philip Marlowe didn't yet exist in 1927, the Special was coming along just in time for both him and the rough 'n' rhetorical private eyes of the Forties who would follow in his gumshoes. According to Colt's literature, this .38-caliber weapon is still the preferred off-duty revolver of most police officers. The gun has a barrel length of 2 inches and is available with either a nickel or blue-metal finish.

Suggested retail prices: $399.96 (blue metal), $449.95 (nickel). Actual selling prices are determined by retailers and may vary.

Colt Firearms Division

P.O. Box 1868
Hartford, CT 06101
Tel. 203/236-6311

M1 Garand Rifle

IN THE darkening period between the wars the United States Ordnance Department kept searching for a reliable, self-loading, semi-automatic design for a U.S. service rifle. John C. Garand, chief civilian engineer with the Springfield Armory, punctuated some thirty years of research at the government arsenal with the invention of a suitable clip-fed, gas-operated self-loading arm that would be officially adopted in 1936 as the "U.S. Rifle Cal .30, M1." To augment government production at Springfield, in 1939 the Winchester Arms Company was awarded a contract to supply the "Garand" to American forces. As the standard infantry weapon of World War II, the M1 saw service in every theater of operations and was lauded by Gen. George S. Patton as "the greatest battle implement ever devised."

The Springfield Armory is today the name of a private concern located in Geneseo, Illinois. It "reincarnates," according to its literature, an M1 Garand rifle "so authentic in appearance and performance and so true to detail, John Garand himself would have trouble telling it from the original." In addition to its status as a historical reproduction, the Springfield Armory's M1 Garand is now sold as a hunting and competition rifle.

Specifications: overall length, 43 inches; barrel length, 24 inches; caliber, .30-06 (with .308 cal. and .270 cal. optional); weight, 9½ lbs.; mechanism, semi-automatic, gas-operated, clip-fed; magazine capacity, 8-round, en-bloc clip; rifling, 6-groove, right-hand twist, one turn in ten; front sight, blade with projecting ears; rear sight, aperture; trigger, two-stage, 5-lb. pull.

Replica M1 bayonets, scabbards, early-issue combo tool, leather rifle sling, grenade launcher stock, prong flash suppressor, field cleaning kit, and other accessories are available.

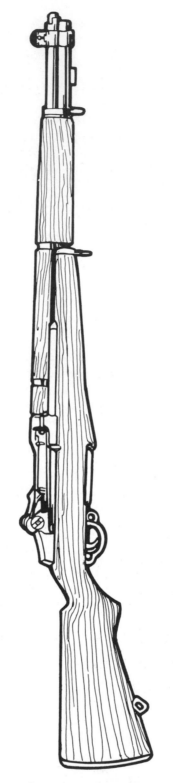

Suggested retail prices begin at $696.

Catalog available.

Springfield Armory

420 W. Main St.
Geneseo, IL 61254
Tel. 309/944-5631

Bill Mauldin's Army

IN THE American pantheon of cultural heroes, there are those men whose friendships—forged in adversity—have obliterated the petty distinctions of race. Among the likes of Hawkeye and Chingachgook, Ishmael and Queeg-Queeg, Huck and Jim, the Lone Ranger and Tonto, and Captain Kirk and Mr. Spock, Bill Mauldin's unshaven pair of World War II buddies, Willy and Joe, share secure quarters.

Joe (or is that Willy?) was a "smart-assed Choctaw Indian with a hooked nose," and Willy (er . . . Joe?) "his red-necked straight man," recalls cartoonist Mauldin in the introduction to this reprint of the 1944 *Army Times* edition of his famous wartime cartoons. Somewhere between boot camp and V-E Day Mauldin switched names on his bedraggled pair, but it makes little difference to the reader who follows them through the mud of wartorn Europe, swearing all the way that this is where M.A.S.H.'s war-is-also-human satire must've been inspired.

For instance: As they crouch in a supply room behind German lines raiding a supply of schnapps reserved for Nazi officers (*Achtung! Fur Offiziere!*), Willy and Joe are suddenly discovered by a hulking enemy guard. As a fellow enlisted man, the German shoulders his rifle and reassures our startled heroes sympathetically: *"Nein, nein—go ahead! I vould not think of interfering."*

For this, the first publication of his cartoons in more than thirty years, Mauldin decided that their evocation of the G.I.'s wartime travails would've been better served by arranging the cartoons in chronological order rather than by subject (like discomfort, rank, weather, food, etc.) as was originally done. But the editors of this Presidio Press edition claimed that authenticity in the reprinting of an early work takes precedence over anything else and refused the author's request to change things.

Prices: for a limited-edition hardcover, $25; for softcover, $12.95 (plus $1.75 each for shipping and handling). The hardcover edition is not available in bookstores.

Presidio Press

31 Pamaron Way
Novato, CA 94947
Tel. 415/883-1373

Normandy Invasion Maps

A landing was made this morning on the coast of France by the troops of the Allied Expeditionary Force. This landing is part of the concerted United Nations plan for the liberation of Europe.
     —GEN. DWIGHT D. EISENHOWER, IN A BROADCAST TO THE PEOPLE OF WESTERN EUROPE ON JUNE 6, 1944, THE MORNING OF THE D-DAY LANDING

ALTHOUGH it won't compare rhetorically to Pershing's "Lafayette, we are here," General Eisenhower's announcement of the invasion of Hitler's Fortress Europe marked the beginning of the end of World War II. It stands not only as the most important action of the war, but as the greatest invasion of all history.

The planning of the Normandy invasion was on an equally gargantuan scale and involved the secret transport and deployment of more than 185,000 Allied troops, 18,000 paratroopers, 13,000 aircraft, 4,000 landing craft, 745 large ships, 20,000 vehicles, and 345 minesweepers, in addition to the support troops and matériel required.

All was in readiness when the forecast of treacherously high winds and rough seas almost forced Eisenhower to delay the invasion. But as nearly 5,000 ships had already moved into position the night before, Ike made the risky decision to proceed—and so at 2 A.M. on June 6, 1944, the "longest day" began.

Along the assigned British beaches and at Utah, the westernmost American landing site, the assault went well. But at Omaha beach, as schoolchildren should know, the story was a different one: there, an elite German division occupying high bluffs studded with pillboxes threatened a massacre of the American invaders, who prevailed to advance inland only by a demonstration of uncommon valor and ingenuity.

The complex planning required for the D-Day invasion is evident in the landing maps that were used by Allied officers. Replicas of these—indistinguishable from the originals—are available in a limited edition from Greg Koyaides of Reston, Virginia. This pair of five-color maps, originally prepared in April of 1944, cover Omaha beach and are rendered in perfect detail.

Price: $24.95 for the set of two.

D-Day Maps

P.O. Box 2309
Reston, VA 22090

Full Length Waterproof Cover

For rifles or shotguns that do not take down or for takedown models that are desired left put together. This case is handy in traveling from point to point in automobiles as the gun can be slipped into the case and thus protected without the bother of frequent taking down and reassembling. Especially made for carbines and bolt action rifles and automatic shotguns.

Cover is tan heavy duck full canvas bound with heavy leather protector opposite the lock and also at muzzle. Leather handle and sling. Flannel lined. Always give manufacturer's name, model and length of barrel and the length over all of your gun or rifle. Shipping weight. 1 pound.
6K910 .... $1.48

Folding Waterproof Gun Case

Tan color canvas, reinforced ends, leather muzzle protector, with sling strap and handle. Flannel lined. For single, double or pump guns with 26, 28, 30 or 32-inch barrels. Mention length of barrel. Shipping wt. 1¾ lbs.
6K917 .... $1.79

Shotgun Cleaning Outfit
Nine Articles

Outfit consists of one hardwood three-joint cleaning rod, one wool swab, one slotted cleaning tip, one wire scratch brush, one Tomlinson gauze, spring center, one gun oil and other articles.

Four Piece Brass Cleaning Rod

Each joint is about 6½ inches long and, when put together the rod is about 30 inches long. Wood handle. Shipping weight.
6K658—32 caliber ....
6K659—For 25, 30 and 30-caliber. State

Brass Rifle Brush

Brass Wire Brush to fit 6K658 and 6K659 Cleaning Rods. Brass shank. Especially made for cleaning rust and burnt powder out of rifles. Shipping weight, 2 ounces.
6K662—22-caliber .... 2 for 19c
6K663—25-caliber .... 2 for 19c
6K664—30-caliber .... 2 for 19c
6K665—32-cal. for .... 2 for 19c
6K666—38-cal for .... 2 for 19c

Hoffman's Gun Blueing Solution

Make your old gun barrels look like new. No experience required and only 20 minutes of your time in your own home will give surprising results. We have tried this blueing in our own gunshop with very satisfactory results. Put up in 4-ounce bottles. Shipping weight, 1 lb.
6K590 .... $1.69

Leather Shotgun Case for Single, Double and Repeating Shotguns

Dark russet leather and fiber reinforced. Canton flannel lined, reinforced bottom seam, leather handle and sling, brass trimmings, inside rod pocket. For single, double and repeating shotguns only. 26, 28, 30 or 32-inch barrels. State length. Shipping weight, 4½ pounds.
6K905 .... $5.79

Flylock Automatic Safety Outdoor Knife
For Hunter, Fisherman, Trapper, Tourist and Camper

Operates with one hand by pressing and sliding button. Locks closed or open. 3¾-inch Crocus polished stainless steel blade, with serrated back for scaling fish. Nickel silver lining, bolster and back. Stag pattern handle, 5 inches long, with hole in end for thong or charm. Often sold elsewhere as high as $2.50. Shipping weight, 5 ounces.
6K7090 .... $1.98

MARBLE'S GUN NEEDS

MARBLE'S GUN NEEDS

Marble's Anti-Rust Rope

When saturated with oil this rope excludes air and moisture, preventing barrels from becoming rusted or pitted. Rope gives a constant pressure of oil against entire inner surface of barrel. One oiling will last a year.
Shpg. wt., 6 oz.
6K551—12-gauge ....49c   6K553—25-caliber ...49c
6K552—16-gauge ....49c   6K556—30 & 32-cal...49c
6K553—20-gauge ....49c   6K557—35 & 38-cal ..49c
6K554—32-caliber ..49c   6K558—45 & 410-cal.49c

Marble's Jointed Brass Rifle Rod

Joints are reinforced steel. Strong and rigid as a one-piece rod. Has strong wood handle. Shpg. wt. 1 lb.
..25-caliber 98c
..30-caliber and larger..98c

Marble's Rifle Cleaner

Made of soft brass gauze, separated by fiber discs. Strung on spiral steel tempered wire. Will not injure rifle or rod. Shpg. wt., 4 oz.
6K568 ...caliber ... 39c
6K569 ...caliber ... 39c   6K572 ..caliber ... 39c
                          6K573 ..caliber ... 39c
                          6K574 ..and 40-cal. 39c
                          6K575 ..caliber ... 39c

Marble's Shotgun Cleaning Rod

Made in three sections of ¼-inch solid light metal. Has end for holding cleaning rag or brush. Strong wood handle. Put up in cloth bag.
6K560—Shpg. wt., 1 lb. 87c

Marble's Shotgun Cleaner

Made in sixteen sections of soft brass gauze, separated by fiber discs. Gives even pressure and will not injure inside of barrel. Cleaner lasts a lifetime. Shipping weight, 6 ounces.
6K562—12-gauge 59c
6K563—16-gauge 59c
6K564—20-gauge 59c

Remington's Dependable Gun Needs

Rem Powder Solvent

A superior dependable solvent for cleaning and removing powder residue from barrels of firearms. Very effective. Shipping weight, 8 ounces.
6K587 .... 24c

Rem Oil

Put up in 3-ounce can. Light oil of superior quality. Lubricates, prevents rust, cleans and polishes. Light enough for the most delicate mechanism. Shipping weight, 8 ounces.
6K588 .... 24c

Rem Gun Grease

A most serviceable rust preventative for firearms and other metals. Put up in soft metal tube. Shipping wt., 4 oz.
6K586 .... 12c

Rem Rust Remover

Removes rust from all metal surfaces. Specially recommended for firearms of all sorts and also good for other metal articles. Shpg. wt., 4 oz.
6K581 .... 19c

Leather Case for Single and Double Barrel or Repeating Shotgun

Good quality leather, fiber reinforced and lined. Brass trimmings, leather handle and shoulder sling. Furnished for 26, 28, 30 or 32-inch barrels. State length of barrel, make and model of gun.
6K919—Shpg. wt., 6¼ lbs. $6.59
6K920—For Remington Automatic Shotguns. State length of barrel......$6.79
6K921—For Winchester Automatic Shotgun $6.79

Victoria Waterproof Gun Case With Bag

Heavy tan color canvas, reinforced with leather, lock and muzzle protector and pocket for cleaning rod; also shell bag to hold fifty shells. For single, double or pump guns with 26, 28, 30 or 32-inch barrels. State length of barrel.
6K914—Shpg. wt. 1¾ lbs. $1.98
Same as 6K914, to fit Remington or Winchester Automatic Shotguns. State length of barrel.
6K915—Shpg. wt. 1½ lbs. $1.98

Light Weight Duck Gun Case

Tan color case for takedown shotgun. Has inside rod pocket. Lined throughout. For single, double or pump guns with 26, 28, 30 or 32-inch barrels. Give length of barrel.
6K916—Shpg. wt., 1 lb. 79c

Gun Cleaning Implements

Made of seasoned hardwood. Brass joints and three implements consisting of swab, scratch brush and wiper. State gauge.
6K650—36 inches long. 10, 12 and 16-gauge. Shpg. wt., ¾ lb. Per set..33c
6K651—36 inches long, 20 and 28-gauge. Shpg. wt., Per set..33c
6K652—45 inches long. 410-caliber. Shpg. wt., 7 oz. Per set 33c
6K663—48 inches long. 10, 12 and 16-gauge. Shpg. wt. ¾ lb. Per set . 39c

Tomlinson Cleaner

Removes lead and powder residue, and gives barrel thorough cleaning without injury. Shpg. wt., 3 oz.
6K639—12-gauge 25c
6K640—16-gauge 25c
6K641—20-gauge 25c

Brass Wire Brush

Wire brush for removing lead, powder caking and rust spots. Shipping weight, 3 ounces.
6K646—12-gauge 37c
6K647—16-gauge 37c
6K648—20-gauge 37c

Hoppe's Nitro Solvent No. 9

Keep Your Guns in the Finest Condition
This well known solvent has been on the market for more than 22 years and is known everywhere for its dependability. It is the original solvent for removing burnt powder from gun barrels. Shpg. wt., 8 oz.
6K591 .... 31c

HUNTERS' CAPS

HUNTERS' CAPS

Duck Cap

Made of khaki color waterproof duck. Body of cap and large cape are warm flannel lined. Excellent rough or cold weather cap. Cape can be folded inside. SIZES—6½ to 7¾. State size. Shipping weight, ½ pound.
6K5189 .... 69c

DeLuxe Hunting Cap

Made of best grade mahogany glove leather with sturdy eye shield and is warm earlaps, which can be let down in cold weather. A practical, fine quality and waterproof hunting cap. Sizes, 6½ to 7¾. State size. Shipping weight, 1 lb.
6K5193 .... $1.98

DeLuxe Sport Cap

A real quality cap for hunting and winter sport. Made of high grade mahogany glove leather and trimmed with the best heavy lambskin, close resembling fur. Visor can be worn up or down. Ear protectors can be tied up when weather is warm. Sizes, 6⅞ to 7¾. State size. Shpg. wt., 1 lb.
6K5192 .... $2.48

Jones Style Waterproof Hunting Cap

This cap is made of good grade waterproof khaki duck with extra strong reinforced brim and shield. Has corduroy lined earlaps, which can be folded back in cap when not in use. Cravat inner lining. SIZES—6¾ to 7¾. State size. Shipping wt., 1 pound.
6K5194 .... 98c

Finger Gloves

Our finger gloves are just the thing for hunting, shooting, driving and all other cold weather outdoor sports. They are as warm as a mitten, yet have the freedom of a glove. Made of soft, pliable glove leather, fleece lined, with close fitting knit wrists.
6K5188—Shipping weight, 8 ounces. $1.79

Safety First DeLuxe Hunting Cap

Reversible Red Lined Cap. Dead grass shade corduroy on outside and scarlet shade warm cotton flannel on inside. Opening on one side at bottom seam allows top part to be pulled over to cover the corduroy and bring scarlet side out. Inside turn-down lined band. SIZES—6¾ to 8. State size. Shipping weight, 1 pound.
6K5196 .... $1.10

All Weather Cap

Improved Hunting and Blizzard Cap. Heavy weight khaki color waterproofed duck, warm, serviceable cotton lining. Has inside band to pull down, lined with warm material. Noiseproof. Detachable warm lined cape so attached that rain or snow cannot run down neck or back. Can be worn as ordinary cap in mild weather, with band over ears in cold weather. SIZES—6¾ to 8. State size. Shpg. wt., 1 lb.
6K5199 .... $1.69

Camping Supplies from the Colorado Tent Company

The Colorado Tent Company was incorporated in 1901 by Robert S. Gutshall, grandfather of Robert C. Gutshall, now the third-generation proprietor. Their catalog contains a good variety of contemporary and traditional camping supplies ranging from wall tents to saddle bags. Below are a few early-twentieth-century examples of their offerings.

Woodsman Wall Tent

"**T**HERE is no business today that is so demoralized as the tent business," bemoaned the Sears, Roebuck catalog of 1908 as it worked itself into a pitch for its own line of Fulton tents. But as the Colorado Tent Company's tents have survived the Fultons, we must assume that whatever the failings of other turn-of-the-century tentmakers, Colorado Tent's pledge to "strive for quality and responsive service" has never faltered.

Nowadays, when there is much overreaching in the design and construction of tents, the traditional wall tent's commonsense approach to shelter still ensures quick run-off and ample snow-load resistance, while providing lots of headroom and floor space. The Woodsman is the Colorado Tent Company's most complete such tent, and is well suited to the company's description of a "comfortable camp headquarters."

Prices for the Woodsman range from $488 for a 42-lb. tent (8 feet wide, 10 feet long, and 6 feet 8 inches at center height) of 12.41-ounce white duck, to $1,502 for a 118-lb. tent (16 feet wide, 20 feet long, and 9 feet 8 inches at center height) of 7.35-ounce camper cloth with a fire retardant finish.

Tepee Tent

THIS TENT is derived from a pattern provided in 1934 by author-artist Ernest Thompson Seton, who had lived among the Indians of the Plains for several years. It is made from white duck fabric that can easily be decorated and has hand-sewn roping both in the main seam and along the edges of the smoke flaps. Guy ropes, wooden stakes, and stake beckets are included; lodge poles are not.

Prices range from $402 for a 33-lb. tent (12 feet in diameter and with a center height of 10 feet 6 inches) made from 12-ounce white duck, to $1,173 for a 135-lb. tent (24 feet in diameter with a center height of 20 feet) made of 14.9-ounce white duck. Zippered door flap and 12-ounce white duck liner are optional.

Colorado Camp Stove

"**S**IMILAR to the sheep herder stove of the early days," says the Colorado Tent Company catalog. "It will produce enough heat to keep a large wall tent comfortable during the winter weather." It's noncollapsible and has no oven. An 8- by 24-inch side shelf is included.

Dimensions: 12 inches wide, 26 inches long, and 8 inches high. Comes complete with four 22-inch pieces of nonstacking stovepipe and steel legs, all of which can be stored inside the stove for transport. Assembled, the top of the stovepipe extends to 9 feet. Shipping weight: 26 lbs.
Price: $150.

Payment of shipping charges (based on weight) is required in advance. Payment with order may be made by personal check, bank draft, or money order. MasterCard or VISA also accepted.

Catalog available.

The Colorado Tent Company
2228 Blake St.
Denver, CO 80205
Tel. 303/294-0924

Lever-Action Rifle

IN THE 1890s true gentlemen looked upon those who hunted for food with disdain. Dr. Elisha Lewis, publisher of the widely read *American Sportsman* magazine, contemptuously declared the "pot hunter" (actually a commercial as well as a traditional hunter of edible game) to be "the most disgusting, the most selfish, the most unmanly, the most heartless" of the hunting fraternity. No turn-of-the-century sportsman could be found shooting deer, duck, or geese without suffering the loss of his credentials as a gentleman, and so he manfully took on diminutive shorebirds and flocks of the tiny sora rail instead. In aid of this, single-shot rifles came to be replaced by repeating arms such as those introduced by the Winchester, Marlin, Bullard, Burgess, Colt, and Savage arms companies during the 1890s. The Savage company's lever-action Model 99 is still in production after more than ninety years, and features a four-round ejector clip that will accept both .243 and .308 Winchester cartridges.

Specifications: overall length, 41¾ inches; barrel length, 22 inches; pull length, 13½ inches. Weight: 8 lbs. Cartridge capacity: 5.

Brochure available.

Savage Industries, Inc.

Westfield, MA 01085

Gamekeeper's Bag

THIS lightweight **game bag** is handcrafted in England of khaki-colored jute and is fitted with brass rings and a leather shoulder strap. The bag expands to carry a load 20 inches by 20 inches by 20 inches.

Price: $49.

Color catalog available, $1.

Banana Republic

175 Bluxome St.
San Francisco, CA 94107
Tel. 415/777-0250 (for orders only, toll free 800/527-5200)

From L.L. Bean

Straight as a New England Jack Pine, Leon L. Bean lived to see the company he founded encompass markets far beyond its Maine watershed. With his famous Maine Hunting Shoe, "L. L." began his mail-order business in 1912, and over the years could claim such of the century's leading figures as Presidents Calvin Coolidge and Franklin Roosevelt, Babe Ruth, Jack Dempsey, John Wayne, Lowell Thomas, and Amy Vanderbilt to be among his loyal customers.

Items from the L. L. Bean catalog, Fall 1933

The Maine Hunting Shoe

HAVING abandoned its original rugged raison d'être to help create contemporary images, the Maine Hunting Shoe has become something of a Jeep CJ of footwear—racking up more miles in the pursuit of downtown game than in hunting the upland variety. For every pair of *these* that now trod the Allagash, a thousand others abide in the walk-in closets of the urban gentry, there to foster the impression that (if only Armani didn't attract black flies) their owners would really rather be out tracking bull moose with a crossbow.

But despite this appeal to the earn-your-age crowd, the L. L. Bean Hunting Shoe is still generally as cool as the beast it was intended to pursue. The offspring of the mating of a rubber overshoe with a cowhide boot, the Bean hunting shoe is perforce a bit silly looking . . . but as anyone truly familiar with moose can tell you, that's just part of its charm.

The Bean Maine Hunting Shoe has uppers made of top-grain cowhide that will not stiffen with wetting and drying. Its bottoms are long-wearing rubber and feature crêpe outsoles permanently vulcanized into the trademark L. L. Bean chain tread.

Bean's Chamois Cloth Shirt

THERE seems to be some confusion up in Freeport regarding the time when "the shirt that Mr. Bean used on his hunting and fishing trips" was first introduced. The 1985 Bean catalog cites 1927 but, as Public Affairs Director Melissa Arsenault informs us, that year rather saw the introduction of the Bean *leatherette* shirt, a far more expensive item that would be replaced by chamois (at $2.15, ppd.) in the fall of 1933. The chamois cloth shirt uses a tightly woven 7-ounce cotton flannel that has been thickly napped on both sides. It features double-needle stitching, two large chest pockets with button flaps, long sleeves, and deep tails. Available in navy, dark green, bright red, sage green, ivory, and slate gray in addition to the natural chamois yellow that authenticity demands.

Prices: men's regular sizes 14½ to 20 (no sizes 18½ or 19½ available), $19.75.

Available in men's whole sizes only, 3 to 14 narrow and medium, and 5 to 14 wide. When in need of a half size, the company recommends that you order the next whole size down.

Prices: with 6-inch uppers (in brown and tan), $44.75; with 8-inch uppers (brown and tan), $48.75; with 14-inch uppers (brown only), $60.75; and with 16-inch uppers (brown only), $64.75.

Both the L. L. Bean Chamois Shirt and Maine Hunting Shoe are registered names of the L. L. Bean Company.

Seasonal catalogs obtainable.

L. L. Bean, Inc.
Freeport, ME 04033
Tel. 207/865-3111

Railroad Items

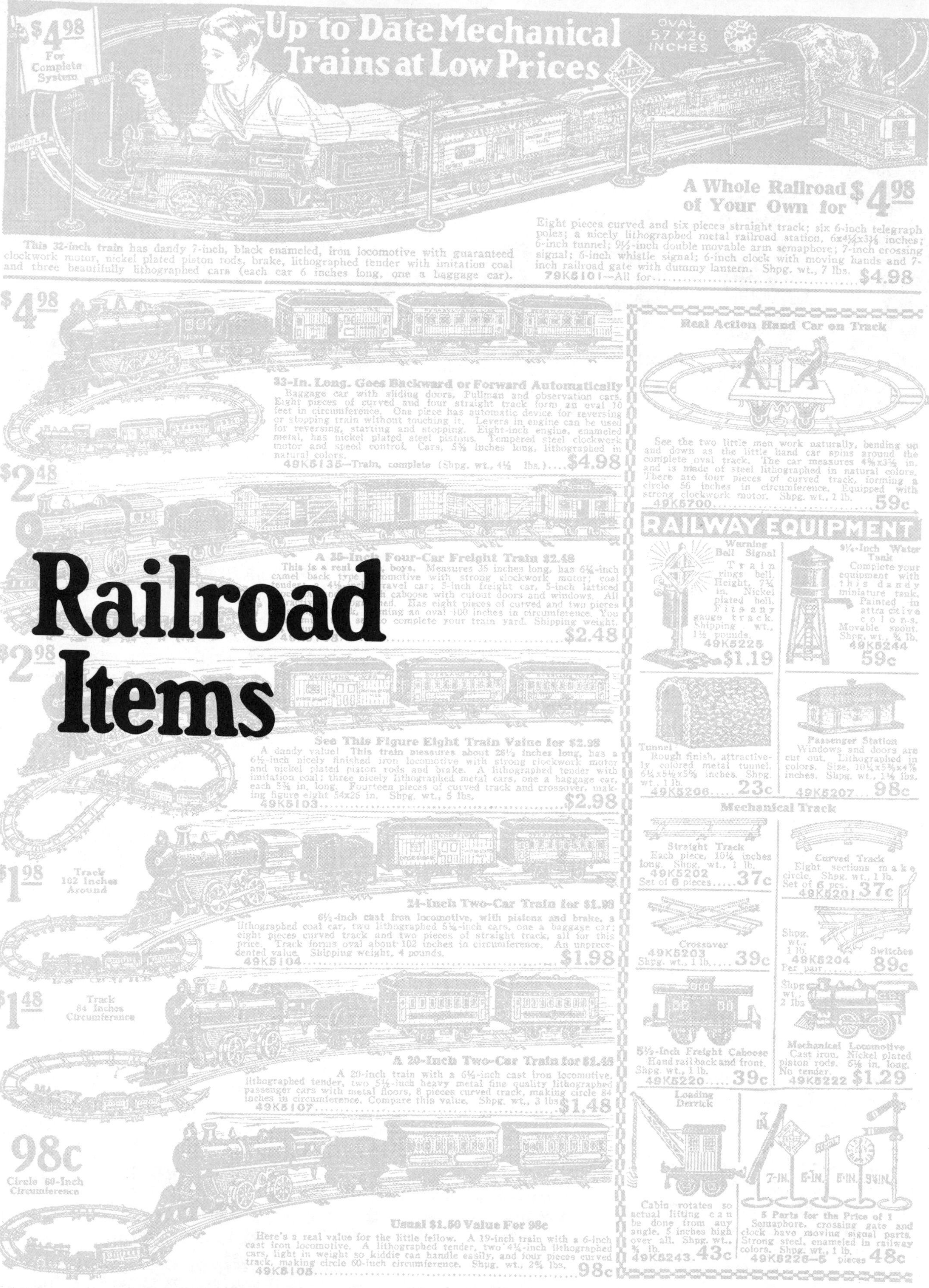

$4.98 For Complete System
Up to Date Mechanical Trains at Low Prices
OVAL 57 X 26 INCHES
WHISTLE
A Whole Railroad of Your Own for $4.98
This 32-inch train has dandy 7-inch, black enameled, iron locomotive with guaranteed clockwork motor, nickel plated piston rods, brake, lithographed tender with imitation coal and three beautifully lithographed cars (each car 6 inches long, one a baggage car).
Eight pieces curved and six pieces straight track; six 6-inch telegraph poles; a nicely lithographed metal railroad station, 6x4¼x3⅛ inches; 6-inch tunnel; 9½-inch double movable arm semaphore; 7-inch crossing signal; 6-inch whistle signal; 6-inch clock with moving hands and 7-inch railroad gate with dummy lantern. Shpg. wt., 7 lbs.
79K5101—All for........................$4.98
$4.98
33-In. Long. Goes Backward or Forward Automatically
Baggage car with sliding doors, Pullman and observation cars. Eight pieces of curved and four straight track form an oval 10 feet in circumference. One piece has automatic device for reversing or stopping train without touching it. Levers in engine can be used for reversing, starting and stopping. Eight-inch engine, enameled metal, has nickel plated steel pistons. Tempered steel clockwork motor and speed control. Cars, 5⅝ inches long, lithographed in natural colors.
49K5135—Train, complete (Shpg. wt., 4½ lbs.)....$4.98
$2.48
A 35-Inch Four-Car Freight Train $2.48
This is a real ..., boys. Measures 35 inches long, has 6¼-inch camel back type ...omotive with strong clockwork motor; coal tender, ... ravel car; 5-inch freight car, 5-inch latticed ... caboose with cutout doors and windows. All ... Has eight pieces of curved and two pieces ... an oval 100 inches in circumference. You ... complete your train yard. Shipping weight.
$2.48
$2.98
See This Figure Eight Train Value for $2.98
A dandy value! This train measures about 28½ inches long, has a 6½-inch nicely finished iron locomotive with strong clockwork motor and nickel plated piston rods and brake. A lithographed tender with imitation coal; three nicely lithographed metal cars, one a baggage car, each 5⅜ in. long. Fourteen pieces of curved track and crossover, making figure eight 54x26 in. Shpg. wt., 5 lbs.
49K5103........................$2.98
$1.98
Track 102 Inches Around
24-Inch Two-Car Train for $1.98
6½-inch cast iron locomotive, with pistons and brake, a lithographed coal car, two lithographed 5⅛-inch cars, one a baggage car; eight pieces curved track and two pieces of straight track, all for this price. Track forms oval about 102 inches in circumference. An unprecedented value. Shipping weight, 4 pounds.
49K5104........................$1.98
$1.48
Track 84 Inches Circumference
A 20-Inch Two-Car Train for $1.48
A 20-inch train with a 6⅛-inch cast iron locomotive, lithographed tender, two 5⅛-inch heavy metal fine quality lithographed passenger cars with metal floors, 8 pieces curved track, making circle 84 inches in circumference. Compare this value. Shpg. wt., 3 lbs.
49K5107........................$1.48
98c
Circle 60-Inch Circumference
Usual $1.50 Value For 98c
Here's a real value for the little fellow. A 19-inch train with a 6-inch cast iron locomotive. A lithographed tender, two 4¼-inch lithographed cars, light in weight so kiddie can handle easily, and four pieces curved track, making circle 60-inch circumference. Shpg. wt., 2¾ lbs.
49K5108........................98c
Real Action Hand Car on Track
See the two little men work naturally, bending up and down as the little hand car spins around the complete oval track. The car measures 4⅝x3½ in. and is made of steel lithographed in natural colors. There are four pieces of curved track, forming a circle 56 inches in circumference. Equipped with strong clockwork motor. Shpg. wt., 1 lb.
49K5700........................59c
RAILWAY EQUIPMENT
Warning Bell Signal
Train rings bell. Height, 7¾ in. Nickel plated bell. Fits any gauge track. Shipping wt., 1½ pounds.
49K5225 $1.19
9¼-Inch Water Tank
Complete your equipment with this dandy miniature tank. Painted in attractive colors. Movable spout. Shpg. wt., ¾ lb.
49K5244 59c
Tunnel
Rough finish, attractively colored metal tunnel. 6¼x5⅛x5⅝ inches. Shpg. wt., 1 lb.
49K5206.....23c
Passenger Station
Windows and doors are cut out. Lithographed in colors. Size, 10¼x5⅜x4⅞ inches. Shpg. wt., 1⅛ lbs.
49K5207... 98c
Mechanical Track
Straight Track
Each piece, 10¼ inches long. Shpg. wt., 1 lb.
49K5202
Set of 6 pieces.....37c
Curved Track
Eight sections make circle. Shpg. wt., 1 lb.
Set of 6 pcs.
49K5201 37c
Crossover
49K5203
Shpg. wt., 1 lb.....39c
Shpg. wt., 1 lb.
Switches
49K5204
Per pair........89c
5½-Inch Freight Caboose
Hand rail back and front. Shpg. wt., 1 lb.
49K5220.....39c
Shpg. wt., 2 lbs
Mechanical Locomotive
Cast iron. Nickel plated piston rods. 6⅛ in. long. No tender.
49K5222 $1.29
Loading Derrick
Cabin rotates so actual lifting can be done from any angle. 5 inches high over all. Shpg. wt., ¾ lb.
49K5243. 43c
7-IN. 7-IN. 6-IN. 6-IN. 9¾IN.
5 Parts for the Price of 1
Semaphore, crossing gate and clock have moving signal parts. Strong steel, enameled in railway colors. Shpg. wt., 1 lb.
49K5226—5 pieces 48c

Steam Freight

ON a stark morning in January 1985, steam engine No. 614 emerged importantly from the Huntington, West Virginia, yard, her huge black wheels turning in time, her smokestack sending up great puffs of steam to disappear into the haze of the surrounding peaks. In an experiment to show the bottom-line efficiency of a return to steam power for the transport of rail freight, the morning seemed dressed appropriately in a business-like black-and-white, the only color present being the emotional kind—inspired by the realization that No. 614 was something more than a performer in a period piece: "Just look at it," breathed one rail buff as the engine rolled majestically past, "the smoke, the pistons—it's alive!"

Engine No. 614 was at the start of her run down to Hinton, an old railroad town located at the confluence of the New and Greenbrier Rivers. Hauling 3,400 tons (equal in weight to about a fifty-car Amtrak train) she began a series of trips on the Chessie System tracks that were the first made since steam was taken out of regular service in West Virginia almost thirty years ago. Even back then, diesel fuel had long before demonstrated its economic efficiency over the coal-fired steam engine; but today, as Ross Rowland, chairman of American Coal Enterprises, claims, the reverse may be true: "The coal is here," he stated, "and it's cheaper to use per energy unit than diesel. We need to reduce our dependence on foreign oil."

Long cognizant of the economic and environmental advantages that an advanced steam engine may hold over diesel as a prime mover of freight, Mr. Rowland bought Engine 614 in 1981, refurbished it, and founded American Coal Enterprises of Lebanon, New Jersey. The engine, built in 1948 by the Lima Locomotive Works of Lima, Ohio (it was one of the last steam locomotives built in this country), was then outfitted by Rowland as a rolling laboratory to assess the thermal efficiency of coal combustion and to produce data leading to the design of an entirely new steam engine. This unit, designated the ACE 3000, is now in the prototype stage.

In appearance, the sleek 3000 suggests a modern diesel engine far more than it does a traditional steam locomotive like the 614. For environmental reasons she will carry no stack, but the ACE 3000 will return the sound of the steam whistle to rail yards and country meadows. Mr. Rowland's optimism over steam's inevitability is shared by one who counts in the railroad business, Hays T. Watkins, chairman of CSX, Chessie's parent company. Mr. Watkins said that he looks forward to buying the first ACE 3000 "when, and not if, it proves itself to be efficient, practical, and economical."

For further information, contact:

American Coal Enterprises

P.O. Box 156
Lebanon, NJ 08833

Engine 614 on the road to Hinton, West Virginia, January 1985

RAILROAD EQUIPMENT

Railfinders of St. Louis, Missouri, is the mail-order division of the Handlan-Buck Company, a railroad equipment supplier since 1856. In the manufacture of their railroad lamps, lanterns, and tinware, Railfinders utilizes original dies and specifications that date back to the mid-nineteenth century. Railfinders' tinware and lamps are handcrafted in the U.S. from brass and galvanized steel.

Oil and Kerosene Lamps

The New York Central Railroad was built by Cornelius "Commodore" Vanderbilt (1794–1877) in 1853 to connect New York City with Buffalo. Through acquisitions, Vanderbilt was able to extend his line to Chicago in the 1860s. This provided the route for the celebrated *Twentieth-Century Limited* to travel beginning in 1902.

Bunk Car Lamp

RAILFINDERS' bunk car lamp is available in either a solid-brass or an antique-brass finish, and is embossed with the Vanderbilt line's "NYCS" brand.

Dimensions: 13 inches by 7 inches.

Price: Railfinder catalog #519, solid brass, $49.95; antique black, $37.95.

Pennsylvania Railroad Caboose Oil Lamp

Dimensions: 21 inches by 5 inches.

Price: Railfinder catalog #529, brass, $69.95; black, $48.95.

Adlake Kerosene Lantern

Price: Railfinders catalog #300, $55.95 with clear, red, or amber globe; $68.95 with blue or green globe.

Switch Lamp

RAILFINDERS' kerosene-fired switch lamp is equipped with red, green, or amber 5⅝-inch regulation lenses with hoods. Dimensions: 19½ inches by 11 inches.

Price: Railfinders catalog #150, railroad black enamel, $116.95; brass or copper, $134.95; for a switch lamp complete with day targets instead of hoods, add $12.

Rear End Marker

THIS CABOOSE tail light is equipped with 5⅝-inch regulation lenses (one red and three green or amber), and is kerosene fired.

Dimensions: 14½ inches by 9 inches.

Price: Railfinders catalog #79, railroad black enamel, $116.95; brass or copper, $137.95.

Railroad Tinware

Long Spout Oiler

Has a 1-quart capacity.
Dimensions: 28 inches by 4 inches.
Price: Railfinders catalog #4, galvanized, $13.95; solid brass, $30.95.

Galvanized Tallow Pot

Has a 3-quart capacity.
Dimensions: 6½ inches high and 14 inches wide.
Price: Railfinders catalog #156, $12.95.

Galvanized Lamp Filler

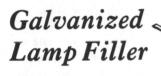

Has a 1-quart capacity.
Dimensions: 4½ inches high and 6 inches wide.
Price: Railfinders catalog #21, $12.95.

Galvanized Oil Can

Has a half-gallon capacity.
Dimensions: 8 inches by 5 inches.
Price: Railfinders catalog #27, $10.95.

Galvanized Journal Oiler

Has a 2-gallon capacity.
Dimensions: 26 inches by 10 inches.
Price: Railfinders catalog #90, $18.95.

Galvanized Dope Bucket

Has a 14-quart capacity.
Dimensions: 10½ inches high, 11½ inches wide at top and 8½ inches wide at bottom.
Price: Railfinders catalog #49, $16.95.

Galvanized Sprinkling Can

Has a 3-gallon capacity.
Dimensions: 12 inches by 9 inches.
Price: Railfinders catalog #47, $21.95.

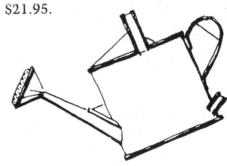

A minimum order of $20 is required, plus 10% for postage and handling.

Catalog available, $2 (refundable with order).

Railfinders
4519 Ridgewood Ave.
St. Louis, MO 63116
Tel. 314/353-1551

Super Chief *China*

Streamlining—the theory of industrial designers that a teardrop-shaped object moves more efficiently through the air—was first advanced by Norman Bel Geddes in his 1932 book *Horizons*. While such things as design theories rarely cause much of a popular stir, in its emotional wallop on the American public streamlining turned out to be the stylistic equivalent of the Lindbergh baby kidnapping.

Nobly proclaiming pure function as their Polaris, Bel Geddes et al. presented their streamlined vehicular designs like the grand viziers of a bright and impending future. Their subliminal message—that economic salvation's sweet chariot would have to have streamlined panels—was not lost on those caught in the Depression's galvanic grip . . . and soon no amount of streamlining ever seemed to be enough.

This meant that not only vehicles, but things with no more mobility than real estate, were to come in for the Bel Geddes treatment: streamlined office equipment, kitchen appliances, belt sanders, and drill presses began to appear wherever you looked. In the mid-1930s a teardrop-shaped meat slicer prepared the sandwiches of the future; a Raymond Loewy-designed pencil sharpener ground lead points unimpeded by the wind; and in a kind of apotheosis of misdirected design, the Oliver Plow Company brought out its streamlined manure spreader. Seeing it all, one might wonder if the Crash of '29 hadn't resulted from too much wind resistance on Wall Street rather than too little in the Dust Bowl.

Many of his colleagues believed that Bel Geddes's ideas about streamlining, while well suited to spreading manure, were in most other ways a joke. Yet few argued with the merits of streamlined design when applied to large vehi-

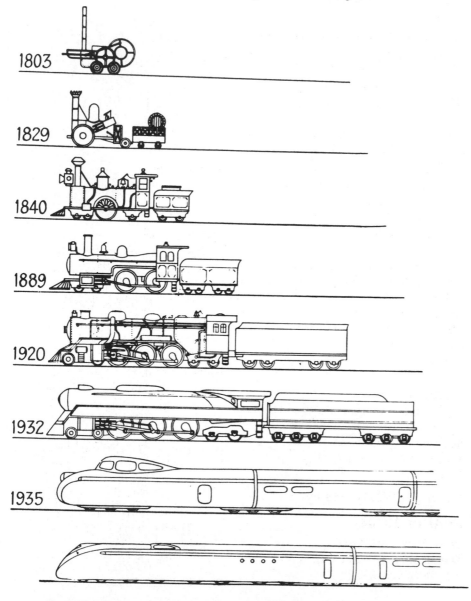

Although streamlining did not survive long after W.W.II, Raymond Loewy's "Evolution Chart of Locomotives" saw it as the pinnacle of design.

cles such as automobiles, boats, buses, and trains. Rarin' to leave hard times behind in machines raked for speed, Americans could hardly wait for the moment when they could board the streamliners and go. While sticker prices for the rakish 1934 Chrysler and DeSoto Airflows were way out of reach for many, by 1939 folks could climb aboard one of Raymond Loewy's streamlined Greyhound buses, or the Santa Fe Railway's *Super Chief* train.

The *Super Chief* wasn't rail's first streamliner (that honor went to the Union Pacific, whose streamliner was introduced at the Chicago World's Fair in 1934), but it was by far the best known. With a solid booking of movie stars and other fashionable types for its Los Angeles–Chicago run, the *Chief* was a hit from the time of its inaugural departure on May 18, 1937.

In many ways the *Super Chief* departed from ordained art deco doctrine as well. Instead of miles of stainless steel switching its way through decorative black enamel, the interior of the train was furnished in a traditional southwestern Indian motif; various native woods replaced steel on the bulkheads, and, drawing upon the Southwest's ancient sources of legend, craftsmanship, and color, interior designers Paul Cret and John Harbeson also furnished the *Super Chief* with Navajo sand paintings, carpets, and hand-hammered silver.

Moreover, every car on the train bore another unpronounceable Navajo name: Hoskini, Betahtakin, Oraibi, and for the diner, Mimbreño.

With the exclusive authorization of the Santa Fe Railway, Nostalgia Station of Baltimore has re-created the *Super Chief*'s beautiful Mimbreño dining car china. Based on the stylized animal design of the ancient Mimbres Indians, the ware is remarkably contemporary in its appeal.

Brochure of Mimbreño china, $1; railroadiana catalog, $2.

Nostalgia Station
1000 Light St.
Baltimore, MD 21230

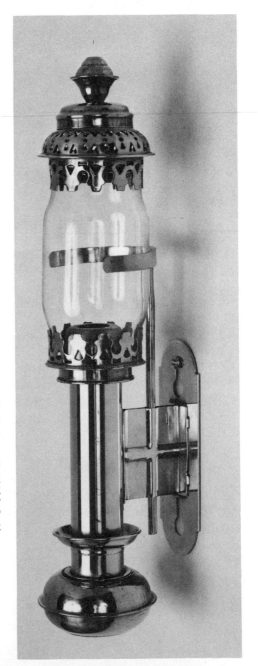

Dining Car Lamp

EARLY - TWENTIETH - century dining cars were run as elegantly as four-star restaurants with lengthy menus and monogrammed silver, glassware, and china. Certain lines became known for specialties in their cuisines, and passengers would be offered the regional delicacies of the states and provinces through which they passed. The Northern Pacific, for instance, which ran through the state of Idaho, was famous for its baked potatoes; and Bostonians riding the New York, New Haven & Hartford could combat their dining car's inevitable winter chill with baked beans served in individual pots.

Jenifer House's dining car lamp replicates one of a nonelectric and Victorian design. A self-adjusting spring mechanism in the lamp maintains its wick at a constant level.

Color gift catalog available.

Jenifer House
New Marlboro Stage
Great Barrington, MA 01230
Tel. 413/528-1500

Canadian Pacific Railway: Dining Car Service

A REPRINT of the manual published in 1926 for Canadian Pacific's dining-car personnel, complete with portion standards, prices, and table service requirements. **Price:** $7.50, 156 pages.

Catalog of collectible railway china, silver, linen, and paper items available, $1.

The Private Car Ltd.

Third and "A" Streets
Belleville, IL 62220

Railroad Pocket Watch

T HE face of Cumberland General Store's railroad pocket watch has large and plain black numerals against a white background. Engraved into the case back is the image of a steam locomotive. It comes in a nickel finish with matching chain.

Dimensions: 2⅛ inches by 2⅝ inches.

Price: $36.95, F.O.B. Crossville, Tennessee.

"Wish and Want Book" available, $3.75.

Cumberland General Store

Route 3
Crossville, TN 38555
Tel. 615/484-8481

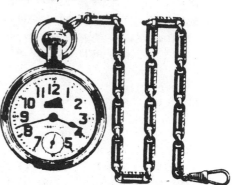

1928 Handy Railroad Atlas of the United States

T HIS reprint of the first railroad atlas produced by the Rand-McNally company shows, by state, America's entire 1928 railroad network. Included are all principal cities, towns, and junction points; interurban lines with their names and mileages; and a reprint of Rand-McNally's 1948 railroad listing—from North Carolina's Alexander Line to the Yreka Western Railroad—with a key to abbreviations. The metro maps that appear are from Rand-McNally's 1937 *Handy*.

Price: $6.25 (plus $1 per order for postage and handling, $1.50 outside the United States).

Kalmbach Publishing Company

1027 N. 7th St.
Milwaukee, WI 53233

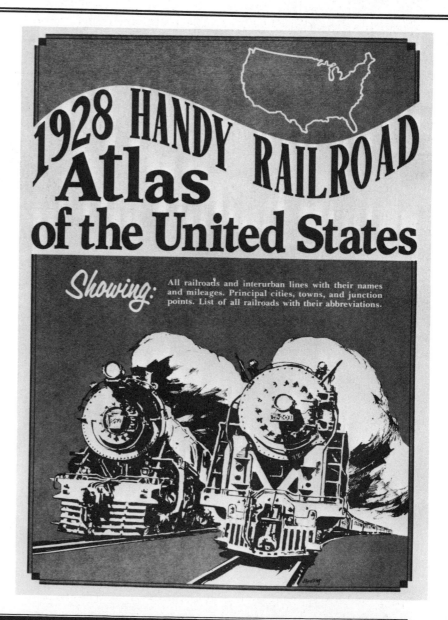

Milwaukee Railroad Locomotive Poster

ORIGINALLY PUBLISHED by the Milwaukee Railroad in **1938**, this poster carries photographs and descriptions of seventeen of the line's steam and electric locomotives. Notable among these is the *Hiawatha*, built in 1935 as one of the first streamliners. The *Hiawatha* is the most famous locomotive ever to have made the Chicago–Minneapolis run, along significant stretches of which it would attain speeds nearing 100 miles per hour.

Price: Vestal stock #R-3, $2 (plus $2 for shipping and handling).

Catalog of book and industrial manual reprints, $2.

The Vestal Press

P.O. Box 97
320 N. Jensen Rd.
Vestal, NY 13850
Tel. 607/797-4872

 90 Years of MILWAUKEE ROAD
Locomotive Progress

Heading for Home

The discharged veteran wears this emblem. Remember his service and honor him.

Know what the railroads are doing—now that the war is over?

They're moving troops! West Coast, East Coast, up and down and across the country—*more troops are moving right now than at any time during the war*—1,300,000 in November with still more coming in December, and it's going to be much like that for several months to come.

But this time they're headed mostly toward home, and although the job of handling so many in such a short time is another challenge, it's a job the railroads tackle with enthusiastic determination. Still in their fighting togs, they will keep right on—as they have done straight through the war—providing 97% of all the transportation for military personnel traveling under orders.

Plans for the future? Yes—the release of material which could not be had during the war has enabled railroads to get started on a large-scale program of improvements all along the line, including new locomotives, new and better cars and trains and more of them. They are looking ahead, and working with foresight and confidence to new high standards of efficient operation and service.

But first of all they're bringing these young men back home.

AMERICAN RAILROADS

—CARRIED MORE THAN 90% OF ALL MILITARY FREIGHT AND PASSENGERS—

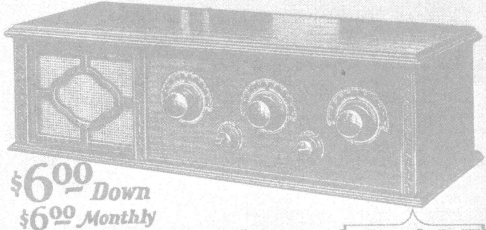

Cylindrical Wax Records

Mr. Garnet came to tea and he took a gramophone out of a black box and put a cylinder on the gramophone and they pushed back the teathings off the corner of the table. Be careful not to drop it now they scratch rather heasy. . . .
—JOHN DOS PASSOS, THE 42ND PARALLEL, 1929

BUT THE WAX cylinders made by Dennis Valente and Peter Dilg of the Electrophone Cylinder Record Company are made of stronger stuff and won't scratch "heasy" at all. From the vantage point of their business restoring and selling old Edison phonographs, Messrs. Valente and Dilg noticed that while there were still plenty of Edison gramophones around, there weren't many of the old cylindrical wax records that they needed to make music, as the last of these were manufactured in 1929. So, after acquiring some of the wax molds from Thomas Edison's original factory, and following much trial and error with a new wax, Valente and Dilg succeeded in reproducing cylindrical records of exceptional durability. In so doing, they found that the trailing edge of social change was not such a bad place to be in the commercial sense: "We are the first generation with an abandoned, once-flourishing, record industry at our disposal," reads their press release.

Electrophone's wax records reproduce not only the authentic sound of early classical, as well as ragtime, jazz, and other popular music, but they are also the best way to do so, according to Dilg, who notes that low-fidelity devices are more faithful to the peculiar tones and pitches of early-twentieth-century music than is today's sophisticated equipment. In addition to accepting two-minute tapes from customers for recording onto the cylinders, Electrophone also sells blank and prerecorded wax records. Among the latter currently available are Al Jolson's "About a Quarter to Nine," "Kansas City Kitty" by Johnny Walker and his Rollickers (1929), and "Turn on the Heat" by Don Neely's Royal Society Jazz Orchestra.

Finally, Electrophone Cylinder has furthered the preservation of original recordings in their original form by recently bringing out an "Everlasting" cylindrical record made of vinyl, a material that will never wear out. Oversize "Busy Bee" gramophone cylinder reproductions are also available.

Prices: shaved wax recording blanks, $8 each ($7 unshaved); vinyl blanks, $8.95 each; prerecorded cylinders, $10 to $20 (those mentioned above are $12 apiece).

Electrophone Cylinder Record Company

32 S. Tyson Ave.
Floral Park, NY 11001
Tel. 516/775-8605

Vintage Radio Programs

Reach for the sky! Lawbreakers always lose! Straight Shooters always win! It pays to shoot straight!
—TOM MIX'S CREDO OF VICTORY, THE "CODE OF THE WEST"

TOM MIX was Hollywood's first clean-living cowboy and, for a time, the greatest hero of them all.

Mix and his Wonder Horse, Tony, began riding the airwaves into Straight Shooters' radio sets in 1933, reminding each little range rider that success in the West also relied upon a nutritious breakfast of Ralston cereal. If "eating at least three bowls of Ralston every week" weren't enough to ensure the humiliation of bad guys (Ralston cereal, incidentally, was a favorite food of the *real* Sundance Kid!), the cereal's boxtops could also bring such treasures as Straight Shooter whistle rings, spurs, pocketknives, flashlights, and even a genuine Tom Mix six-shooter.

The Tom Mix adventure serials are just one of more than 700 old-time radio shows that have been recorded on one-hour cassette tapes by BWP Radio of Gainesville, Florida. These shows were broadcast over a period ranging from the Thirties through the Fifties and include such favorites as the "Aldrich Family," "Amos and Andy," "Boston Blackie," "Buck Rogers," "Captain Midnight," "The Cisco Kid," "The Fat Man" ("There he goes now, into that drugstore. He's

stepping on the scale. Weight? Two hundred thirty-nine pounds. Fortune? Danger!"), "Grand Ole Opry," "The Green Hornet," "Jack Benny," "The Lone Ranger," "Mr. and Mrs. North," "Our Miss Brooks," "Phillip Marlowe," "Sergeant Preston of the Yukon," and "The Whistler."

Prices: 1 to 10 cassettes, $5 each (plus $4 for postage); 11 to 20, $4.50 each (plus $5 for postage); 21 or more, $4 each (plus $6 for postage). Canadian residents must add $1 per cassette ordered.

Catalog available, $2.

BWP Radio, Inc.

Suite 9-E
1105 N. Main St.
Gainesville, FL 32601

Silent Film Comedies

LTHOUGH D. W. GRIFFITH is remembered as America's early film genius, it was Mack Sennett who, with his Keystone Comedies, first made us a nation of moviegoers. Sennett, a former circus and burlesque performer, began his movie career as a writer and actor for New York's Biograph Studio in 1909. He followed Griffith and the burgeoning silent-film industry to California in 1912 where, at the age of twenty-eight, he opened his famous Keystone Studio in the Los Angeles suburb of Glendale.

Of such players made famous by Sennett as Buster Keaton and Ben Turpin, Laff-O-Graph Studios' Bill Shelley says, "As a kid, I loved these old-time comedians and wished I could be like them. Now my dream is coming true!"

Villain Russ Rieley (right) with Laff-O-Graph's Bill Shelley between takes on the set of "Blacker Daze."

Mr. Shelley, whose Laff-O-Graph is the only studio in the world producing new silent-film comedies, is likely making the dreams of others come true in the process.

Laff-O-Graph began in 1981, when Mr. Shelley was only twenty. He describes its first hit as "the simple story of a boy who takes a waiter's job in a restaurant to win the hand of a girl. He seems to goof everything up, causing havoc with customers, starting a pie fight, and eventually blowing the place up with a hidden stick of dynamite!" This comedy is called *Blacker Daze,* and its cast includes (besides Mr. Shelley) comedienne Miss Jeanne Dickey and "a host of comics who can take pratfalls, tumbles, and a well-timed pie in the face." *Blacker Daze* has been shown, along with such other Laff-O-Graph comedies as *Waiting for Sweetie,* on Manhattan Cable TV and in New York's Orpheum and Beekman Theaters. Each film runs from five to ten minutes (known during the Twenties as a "split-reel," or "one-reeler") and authentically uses period automobiles, costumes, furniture, and a hand-cranked 16-mm camera specially altered "to give the right projected speed." Laff-O-Graph's comedies depart from absolute purity in that they employ soundtracks—but the sounds thereon have been limited to those made by old 78-r.p.m. records, player-piano rolls, and, in some cases, new bands playing old music. Mr. Shelley is presently discussing production of his first "talkies" with Peter Dilg, whose Electrophone Recording Studios are described above.

Clara Bow was pretty, but Miss Jeanne Dickey could be the "It" girl of the Eighties.

Mr. Shelley has made *Blacker Daze* available for purchase, lease, or rental, both privately and by television stations. In addition, "Laff-O-Graph Classics," videotape recorded versions of silent comedies from Mr. Shelley's private collection (speeds have been corrected and vintage music added) are also available from Mr. Shelley by mail order.

Kitchen set for "Blacker Daze" reflects Laff-O-Graph's attention to authentic period detail.

Laff-O-Graph Studios

c/o Mr. Bill Shelley
2307 Harrison Ave.
Baldwin, NY 11510
Tel. 516/868-7379

Wurlitzer "Bubble-Tube" Jukebox Cabinets

THE WORD "jukin" wound down to us from African roots to mean "raising hell," and making the rounds of dives and roadhouses to do it. By the early Forties these places began to be called "juke joints," and their dance music was played by record machines called "jukeboxes." As the following item duplicates a 1946 jukebox cabinet, it replicates something outside the official (1900–1945) scope of this book. But something like a bubble-tube Wurlitzer is just too good to pass up, particularly when it's accompanied by such excellent lore as has been provided by Ken Wojdyla of the Antique Jukebox Emporium:

> In 1946 the Rudolph Wurlitzer Company pulled out all the stops to produce a jukebox that had the pizzazz people were looking for after the war. Complete with side color wheels, new die castings, formed plastics, and the bubble tubes that made it famous, the Model 1015 was the most popular jukebox of the "light-up" era. Wurlitzer's Paul Fuller designed this machine—the best known and loved jukebox of all time.
>
> During the period from 1946 to 1947, the shipment of 56,000 Model 1015s was accompanied by the largest promotional campaign in jukebox history. In the age and time when the name of a jukebox could determine the success of a bar or restaurant, napkins, swizzle sticks, coasters, decals, tablecloths, magazines, and billboards together raised the chorus that "Wurlitzer *is* Jukebox."

When it was first manufactured the 1015 sold to distributors for about $750, less quantity discounts that could range up to 40%. Prices fluctuated downward during the next twenty years, and in the 1960s original Model 1015s could be found for as little as $35. Yet ten years later the same jukebox would sell for close to $300, and in 1985 a Model 1015 in restored condition would bring as much as $7,500.

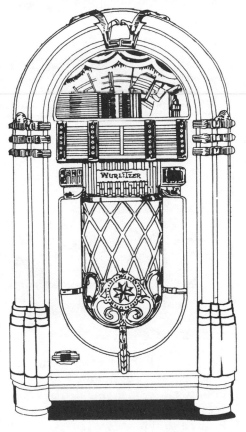

Jukeboxes seem to have sentimental value for all kinds of people—movie producers, doctors, rock and roll stars, oldtime hipsters, lawyers, assembly-line workers—and others from almost every walk of life. All seem to want to bring back a bit of the jukebox's Golden Age, and to relive some of their own by-gone days.

Mr. Wojdyla's Wurlitzer Model 1015 cabinets are not restored antiques but newly replicated items. Each has been fully veneered, stained, finished, and predrilled.

Information on models complete with hardware available.

Price: $1,795 (plus shipping).

Antique Jukebox Emporium

7S. 066 Suffield Court, #202
Westmont, IL 60559
Tel. 312/968-0176 or 863-0034

FROM THE VESTAL PRESS

Rock-Ola Poster

A REISSUE of the Rock-Ola Corporation's 1933 jobber-mailer to operators (those men who owned "routes" of machines), the poster shows the then-current Mills, Jennings, Watling, Pace, and Caille lines. Black-and-white printing on heavy cream stock, 18 by 24 inches.
   Price: Vestal Press stock #A-263, $6.

Radio Equipment and Supplies

A REPRINT OF A 1922 catalog of radio receivers, receiving accessories, transmitting equipment, and general information about the field of radio transmission. 168-pages, 8½ by 11 inches, heavy slick stock, illustrated.
   Price: Vestal Press stock #K-28, $12.50.

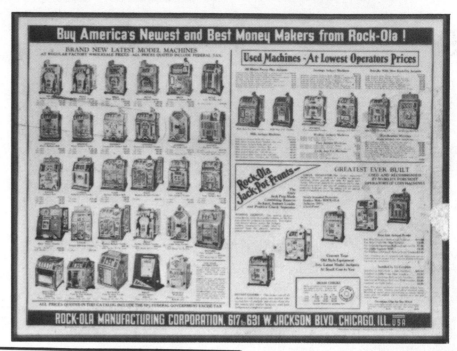

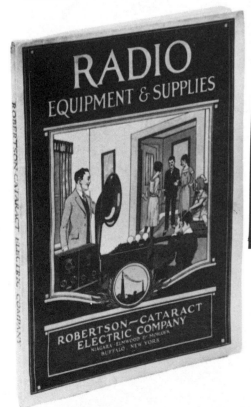

Phonograph Postcards

A SET OF nine early-twentieth-century postcards featuring phonograph machines that have been replicated from rare originals. Printed on postcard stock in sepiatone.
   Price: Vestal Press stock #A-270, $2.50.

Radio Enters the Home

A FACSIMILE edition of the book published by the Radio Corporation of America for its 1922 entry into the domestic U.S. market. In it, the 1922 line is set amid glowing depictions of family life. This book is now exceedingly rare in its original form. Paperback, 8½ by 11 inches.
   Price: Vestal Press stock #K-26, $12.50.

Crosley Radio Catalog

READ ALL ABOUT the Crosley Manufacturing Company's Condenso and Duo-Amplo units, as well as the Harko series, circa 1923. Paperback, 32 pages.

Price: Vestal Press stock #K-25, $4.

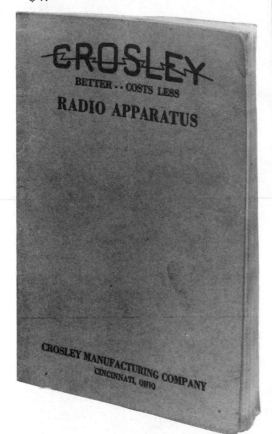

The Victor

V ictor Aux-e-to-phone
Price $500

From "The Victor," 1911

TAKEN from the Victor Talking Machine Company's 1911 catalog, this reprint features several of the firm's phonograph machines, Victrolas, and the theatrical Victor Aux-e-to-phone with their descriptions and prices. Included are testimonials from such luminaries of the musical world as Enrico Caruso, Nellie Melba, and Louise Homer.

Price: Vestal Press stock #A-154, $3.

Include $2 to cover the cost of postage and handling on all orders.

Catalog of period industrial book and manual reprints, $2.

The Vestal Press

P.O. Box 97
320 N. Jensen Rd.
Vestal, NY 13850
Tel. 607/797-4872

Original Movie Posters

BERGMAN'S *For Whom the Bell Tolls*, Bogart's *They Drive by Night*, Reagan's *Million Dollar Baby*, and hundreds more from the days of the Hollywood studio system.

Catalog available, $3.

Cine Monde

1916 Hyde St.
San Francisco, CA 94109

$29⁹⁵

Belber's
Guaranteed TRUNKS
as Low as $19⁷⁵

Belber's Wardrobe
$53⁹⁵ Equipped with Belber's Patented Safelock

$41⁹⁵

"Stratford" Wardrobe Trunk
Made by Belber

Box of three-ply veneer wood covered and interlined with vulcanized fiber. Open top. Wide vulcanized fiber binding. Four drawers including large bottom drawer with removable hat form. Shoe box, laundry bag, eight hangers, steel drawer locking bat.
6K9514¼—Size, 40x21½x20 inches. **$29.95**
Shipping weight, 82 pounds.

Steamer Size Trunk

Same style as above, excepting it has three drawers including one large tumbler drawer, shoe pockets, no locking bar. Six hangers.
6K9515¼—Size, 40x21½x14 inches. **$24.85**
Shipping weight, 68 pounds.

"Cadillac" Box Trunk

Vulcanized Fiber Covered Five-Ply Construction

Five-ply construction. This means three-ply basswood veneer covered and interlined with vulcanized fiber. Popular round edge style with metal skids which run lengthwise of the trunk, on the top and front. Deep top tray, full covered, and an extra dress tray. Brass plated lock and draw bolts. The body and binding are black. Lining is a neat pattern of good quality. Will positively give a great deal of service, as the construction is of the best.
6K9560¼—Size, 32x19x21 inches. **$12.95**
Shipping weight, 55 pounds.
6K9561¼—Size, 36x20½x23 inches. **13.95**
Shipping weight, 60 pounds.
6K9562¼—Size, 40x22x24¼ inches. **14.95**
Shipping weight, 65 pounds.

For Package Carrying Straps, See Page 1056

Large Size
Special Features

1. Good patented safe tumbler lock which locks or unlocks trunk in one operation, and does away with the draw bolts.

with removable hat form. Nickel trimming on drawers, and two large nickel drawer pulls. Steel bar drawer locking rod.

Removable ironing board, iron holder.

Sateen laundry bag with silk cord.

Patented shoe box which works in channel.

Box constructed of three-ply veneer wood covered and interlined with vulcanized fiber. All round edged, covered with closely nailed vulcanized fiber binding, steel runner. Open solid dome top with plush facing, with nickel hinge. Substantial brass plated steel hardware ... Open top and three heavy ... inches. Shipping ... **$53.95** ... packed as closely. ... has open dome top. Pat-... holds the clothes in place ... any hard pre-... **Shipping $46.95** ... weight, 95 pounds.
6K9512¼—Size, 42x ... inches. **$38.95**

Same as 6K9512¼, but has four drawers with neat pattern cloth lining. Patented clothes retainer which holds the clothes in place without any hard pressure. 8 hangers.
6K9511¼—Size, 42x21½x20 inches.
Shipping weight, 94 pounds. **$38.95**

Wardrobe Trunk
Made by Belber

Five-ply construction, which means three-ply veneer wood with vulcanized fiber covering and inter lining. Fitted with Belber patented massive hardware; riveted throughout. Patented new dustproof valances which prevent the dust from getting into the trunk. Soft curtain clothes retainer, ironing board, iron holder. Drawer locking device. This comprises all the necessary fittings to make a high grade wardrobe trunk. Lined with blue cloth with gold figures. An extremely durable as well as beautiful trunk. Size, 43x21½x22 inches. Shipping weight, 90 pounds.
6K9506¼. **$41.95**

"Sherman" Box Trunk

$14⁹⁵ 32-In.
Vulcanized Fiber Five-Ply Construction

Our best quality box trunk of five-ply construction, which means three-ply basswood veneer covered and interlined with vulcanized fiber. Round edges. Heavy hardware, partly hand riveted. Full cloth lined. Deep top tray with division for hat box. Extra dress tray. Has three double nailed fiber center bands which make it very strong and beautiful. Black body with blue center band, forming a beautiful contrast. Has high grade lock and draw bolts of superior quality. Leather handle at each end. Any traveler or tourist will be proud of this trunk.
6K9524¼—Size, 32x19x21 inches. **$14.95**
Shipping weight, 52 pounds.
6K9525¼—Size, 36x20½x22 inches. **15.95**
Shipping weight, 58 pounds.
6K9526¼—Size, 40x22x24½ inches. **16.95**
Shipping weight, 68 pounds.

For Trunk Straps, See Page 1057

$9⁷⁵ 32-In.
Lincoln Box Trunk, Metal Covered

Box of well seasoned lumber and covered with strong metal covering. Has two iron bands riveted at hinges and draw bolts, these bands completely encircle the trunk when draw bolts are fastened. The corners and all edges are protected with iron angles. Heavy brass plated draw bolts and spring lock. Has four hardwood slats on top and bottom and two all around body. Two leather handles. Fancy pattern paper lining, one tray, one end of which forms covered hat compartment.
6K9545¼—Size, 32x19½x21½ inches. **$9.75**
Shipping weight, 58 pounds.
6K9546¼—Size, 36x21½x23½ inches. **10.85**
Shipping weight, 70 pounds.
6K9547¼—Size, 40x22x24 inches. **11.95**
Shipping weight, 80 pounds.

$24⁴⁵ Regular Size
"Waldorf" Wardrobe Trunk
Made by Belber

Box of three-ply veneer wood with wide vulcanized fiber binding. Closed top with all round edges. Substantial brass plated steel hardware including snap lock, draw bolts, and three hinges in back. Neatly cloth lined, with shoe pockets and laundry bag to match. Extension clothes trolley, four drawers with removable hat form in large bottom drawer. Eight hangers.
6K9517¼—Regular size, 40x21½x20 inches. Shipping weight, 75 pounds. **$24.45**
As above, with three drawers including one large tumbler drawer. Six hangers.
6K9518¼—Size, 40x21½x14 inches. **$19.75**
Shipping weight, 60 pounds.

$7⁴⁸ 28-In.
"Harvey" Low Priced Trunk
Metal Covered—Leather Straps

Strong enough for all practical purposes. Box made of well seasoned lumber with metal covering, and bindings, with one slat all around body and three slats on top, leather handles at each end. The feature of this trunk is the two leather straps all around. Brass plated hardware including corners, lock and end catches. Very neatly lined. One dress tray and covered hat box at one end of tray. Especially suitable for home use to store wearing apparel and linens.
6K9551¼—Size, 28x17½x21 inches. **$7.48**
Shipping weight, 43 pounds.
6K9552¼—Size, 32x19x22 inches. **7.95**
Shipping weight, 55 pounds.
6K9553¼—Size, 36x20½x23 inches. **8.95**
Shipping weight, 65 pounds.

Travel and Lodging

Steamer-Class™ Cruises

YOU'LL NOTICE that these cruises, offered by the Coastwise Cruise Line of Hyannis, Massachusetts, are steamer-class ones. Steamer *class?* Now there's a suspicious-looking qualifier. Just what gives here? In December of 1984 Coastwise put the *Pilgrim Belle* into service. Its mission: To re-create "life as it was lived aboard the great coastal steamers of the 1880s to the 1920s." Unfortunately, as it turns out, the *Belle's* not really a steamship at all. In fact, if Dos Passos' character Mac McCreary had fallen in love (as he does above) aboard *her,* he wouldn't be quivering to steam engines, but to the throb of a couple of 1,055-h.p. diesel cats.

As it is with trains, there's a big difference between steam and diesel in the romance-of-the-past department. But while living-history purists may turn up their noses at the *Pilgrim Belle,* it should be allowed that Coastwise's attempt to at least replicate the *look* of an early-twentieth-century coastal steamer is a very interesting undertaking, even if compromised by various commercial considerations.

For one thing, the *Belle* was built for cruises, not the point-to-point transportation that was provided by the steamers she emulates. Therefore, a voyage aboard her necessarily begins with a brochure that itself churns with hyperbole, refusing to concede any trade-off between authenticity ("authentic period reproductions" abound onboard), luxury ("interior accents in beige, rose coral, and, of course, mahogany"), and all the modern amenities "expected by today's vacationer." Naturally, the fares for a cruise run to the modern as well: the cost of a seven-day voyage is a minimum of $875 per person, including onboard accommodations and ship's entertainment and meals.

The *Pilgrim Belle* departs from Hyannis for eight days from June through September for her New England cruise, and for seven days during October for the "Fall Foliage Spectacular." The Chesapeake Bay cruise lasts for seven days during October, November, April, and early May, departing from Alexandria, Virginia. For ten days in late November, early December, and April, the Virginia–Florida "Intracoastal Waterway and Colonial South" cruises are available. And for seven days in January, February, and March, the *Belle* embarks upon her Florida east coast cruises. In addition to these, a New England and a Floridian 3½-day mini-cruise are each available for booking.

For further information, contact:

Coastwise Cruise Line

P.O. Box 1630
36 Ocean St.
Hyannis, MA 02601
Tel. 617/778-6996

By Thanksgiving Mac had beaten his way to Sacramento, where he got a job smashing crates in a driedfruit warehouse. By the first of the Year he'd saved up enough to buy a suit of dark clothes and take the steamboat . . . to San Francisco. . . .

"Sure," said Mac. He walked on round the deck, his heart beating hard. He could feel the pound of the steamboat's engines and the arrow-shaped surge of broken water from the bow and he felt like that.

—JOHN DOS PASSOS,
THE 42ND PARALLEL, 1929

Sagamore Lodge and Conference Center

THE Adirondack forest followed Newport as the favored retreat of the northeastern business aristocracy at the century's turn. Here, rough-hewn palaces known as Adirondack Great Camps provided a suitable atmosphere for Whitneys, Vanderbilts, Astors, and other wealthy clans to rusticate in splendor both natural and man-made.

The Sagamore Lodge was first built in 1897 by William West Durant. From 1901 to 1954 (when it was donated for a time to Syracuse University) Sagamore was the Adirondack hermitage of Alfred G. Vanderbilt and his widow, Mrs. Margaret Emerson. It is now considered to be an outstanding example of Great Camp architecture and is listed in the National Register of Historic Places.

Situated on mile-long Sagamore Lake and surrounded by hundreds of thousands of acres of New York's boreal forest preserve, Sagamore in its day played host to this century's leading figures from the world of politics, entertainment, sports, high society, and, of course, finance. Today the lodge and surrounding log buildings will accommodate up to 100 "recreational weekend" guests in a setting that includes twenty-six stone fireplaces, a lakefront dining room, a blacksmith's shop, furniture shop, sugar house, many original turn-of-the-century furnishings, and an excellent library. Canoeing, rowing, swimming, bowling, badminton, tennis, horseshoes, eighteen miles of cross-country skiing, and "unlimited" hiking and mountain climbing are the recreational activities available.

Two-hour tours of Sagamore begin at 10 a.m., 1 p.m., and 3 p.m. daily from July 1 to October 15. These include a 45-minute slide presentation on the history of Sagamore and other Great Camps, and a walking tour of the buildings and grounds.

For additional information, contact:

Sagamore Institute

Sagamore Road
Raquette Lake, NY 13436
Tel. 315/354-5311

Hotel Algonquin

BUILT in 1905 on Manhattan's West 44th Street, the Hotel Algonquin is a beaux arts bastion of tradition.

Not straitlaced tradition mind you, emphatically not. For like the *New Yorker* magazine it helped spawn back in 1925 (and which guests receive free with breakfast), the Algonquin enjoys providing a predictable setting for the unpredictable to take place.

The hotel's immutability is key to this, and closely watched over by patrons. When Ben Bodne, the present owner (he bought the Algonquin in 1946), first undertook to replace the hotel's worn carpets, sofas, chairs, and beds, he had to do so stealthily, and by dark of night. "Here I was spending a fortune to make the guests more comfortable," he once recalled, "but couldn't let them find out."

Through this setting passes a variety of types: businessmen, lawyers, agents, a couple of Supreme Court Justices, as well as the many playwrights, novelists, and moviemakers for which the hotel has become a well-known shelter. Some among this last batch are every bit as colorful as the characters they've created.

Here, had he actually lived, is where Hercule Poirot might've charmed the curmudgeonly H. L. Mencken, or, were he both visiting New York and nonfictitious, where

Palmer House Hotel

LOCATED ON Main Street of Sauk Centre, Minnesota, the Palmer House has been restored to the 1901 appearance it had when novelist Sinclair Lewis worked there as a boy. The hotel has thirty-seven rooms, with baths located down the hall. A restaurant offering home-cooked meals is located on the premises.

Rates: single room, $13 to $20; double room, $18 to $27. No credit cards accepted.

Palmer House

500 Sinclair Lewis Ave.
Sauk Centre, MN 56372
Tel. 612/352-3431

Gulley Jimson could've been found regaling Tallulah Bankhead between quick shots of Napoleon Brandy. It is in fact where William Faulkner first met Thornton Wilder on an elevator; where James Thurber, Bette Davis, George M. Cohan, and Boris Karloff always stayed; and where Hamlet, the hotel's live-in cat, can still be found curled atop a stack of newspapers in the lobby.

The lobby is oak-paneled and nearly as wide as the narrow building itself. In it, couches, tables, divans, and armchairs are set asymmetrically into intimate clusters suggesting nothing so much as a cozy parlor. The lobby leads in its distinctly unceremonious fashion to the Oak Bar, where Brendan Behan put his bouts with sobriety to the test; to the Blue Room, which actually hasn't been blue for years; and to the Chinese Room, somewhat incongruous in a hotel named for an aboriginal northeast woodland linguistic group, but in keeping with its dotty English atmosphere.

The Algonquin's genteel tradition was greatly undercut by its famous Round Table group, the cluster of New York literati who met there every day in the Twenties to determine the precise status of everyone else in American culture. The Round Table's Arthur, the autocratic New York drama critic Robert Benchley, dined with George S. Kaufman, Heywood Broun, Dorothy Parker, Marc Con-

nelly, Franklin Adams, Robert E. Sherwood, and Harold Ross, and together their waspish dissection of others in the world of the arts also gave them the name of the Vicious Circle. Treading uncharacteristically near an apology, Dorothy Parker blamed the Round Table's ways on the times: "Silly of me to blame it on dates," she explained, "but so it happened to be. Dammit, it was the Twenties, and we had to be smarty."

In similar fashion, the Algonquin's celebrated sedateness is also sometimes allowed to slip. This is never more evident than at midnight each New Year's Eve when, following a tradition that erupted spontaneously a generation ago, the hotel's entire staff marches through the lobby, banging huge kitchen pots with spoons and ladles like a Chinese New Year and fire drill combined.

Perhaps it's whimsy, then, that saves the Algonquin from any expression of self-importance. In "the

unicorn of big-city hotels" there are no little historic sites, no F. Scott Fitzgerald or Edna Ferber Memorial Guest Rooms. True, a cadre of regulars known as "friends of the house" are used to having their wishes anticipated by the staff, but first-timers and bigwigs alike are always catered to as if by family—one effusively happy to have them as guests, but too dignified to show it overmuch. For, as sure as chimes announce cocktails at the Algonquin, warmth and camaraderie are fostered there too. As *New Yorker* magazine theater critic Brendan Gill put it, the Algonquin's "a place that makes one feel happy among strangers."

Open all year, serving breakfast, lunch, and dinner.

Hotel Algonquin
59 W. 44th St.
New York, NY 10036
Tel. 212/840-6800; Telex 66532;
Cable ALGONQUIN, New York

Plaza Hotel

Several times he turned his head and looked for their car, and if the traffic delayed them he slowed up until they came into sight. I think he was afraid they would dart down a side street and out of his life forever.

But ·they didn't. And we all took the less explicable step of engaging the parlor of a suite in the Plaza Hotel.

—F. SCOTT FITZGERALD,
THE GREAT GATSBY, 1925

WHEN the Plaza Hotel opened in October of 1907, it was acclaimed not only as an engineering marvel (the Plaza boasted ten elevators, twelve electric dumbwaiters, nine steam dynamos, and an early form of air conditioning), but with its specially imported Aubusson tapestries, Ravenna mosaics, Savonnerie rugs, and other custom-designed appointments, it was undeniably the epitome of a lavish Edwardian hostelry. When one reads of the Vanderbilts, Dukes, Harrimans, and Wanamakers who moved in the first day, one half expects the Plaza to hit an iceberg and sink beneath the cobblestones of Manhattan's Grand Army Plaza.

But despite all the monied elegance, architect Henry Hardenburgh's design for this French renaissance château on Central Park South and Fifth Avenue has invested the place with a relaxed and cheerful atmosphere for more than three-quarters of a century. This may be why as early as 1908 the *New York World* dubbed it the "Pa-La-Za"; why, like Fitzgerald, many artists and writers have expressed their affection for it in their work; and why even Frank Lloyd Wright once gushed forth with the confession that he liked it almost as much as if he'd built it himself.

Rates: singles, $125 to $160 standard, $230 medium, $305 deluxe, and $330 park view; twins and doubles, $190 standard, $250 medium, $305 deluxe, and $330 park view; one-bedroom suites, $415 standard, $570 medium, and $700 deluxe; two-bedroom suites, $880; and the Plaza Suite, $900.

Plaza Hotel

Fifth Avenue at 59th Street
New York, NY 10019
Tel. toll free 800/228-3000, or 212/759-3000

Copley Plaza Hotel

THE **"Grande Dame" of Boston,** the Copley Plaza Hotel formally opened on August 19, 1912, when Mayor John F. Fitzgerald ("Honey Fitz," grandfather of President John Kennedy) led civic leaders, captains of industry, stars of stage and screen, and more than 1,000 guests to what one newspaper termed "one of the most colorful and brilliant pictures the city has ever seen."

Designed by Henry H. Hardenburgh, who was also the architect of New York's Plaza Hotel, the Copley Plaza has hosted every president since William Howard Taft, as well as royalty from throughout the world. History's lesser lights attended the popular Thirties tea dances that were held in the Oval Room (where more people have been married than in Trinity Church, next door); and debutantes in gardenia corsages and their escorts once nicknamed the place the "Costly Pleasure," while from the dance floor Rudy Vallee crooned to them of love everlasting in a world west of war.

Open all year, serving breakfast, lunch, and dinner.

The Copley Plaza

138 St. James Ave.
Copley Square
Boston, MA 02116
Tel. toll free 800/225-7654, or 617/267-5300

Steam Rail Excursions

Cass Scenic Railroad

AN early-twentieth-century logging road that for sixty years hauled lumberjacks from the company town of Cass deep into the Appalachian Mountains, the Cass line was taken over by the state of West Virginia and more recently listed in the National Register of Historic Places. Passengers ascend steep grades through the wilderness in former logging cars and cabooses that are pulled by steam locomotives. The 22-mile trip takes 4½ hours to complete.

Operates from May through October.

For further information, contact:

Cass Scenic Railroad
Cass, WV 24927
Tel. 304/456-4300

Edaville Railroad

THE Edaville's 5½-mile line originally labored in the harvesting of more than 200 acres of cranberry bog nearby Cape Cod, Massachusetts. Today the bogs are still visible to tourists as they take the railroad's 30-minute trip over a narrow-gauge road. The Edaville's locomotive dates from 1913, and its vintage cabooses and coaches feature wrought-iron and leather appointments and mahogany seats.

Operates from May through January each year.

For further information, contact:

Edaville Railroad
P.O. Box 7
South Carver, MA 02566
Tel. 617/866-4526

Rustic Roads of Wisconsin

INVISIBLE from the Interstate, Wisconsin's Rustic Roads emerge from the industrial haze like the byways of Brigadoon. A special state board now protects some 300 miles of these specially selected roads—a sinewy historical site winding its way through rural dairyland.

Board chairman Earl Skagen was once the highway commissioner of Racine County. As such, he may seem a renegade Babbit to some when he describes the vision that has made him the driving force behind this "positive step backward." But there's a spirit in what he says with the potential to quiver the collective wattles of the most old-school (and pro-development) Chambers of Commerce. "I want to see the roadsides grow up wild," he explained in Emersonian tones, "to see the woods go untouched, and the character of the farmland remain unchanged." Motoring at the required 45 m.p.h. through this endangered landscape of tree tunnels, grazing livestock, wildflowers, winding streams, and early-twentieth-century barns fosters a contagion of this sentiment, and with it a feeling that it's a sensible (including business-sensible) as well as a noble one. "There is a need for high-speed highways," the former county commissioner went on, "but there's also one for preserving these beautiful roadsides where people can enjoy themselves."

And this they do. For while a trip down Wisconsin's Rustic Roads isn't as exciting as threading the pylons at the Nevada Air Races, you don't need to be blue-haired to be won over by the charm, living history, and sense of balance between man and nature it offers.

Brochure and maps available.

Rustic Roads
Wisconsin Department of Transportation
P.O. Box 7913
Madison, WI 53707
Tel. 608/266-2972

A new old-fashioned Brigham's

Brigham's Restaurants

BRIGHAM'S, **a Massachusetts restaurant chain,** began as the Durand Company on Boston's Post Office Square in 1914. Until America entered World War I, Durand produced all of its candy right down in the basement.

But during the Twenties the Jazz Age brought with it an acceptance of headier pleasures, and the per-capita consumption of candy declined. Now, women in particular would sooner "reach for a Lucky instead of a sweet," and bootlegging would make bathtub gin as easy to come by as pecan truffles.

Durand compensated by expanding its line to include ice cream, and brought in Edward Brigham, a maker of quality ice cream, in 1929. The new shop, named Brigham's, has since expanded to include seventy-eight restaurants (meals are now also served) throughout the state. But what customers still remember most is Brigham's old-style ice cream.

Not the least of all that's changed about Brigham's over the decades has been the decor, which since the Bicentennial has been a glaring red, white, and blue affair doing as little for your appetite as it does for your patriotism. But today, thanks to the efforts of new owners Fred and Richard Johnson, this setting is being replaced with one that's ideal for savoring Brigham's 1920s-style ice cream. The old-fashioned decor is *new* stuff—not a restoration—and it is the result of diligent research by the new Brigham's designers. Now, according to Richard Johnson, when customers enter a redesigned store they'll often exclaim, "This is what the old Brigham's was."

Miami Beach's Art Deco Hotels

MIAMI, Florida's fortunes are about as curvilinear as some of its architecture. Although until World War I the place consisted mainly of mangrove jungle and malarial swamp, the density of the flora could not disguise Miami's potential from developers like Carl G. Fisher. Fisher arrived early in the Twenties, and with his partners, cleared jungle, drained swampland, connected beach with mainland, and promoted a land boom that would become as fevered as the Gold Rush. Due to the enterprise of Fisher and men like him, by 1925 the "Magic City" had grown from

esque-Gothic-Renaissance-Big-Bull-Market-and-Damn-the-Expense''* amalgam that begged for transient status anyway. But in the decade that followed, Miami's reemergence would bring with it the remarkable outcropping of art deco architecture for which a part of Miami Beach has again become famous.

This architecture—also known as Streamline Moderne, Mediterranean Revival and Tropical Deco—comprises Miami Beach's Art Deco District, an area that extends roughly between 6th and 21st Streets, and which was the first twentieth-century district to be incorporated into the National Register of Historic Places.

The buildings of the Art Deco

tion League to spare it from becoming mere textbook history at the hands of Florida's traditionally powerful developers.

The Art Deco District's neighborhood of surprisingly small buildings is made all the more charming by their ambitiously soaring facades and gulf-streamlined profiles. Amid the district's palette of tropical pastels now swarm deco aficionados from all over the world, their presence enhancing the neighborhood's Cole Porter lyricism.

An important part of the engine driving the Art Deco District's resurgence have been the Art Deco Hotels, a fully restored group of six of the area's most moderne old houses offering period accommodations. Flagship of the Art Deco

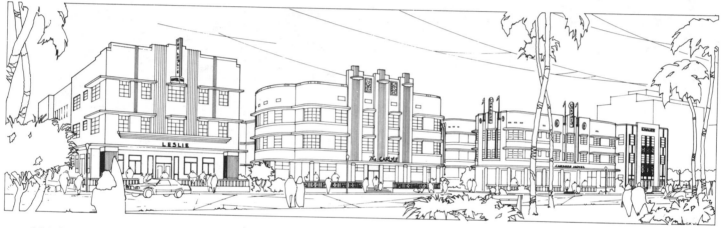

an 1896 population of 60 persons to more than 60 *thousand* souls. Some of the earlier settlers (like William Jennings Bryan, who arrived in Miami in 1912 and eight years later was able to sell his modest home for $250,000) got rich, while late-comers, lured by the promise of easy money, got fleeced by a new generation of swamp pirate.

Then, in September of 1926, all were blown away by a hurricane that swept the city with gales reaching 130 miles per hour. The winds, which heaved thousand-ton ships up onto the streets, left 40,000 homeless and caused $300 million in damages.

Naturally, this storm was also rough on the architecture, a "Bastard Spanish-Moorish-Roman-

District were constructed during the period between the hurricane of 1926 and the beginning of World War II while Miami Beach was attracting its second wave of northerners. The war, which exposed many Americans to new paradises in California and Hawaii, ended the building boom, as even Florida vacationers began to abandon Miami Beach for places farther up the Gold Coast. By the middle 1950s Miami Beach had declined into a low-rent ghetto for the aged.

The Art Deco District's placement in the National Register (and concomitant revitalization) in 1982 climaxed a five-year struggle on the part of the Miami Design Preserva-

Hotel fleet is the seventy-room Cardozo, built in 1939 and named for Justice Benjamin Cardozo (1870–1938), the first Jewish member of the United States Supreme Court. The Hotel Cardozo's sisters include the Carlyle (1941), the Cavalier (1936), the Leslie (1937), the Senator (1939), and the Victor (1937).

For further information, contact:

Art Deco Hotels

*Ocean Drive and 13th Street
Miami Beach, FL 33139
Tel. toll free 800/327-6303 outside Florida (305/534-2135 within Florida)*

*John Burke, *Rogue's Progress* (New York: G. P. Putnam's Sons, 1975), p. 212.

Santa Claus' Catalog Starts Here
With World's Greatest Stocking Value

For Girls

For Boys

We Defy Competition

Are you comparing these values with others? Read this before you make your selection. Compare the size of each article. Do not be misled by the number of pieces offered.

For many years we have compared and examined Christmas Stockings offered by others and we have yet to find values that are anywhere near the tremendous values we offer. We could put twice as many pieces in each assortment but they would be cheap, worthless, tiny, paper or tin toys. Our assortments have practical toys. Due to the large quantity we buy we are able to offer these wonderful assortments at these prices. Compare our beautifully dressed 10-inch full jointed sleeping doll with the dolls offered by others, or the 17-inch break action, metal barrel popgun against the small wood popguns usually offered.

Two Assortments for Boys—Two for Girls

Guns, toys, watches, horns in the boys' stockings. Toy dishes, story books, dolls, cut-outs for the girls.

Christmas Items

We prefer to give you Quality rather than a large number of cheap items

98¢

98¢

$1.98

$1.98

Girls
25 Toys— If Bought Separately Would Cost $3.00 to $3.25

Ten and one-quarter-inch beautifully dressed doll with real bobbed hair, and colored ribbon, sleeping eyes, movable head, arms and legs, shoes and stockings, nice dress. Doll alone frequently sells elsewhere from 75c to $1.00. Pretty 11-piece dolly tea set; 9-inch washable stuffed animal; flexible toy wrist watch; transparent drawing slate; hardwood sliding cover pencil box; box each of fresh Cracker Jack and stick candy; set of jacks and ball; noise makers, including horn, cricket, blowout and baby cry; games of Donkey Party, Old Maid and Clown Ring Toss; 3 sets of cut-out toys; two good books; box of crayons and 10 paints in box, 9¼x5 inches, and two other girls' toys. 25 toys, packed in box with bright red net stocking, 34 inches long and 10 inches wide, and ribbon for tying. Shipping weight, 4½ pounds.

69K9916 .... **$1.98**

For Little Sister
20 Toys. If Bought Separately Would Ordinarily Cost $1.30 to $1.40.

Twelve-inch red rubber clown doll; varnished hardwood sliding cover pencil box; 10 paints in box, 8½x5 inches; box each of fresh Cracker Jack and pure stick candy; two good books and a box of crayons; set of jacks and ball, games of old maid and donkey party, noise makers, including horn, blowout, cricket, baby cry and hummer; a bubbler outfit; two cut-out toys and one other girls' toy. 20 toys packed in box with bright red net stocking, 30 ins. long and 9½ in. wide, and ribbon for tying. Shipping weight, 3 pounds.

69K9919 .... **98¢**

For Little Brother
26 Toys. If Bought Separately Would Ordinarily Cost $1.30 to $1.40.

Real mouth organ and flute; compass to guide you; varnished hardwood sliding cover pencil box; 10 paints in box, 8½x5 inches; box each of fresh Cracker Jack and pure stick candy; games of Donkey Party and Old Maid; two good books, and box of crayons; noise makers, including horn, cricket, blowout, baby cry and hummer, a bubbler outfit and two other good toys; 26 toys packed in box with bright red net stocking, 30 inches long and 7¾ inches wide, and ribbon for tying. Shipping weight, 3 pounds.

69K9911 .... **98¢**

Boys'
32 Toys— If Bought Separately Would Ordinarily Cost $3.00 to $3.25

Six-inch wood sailboat with cloth sails, 9 inch black enameled wood 4-key saxophone. 28-cent 17-inch break action, metal barrel popgun. Ticking toy watch with chain. 25-cent mechanical automobile 6 inches long with strong spring. Glass drawing slate. Hardwood pencil box. 10 paints in box, 9¼x8 inches. A real compass, and soft rubber baseball. Box each of fresh Cracker Jack and stick candy. Games of Donkey Party, Dominoes, Old Maid and Clown Ring Toss, mouth organ, flute and top; noise makers, including horn, paper blowout, baby cry, hummer and a wood cricket; two books; box of crayons and five other boys' toys. 32 toys packed in strong carton with bright red net stocking, 34 inches long and 10 inches wide, and ribbon for tying. Shipping weight, 5 pounds.

69K9912 .... **$1.98**

Decorations and Stocking Stuffers

B. SHACKMAN & COMPANY has been doing business at the same Fifth Avenue location since 1897, and sells many novelty items reminiscent of that time. Their Christmas catalog contains a wonderful array of paper and tinsel Victorian Santas, angels, tree decorations, and cards.

A minimum $10 order is required.

B. Shackman & Company
85 Fifth Avenue at 16th Street
New York, NY 10003
Tel. 212/989-5162

From the Henry Ford Museum and Greenfield Village
Christmas Tree Ornaments

THESE hand-painted ornaments are adaptations of the carved wooden animals to be found on the 1913 Herschell-Spillman carousel located in Suwanee Park in historic Greenfield Village.

Styles: Henry Ford Museum Store catalog #92-0112, goat; catalog #92-0113, horse; catalog #92-0114, frog; catalog #92-0124, rooster; catalog #92-0125, stork; and catalog #92-0126, camel.

Price: $4.50 each (plus 50¢ each for shipping and handling); set of all six (catalog #92-0076), $23.95 (plus $2 for shipping and handling).

Roly-Poly Santa

"**A** papier-mâché reproduction of one enjoyed by children in the early 20th century," cites the Henry Ford Museum Store catalog. The original Santa was displayed in the toy collection of the Henry Ford Museum. Approximately 3¾ inches high.

Price: Henry Ford Museum store catalog #92-0098, $5.95 (plus 75¢ for shipping and handling).

Gift catalog available.

The Edison Institute
Henry Ford Museum and Greenfield Village
Museum Store
P.O. Box 1970
Dearborn, MI 48121

King Leo Stick Candy

ALTHOUGH the can is from a later period, King Leo Stick Candy has been a Christmas tradition in Tennessee since 1901. The candy is available in four "strong" versions of peppermint, clove, lemon, and vanilla. All are real flavorings, with peppermint preferred four to one.

Prices: first 2-lb. tin, $5.50; each additional tin, $4.35. A case of 12 tins is available for $45.95. Indicate flavors desired as only one flavor is available per tin.

Standard Candy Company
Mail Order Department
715 Massman Dr.
Nashville, TN 37210

Christmas Postcards

REPLICAS OF turn-of-the-century Christmas postcards (and reprints of period cards on a variety of other subjects) are available from both Evergreen Press and the R. J. Fish Publishing Company.

Brochures and order forms available.

R. J. Fish Publishing Company

P.O. Box 1771
Reseda, CA 91335

The Evergreen Press

P.O. Box 4971
Walnut Creek, CA 94596
Tel. 415/825-7850

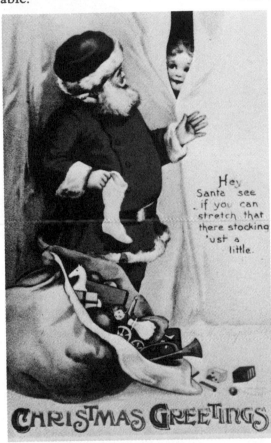

Glass Christmas Globe

UNLIKE THE CHEAP plastic ephemera we're now used to, this is the genuine crystal snow-storm-under-glass that anyone who can remember real reindeer at Macy's will also recall. It's 4½ inches tall with a 3-inch-diameter globe enclosing a Christmas tree. Shipping weight: 2 lbs.

   Price: Vermont Country Store catalog #13934, $12.

Delivery charges (based on shipping weight) required in advance.

Seasonal catalog available from The Vermont Country Store, Catalog Request, Route 100, Weston, VT 05161.

The Vermont Country Store

Mail Order Office
P.O. Box 3000
Manchester Center, VT 05255

If you are interested in receiving periodically updated mail-order information on these and other early-twentieth-century-style items, address your request to American Historical Supply, P.O. Box 15428, Springfield, MA 01115.

Index

Index of Suppliers and Manufacturers

Heller-Aller Company, Inc.　68
Corner of Perry & Oakwood
Napoleon, OH 43545
Tel. 419/592-1856 or 592-3216

Hershey Foods Corp.　100
P.O. Box 800
Hershey, PA 17033
Tel. 717/534-7500

Historic Newspaper Archives　89
1582 Hart St.
Rahway, NJ 07065
Tel. 201/381-2332

Historical Aircraft Corporation
169-171
P.O. Box 2218
Durango, CO 81301
Tel. 303/259-1037

Hotel Algonquin　201
59 West 44th St.
New York, NY 10036
Tel. 212/840-6800

Hugh Lauter Levin Associates　101
130 West 17th St.
New York, NY 10011
Tel. 212/242-1405

Hunter's Frontier Times　89
P.O. Box 665
Perkins, OK 74059
Tel. 405/547-2473

ICF Inc.　33
305 E. 63rd St.
New York, NY 10021
Tel. 212/750-0900

Indian Motorcycle News　141-144
P.O. Box 455
32606 Hartley
Lake Elsinore, CA 92330
Tel. 714/678-1583

James & Son Military Clothiers
159-160
1230 Arch St.
Philadelphia, PA 19107
Tel. 215/963-9937

Jenifer House　58-59, 128, 187
New Marlboro Stage
Great Barrington, MA 01230
Tel. 413/528-1500

John Wright, Inc.　42
North Front St.
Wrightsville, PA 17368
Tel. 717/252-3661

Kalmbach Publishing Company　188
1027 N. Seventh St.
Milwaukee, WI 53233

L.F. Deardorff & Sons　130-131
315 S. Peoria St.
Chicago, IL 60607
Tel. 312/829-5655

L.L. Bean, Inc.　181
Freeport, ME 04033
Tel. (for orders only) 207/865-4761

Laff-O-Graph Studios　194
c/o Mr. Bill Shelley
2307 Harrison Ave.
Baldwin, NY 11510
Tel. 516/868-7379

Lamp Light　25
135 Yorkshire Court
Elyria, OH 44035
Tel. 216/365-4954

Lehman Hardware & Appliances
46-47
4779 Kidron Rd.
Kidron, OH 44636
Tel. 216/859-5441

Les Paul Collector Trucks　119
R.R. #2, Box 309
Winamac, IN 46996

Liberty-Ramsey Imports　99
66 Broad St.
Carlstadt, NJ 07072
Tel. 201/935-4500

Lodge Manufacturing Company　42
P.O. Box 380
South Pittsburgh, TN 37380
Tel. 615/837-7181

Louisville Art Glass Studio　17
1110 Baxter Ave.
Louisville, KY 40204
Tel. 502/585-5421

Louisville Tin & Stove Company
70
P.O. Box 1019
Louisville, KY 40201

Manhattan Special Bottling Company
98
342 Manhattan Ave.
Brooklyn, NY 11211
Tel. 718/388-4144

Margaret Woodbury Strong Museum
59, 116
Museum Shop
One Manhattan Sq.
Rochester, NY 14607

The Maytag Co.　52
Newton, IA 50208
Tel. 515/792-7000

Gene Morris　87
1555 Chambers Rd.
McDonough, GA 30253

Murphy Door Bed Company　31
40 East 34th St.
New York, NY 10016
Tel. 212/682-8936

Nabisco Brands　99
Nabisco Brands Plaza
Parsippany, NJ 07054
Tel. 201/898-7100

Nader the Hatter, Inc.　74-75
340 Worthington St.
Springfield, MA 01103
Tel. 413/736-8081

National Trust for Historic
Preservation　37
Preservation Shops
Dept. AH
1600 H. St. NW
Washington, D.C. 20006
Tel. 202/673-4200

Nostalgia Decorating Company　126
P.O. Box 1312
Kingston, PA 18704
Tel. 717/288-1795

Nostalgia Station　186-187
1000 Light St.
Baltimore, MD 21230

Original Music Company　102-103
18108 Redondo Circle
Huntington Beach, CA 92648
Tel. 714/848-9823

Orvis　25
Manchester, VT 05254
Tel. 802/362-1300

Palmer House　200
500 Sinclair Lewis Ave.
Sauk Centre, MN 56372
Tel. 612/352-3431

The Paper Potpourri　135
P.O. Box 698
Oakland Gardens, NY 11364

Parker Brothers　122
P.O. Box 1012
Beverly, MA 01915
Tel. 617/927-7600

Past Patterns　76-79
2017 Eastern, S.E.
Grand Rapids, MI 49507
Tel. 616/245-9456

Paul K. Guillow, Inc.　119
P.O. Box 229
Wakefield, MA 01880
Tel. 617/245-5255

Philip Morris Company　106
Richmond, VA 23261

The Pioneer Place　48-49
Rte. 2, 9938 County Rd. 39
Belle Center, OH 43310

Plaza Hotel　202
Fifth Ave. at 59th St.
New York, NY 10019
Tel. toll free 800/228-3000 or
212/759-3000

Pocket Books　84-85
1230 Ave. of the Americas
New York, NY 10020
Tel. 212/246-2121

Pool Tables by Adler　112
820 S. Hoover St.
Los Angeles, CA 90005
Tel. 213/382-6334

Portland Stove Company　63
P.O. Box 377
Fickett Rd.
North Pownal, ME 04069
Tel. 207/688-2254 or 775-6424